REAL ESTATE FINANCE

IN A NUTSHELL®

SEVENTH EDITION

VADA WATERS LINDSEY
Associate Professor of Law
Marquette University Law School

WEST ACADEMIC PUBLISHING

444 Cedar Street, Suite 700
St. Paul, MN 55101
1-877-888-1330

Printed in the United States of America

ISBN: 978-1-68328-263-1

To my wonderful daughter
Alexis Taylor Lindsey

PREFACE

The seventh edition of this book examines the law of real estate finance. It is intended to be used as an introductory guide for lawyers and a general reference for law students who are enrolled in law school classes that address real estate finance issues. It discusses the fundamental rules related to various types of mortgage instruments, priority of encumbrances, loans in default and foreclosure. This book summarizes the law and relies on case and statutory law from various states to provide context to the application of rules that are fundamental to real estate finance.

The seventh edition greatly expands the federal government's involvement in real estate finance resulting from the subprime loan crisis and the Great Recession that was in its early stages when the prior edition of this book was written. The seventh edition includes a discussion of the changes in the regulatory landscape, including the enactment of the Dodd-Frank Wall Street Reform and Consumer Protection Act of 2010.

The tax consequences of issues related to real estate finance are critical. Therefore, this edition discusses various tax issues related to mortgages and real estate finance. It discusses the tax consequences of loan modifications, deeds in lieu of foreclosure and short sales. In addition, this edition includes a new chapter on advanced tax issues. That chapter outlines the fundamental tax issues, including the tax issues related to the inclusion of debt in an owner's adjusted basis, depreciation, disposition of real property encumbered by a mortgage, form of ownership, limitations on deductions and character of gain or loss. This chapter also addresses the tax treatment of like kind exchanges, installment sales and sale and leaseback transactions.

Several people played significant roles in helping me write the seventh edition of this book. First, Vanderbilt Law School Professor of Law Emeritus Jon W. Bruce, the author of the first six editions of this book, provided me with a great foundation. In addition, I am grateful to Professor Carol N. Brown, a professor of law at the University of Richmond School of Law, for recommending me to West Publishing Co. to become the new author of this book. I also owe a thank you to Elana Olson, director of the Eckstein Law Library at Marquette Law School for her research support. Finally, I want to thank my three talented and dedicated research assistants, Edona Ajvazi, Matthew Carlson and Emily Greene, for their excellent research.

VADA WATERS LINDSEY

September 2017

OUTLINE

TABLE OF CASES

References are to Pages

REAL ESTATE FINANCE

IN A NUTSHELL®

SEVENTH EDITION

CHAPTER 1

INTRODUCTION TO LAW OF REAL ESTATE FINANCE

This introductory chapter presents an overview of the fundamentals on real estate finance. Because the mortgage is the cornerstone of real estate finance, it is the focal point of this chapter and for that matter the entire book.

I. MORTGAGE CONCEPT

A. FUNDAMENTALS AND REQUIREMENTS

A mortgage is the transfer of an interest in real estate as security, usually for the repayment of a loan, but occasionally for the performance of another obligation. The typical mortgage transaction is relatively uncomplicated. An individual borrows money from a lender and enters into a written agreement with the lender that the individual's real estate is collateral for the loan. In legal terminology the individual is a mortgagor, the lender is a mortgagee, and the agreement is a mortgage. If the mortgagor defaults on the mortgage loan, the mortgagee may enforce its security interest by using appropriate foreclosure procedures to have the mortgaged real estate sold to satisfy the loan. A fundamental requirement of all mortgages is that the mortgagor must have the equitable right to redeem the mortgaged real estate prior to foreclosure by paying the outstanding loan balance and interest. In many jurisdictions, the mortgagor has the right to statutorily redeem the real estate after it has been sold to a purchaser by paying the foreclosure sales price to the purchaser.

A mortgage will be an effective lien on the security if it is executed pursuant to the state's requirements. In general, a mortgage must identify the mortgagor and mortgagee, describe the loan amount or underlying obligation, state the maturity date and describe the mortgaged property. It also provides other important information, including the meaning of default under the mortgage and the mortgagee's remedies upon the default.

B. REDEMPTION RIGHTS

1. Equity of Redemption

At early English common law, when a mortgagor granted a mortgage to a mortgagee to secure a loan, the mortgagor conveyed a defeasible fee in the property to the mortgagee. If the debt was repaid at maturity, or "law day" in common law parlance, the mortgagee's estate terminated, and the mortgagor again owned the property. If, however, the debt was not paid at maturity, the mortgagee's defeasible fee became a fee simple absolute. Because the law courts strictly enforced the time for payment, the mortgagor lost the land even if the mortgagor tendered payment just a day late.

In order to mitigate the harsh results of the common law approach, equity courts intervened. If a mortgagor established a sound reason for failing to perform as agreed in the mortgage, equity would permit the mortgagor to recover the property by paying the debt after the maturity date. Originally, the mortgagor's right to recover the property was open-ended and left title unclear for years. *In re* Braker, 125 B.R. 798, 799 (9th Cir. BAP 1991). Equity courts began imposing deadlines for a mortgagor to recover the property from the mortgagee. Id. The deadline imposed was the date of foreclosure. Id. The right to recover the property before the foreclosure became known as the equity of redemption. Id. Under the Restatement, "[f]rom the time the full obligation secured by a mortgage becomes due and payable until the mortgage is foreclosed, a mortgagor has the right to redeem the real estate from the mortgage. . ." Restatement (Third) of Property, Mortgages § 3.1(a) (1997).

Equity courts have always zealously preserved the mortgagor's equity of redemption. Any clause in the mortgage or in a contemporaneous agreement that has the effect of eliminating or impairing the mortgagor's equitable right to redeem is termed clogging and is prohibited. *See* Restatement (Third) of Property, Mortgages § 3.1(b) (1997) (stating that any agreement that impairs the mortgagor's equity of redemption is invalid). Otherwise a mortgage could be transformed into a defeasible fee by the use of a simple waiver clause. The courts' protective approach in this regard gave rise to the maxim: "once a mortgage, always a mortgage."

A mortgagee is not able to eliminate the mortgagor's equitable redemption rights by disguising the true substance of a transaction. For example, if a mortgagor executes a mortgage in favor of a mortgagee and at the same time, the mortgagor gives the mortgagee an option to purchase the mortgaged land for a nominal sum upon the mortgagor's default, the option is unenforceable as a contemporaneous clog on the mortgagor's equity of redemption. It is really a disguised waiver.

2. Statutory Redemption Rights

Statutes in numerous jurisdictions give the mortgagor an opportunity to redeem the mortgaged property after the mortgagor's right to equitably redeem the property has ended and the property has already been sold at a foreclosure sale. This right, referred to as statutory redemption, exists in about one-half of the states. Statutory redemption offers the mortgagor a set period of time after the foreclosure sale to pay the foreclosure sales price and redeem the property. For example, New Jersey has a six-month redemption period. N.J. Stat. Ann. § 2A:50–4 (2017). Kansas has a one-year redemption period. Kan. Stat. Ann. § 60–2414 (2017). Generally, Minnesota has a six-month redemption period, but allows for a 12-month period in certain situations, such as the foreclosed mortgage was a reverse mortgage or the mortgage was executed prior to July 1, 1967. Minn. Stat. Ann. § 580.23 (2017). Tennessee has a very long statutory redemption period by allowing mortgagors to redeem within two years of the foreclosure sale. Tenn. Code Ann. § 66–8–101 (2017).

C. OBLIGATION/SECURITY DISTINCTION

A mortgage exists solely as security for an underlying obligation, ordinarily a promissory note. Consequently, every mortgage lives, travels, and dies with the obligation it secures. A security interest cannot have an independent existence separate from the underlying obligation that it secures. Jackson v. Mortgage Elec. Registration Sys., 770 N.W.2d 487, 494 (Minn. 2009).

If the promissory note is assigned to an assignee, the mortgage follows the note into the assignee's hands by operation of law. For example, assume that a mortgagor executes a promissory note and a mortgage to a mortgagee. The mortgagee assigns the note to an assignee, but through inadvertence fails to assign the mortgage to the assignee. Nonetheless, the assignee can enforce the mortgage upon the mortgagor's default because it follows the note.

In addition, the security interest created by the mortgage lapses when the underlying debt is satisfied. Assume that a mortgagor executes a promissory note and mortgage in favor of a mortgagee. The mortgagor pays the mortgagee in full. The mortgagee returns the note to the mortgagor but does not release the mortgage. Even though the mortgagee failed to officially release the mortgage, the mortgagee has no further rights under the mortgage.

D. STATUTE OF FRAUDS

A mortgage, as the transfer of an interest in land, falls squarely within the scope of the Statute of Frauds. Thus, mortgages, as well as agreements to execute mortgages, must be in writing to comply with the Statute. For example, assume that a man asks a lender for a loan to pay several bills. The lender makes the loan upon the man's oral pledge that man's farm is security for the loan. The man defaults on the loan. The lender seeks to foreclose and have the farm sold. The lender has no right to do so, because the man's oral pledge is unenforceable. As a general rule, simply lending money does not constitute sufficient part performance to take an unwritten security arrangement out of the Statute of Frauds. Hence, the loan is unsecured.

Equitable principles, however, may dictate that a mortgage arises by operation of law or is enforceable even though it is unwritten. Assume that a debtor asks a creditor for a loan to purchase a specific parcel of real estate. The creditor makes the loan upon the debtor's oral promise to give the creditor a mortgage on the property to be purchased. The debtor uses the loan proceeds to purchase the property, but refuses to execute a mortgage to the creditor as promised. The debtor defaults on the loan, and the creditor seeks to foreclose and have the land sold. The creditor generally may do so because an equitable mortgage arises by operation of law in order to permit the creditor to obtain payment out of the product of the creditor's loan. Such a mortgage is not subject to the Statute of Frauds. The creditor also may prevail on another ground. Hardship on the creditor, advancement of the loan proceeds, and their use to purchase the property may be considered to constitute sufficient part performance to satisfy the Statute of Frauds, rendering the debtor's oral promise enforceable.

II. HISTORICAL DEVELOPMENT OF MORTGAGE

Real estate finance is best understood by one who is thoroughly acquainted with the development of the mortgage concept. An abbreviated jaunt through legal history, therefore, is in order. During this excursion, note how the legal pendulum swings first in the mortgagee's favor, then in the mortgagor's direction, and so on, back and forth, throughout history.

A. FORECLOSURE

1. Strict Foreclosure

The creation of an immutable equity of redemption placed the mortgagee in a difficult position. The defaulting mortgagor's right to redeem effectively prevented the mortgagee from selling or improving the mortgaged property. The English equity courts thus came to the aid of mortgagees by developing the concept of foreclosure of the equity of redemption. After default and at the mortgagee's request, the equity courts set a time period within which the mortgagor was required to pay the debt or lose the right to redeem. If the mortgagor failed to pay within the period specified, the mortgagee obtained a fee simple absolute. This method of terminating the mortgagor's equity of redemption became known as strict foreclosure.

2. Foreclosure by Sale

Strict foreclosure was inherently unfair to the mortgagor because the value of the mortgaged land acquired by the mortgagee frequently exceeded the debt. The legal pendulum, consequently, began to swing back in favor of mortgagors. This time our state courts played an active role. The rest of this chapter deals exclusively with the evolution of real estate finance law in this country.

Equity again readjusted the conflicting interests of the parties by requiring foreclosure of the mortgagor's equity of redemption via public sale. The proceeds of the foreclosure sale were distributed pursuant to equitable considerations. The funds were employed first to satisfy the mortgage debt. Any surplus was given to the mortgagor. If the funds were insufficient to pay off the debt, the mortgagee was permitted to recover a deficiency judgment against the mortgagor.

In the United States, foreclosure by sale is the primary method of terminating the mortgagor's equity of redemption. Strict foreclosure is not widely available.

Two variations on the foreclosure by sale theme exist—foreclosure by judicial sale and foreclosure by power of sale. Foreclosure by judicial sale involves a court-supervised procedure that is often complex, protracted, and expensive. Nonetheless, because judicial supervision protects the mortgagor, foreclosure by judicial sale is available in all states and is the exclusive method of foreclosing the mortgagor's equity of redemption in a substantial number of jurisdictions.

Power of sale foreclosure derives its name from the fact that in many jurisdictions the mortgage may include a provision granting the mortgagee the power to sell the mortgaged property without court supervision. Where this type of foreclosure is available, lenders frequently employ a special kind of mortgage known as a deed of trust. The deed of trust provides that a trustee will conduct the foreclosure sale outside the judicial system.

III. MORTGAGE THEORIES

Although it is commonly recognized that a mortgage is a transfer of a security interest in land, controversy exists regarding the precise nature of the mortgagee's interest. During the evolution of the mortgage from a defeasible conveyance to a security device, courts did not adequately deal with the interrelated problem of possession. Today states handle this unresolved possession problem based on three theories of mortgages. These theories are known as "title," "lien" and "intermediate."

A. TITLE THEORY

Some states, referred to as title theory jurisdictions, follow a diluted version of the original common law view that a mortgage conveys legal title to the mortgagee. Predicated on the concept that possession follows legal title, the mortgagee in these jurisdictions receives the right to possession of the mortgage property when the mortgage is executed. Most title theory states lie in the eastern part of the country where early common law had the greatest impact. Use of the term title theory to describe the mortgage law of these jurisdictions, however, is somewhat misleading. Title theory states have departed from most aspects of the traditional English theory of mortgages, retaining it primarily with respect to possession. As a general rule, these jurisdictions consider the mortgagee's "title" to be in the nature of a security interest, rather than fee ownership. In title theory jurisdictions, the mortgagee holds legal title to the property and the mortgagor holds an equitable title. Nat'l City Mortgage Co. v. Stoecker, 92 Conn. App. 787, 792, 888 A.2d 95, 99 (Conn. App. Ct. 2006); MERS v. Saunders, 2 A.3d 289, 294 (Me. 2010). The mortgagee's fee simple interest is defeasible, and it reverts to the mortgagor upon satisfaction of the mortgage conditions. Id. at 793. However, the conveyance of a fee in a title theory jurisdiction is not inconsequential. In Faneuil Investors Group, Ltd. Partnership v. Board of Selectmen, 933 N.E.2d 918 (Mass. 2010), a town conveyed land to a housing authority. Id. at 920. The deed contained a clause that the land would revert to the town if the housing authority conveyed it without the consent of the town. Id. After the conveyance, the housing authority granted a mortgage to a bank. Id. The court concluded that the town properly invoked the reverter clause because the jurisdiction followed the title theory of mortgages. Id.

In a title theory jurisdiction, a mortgagee is not responsible as an owner to maintain the mortgaged property even if the mortgagor has abandoned it. The mortgagor continues to bear the responsibility of maintaining the property until the mortgagee obtains possession or forecloses. *In re* Cormier, 434 B.R. 222, 226–227 (2010) (stating that even though Massachusetts is a title theory state, the mortgagor remains the owner and cannot require the mortgagee to maintain and preserve the property).

Another consequence of the title theory of mortgages is where a joint tenant grants a mortgage to a mortgagee. One of the fundamental attributes of joint tenancies is the right of survivorship. Under the right of survivorship principle, upon the death of a joint tenant, that joint tenant's interest automatically passes to the surviving joint tenants by operation of law. In a title theory jurisdiction, when a joint tenant grants a mortgage on the joint tenant's interest in the property, it severs the joint tenancy and converts it to a tenancy in common for the mortgaging joint tenant. Stewart v. AmSouth Mortgage Co., Inc., 679 So.2d 247, 249 (Ala. Civ. App. 1995).

B. INTERMEDIATE THEORY

A few states still recognize the mortgage as a conveyance of a form of legal title, but limit the mortgagee's right to possession in a manner consistent with the view that the mortgage creates merely a security interest. These states, called intermediate theory jurisdictions, give the mortgagor the right to possession until default and the mortgagee the right thereafter. Restatement (Third) of Property, Mortgages § 4.1 cmt. a (1997).

C. LIEN THEORY

In the majority of states, the mortgage is viewed as giving the mortgagee a lien on the mortgaged property, not legal title. Thus, in these lien theory jurisdictions, the mortgagor retains the right to possession until foreclosure. A mortgagee is not entitled to immediate possession upon the mortgagor's default.

D. PRACTICAL SIGNIFICANCE OF MORTGAGE THEORIES

It is important to emphasize that even in title and intermediate theory states, the mortgagee's rights as erstwhile legal titleholder generally have been eliminated where unnecessary to protect its security interest. The primary distinction among the title, intermediate and lien theories, therefore, is with respect to the right to possession. Even this difference is often obscured by a mortgage clause that spells out the rights of the parties regarding possession.

The most important practical difference between the theories occurs upon the mortgagor's default. It is much easier for a mortgagee to take possession of the mortgaged property in a title theory or intermediate theory jurisdiction. In a lien theory jurisdiction, there must be some basis for the mortgagee to take possession of the mortgaged property. For example, if the mortgagor commits waste on the mortgaged property or abandons it, courts will permit the mortgagee to take possession of it.

IV. MODERN FINANCING FORMATS

Although the mortgage is still the foundation of real estate finance, many sophisticated financing variations exist today. The complex financing formats that have evolved over the past several decades may employ a combination of mortgages, leases, installment land contracts, outright conveyances, or other arrangements. In subsequent chapters, you will become well acquainted with fundamental mortgage law and will be introduced to a wide variety of other real estate financing devices. The tax implications are critical in determining the best approach to structure a transaction. These tax implications will be addressed in this book because they are important for the purchaser, lender and seller of the property to consider.

V. OBTAINING REAL ESTATE FINANCING

A. KEY PREFINANCING CONSIDERATIONS

There are several important considerations in deciding the best way to finance the acquisition of real estate. These are important considerations that musts be carefully weighed before a mortgagor agrees to the loan.

1. Leverage and the Loan-to-Value Ratio

Most people who purchase real property take out loans to finance a portion of the purchase price. This is known as leverage. The level of leverage is dependent on the loan-to-value ratio required by the lender. If the lender requires a loan-to-value ratio of 80% and the property costs and is worth $100,000, the mortgagor must come up with a down payment of $20,000 and take out an $80,000 loan. The difference between the fair market value of the property and the outstanding balance of all mortgages is the mortgagor's equity. Generally, loans are riskier where the mortgagor has little equity in the property.

If a homeowner purchases a home using conventional financing with a loan-to-value ratio greater than 80 percent, the homeowner will have to pay private mortgage insurance, known as PMI. PMI protects the lender from the additional risk caused by low down payments. The mortgagor pays PMI either with the regular mortgage payments as a premium, as a one-time, upfront premium paid at closing or a combination of both approaches. In either case, PMI is paid to private insurance companies, and the amount of PMI is noted on forms known as the Loan Estimate and Disclosure Statement. The growth of PMI made high loan-to-value (e.g., with 95% leverage) conventional home mortgage loans broadly available. Today, PMI companies dominate the residential mortgage insurance business.

The Homeowners Protection Act of 1998 (12 U.S.C.A. § 4901 *et seq.*) allows mortgagors to cancel PMI on post-July 28, 1999 residential mortgage transactions upon written request if the mortgagor is current on payments and has a good payment history (as defined under U.S.C.A. § 4901(4)), there are no junior liens, the outstanding balance of the mortgage loan is 80% of the original value of the home and the value of the home has not declined below its original value. 12 U.S.C.A. § 4902(a) (2017); 12 U.S.C.A. § 4901(2) (2017). Moreover, the Act generally requires automatic termination of PMI on such mortgages whenever the mortgage debt declines to 78% of the mortgaged property's date-of-mortgage-execution value. 12 U.S.C.A. § 4902(b) (2017); 12 U.S.C.A. § 4901(18) (2017). Finally, the Act imposes extensive disclosure requirements on mortgagees. *See* 12 U.S.C.A. § 4905 (2017). This legislative measure was designed to relieve homeowners of the obligation to continue to submit premiums for insurance no longer needed by mortgagees.

2. Amortization

Amortization is the repayment of a loan in accordance to a schedule. The amortization table sets forth the mortgagor's payment of principal and interest only. It does not reflect the mortgagor's actual payments because they may include escrow payments for property taxes and insurance.

Under a level payment amortization, the payment amount does not change during the term of the loan; however, the amount allocated to principal and interest changes with each payment. During the early stages of amortization, a greater portion of each payment is allocated to interest and a lesser amount is allocated to principal. After each payment, the amount payable for interest decreases and the amount payable for principal increases. This is important for several reasons. The mortgagor is entitled to deduct mortgage interest, and the mortgagee is required to include mortgage interest in income. During the early years of amortization, the mortgage interest deductions will be higher than in the later years. Hence, from the mortgagor's perspective, there is a greater tax savings. But, the mortgagee must recognize a greater amount of interest income during the early years of amortization. Another important consideration is the impact of refinancing on the amortization of a mortgage loan. When a mortgagor refinances a loan, a new loan replaces or substitutes the original loan. This means that the amortization clock restarts, and the overwhelming majority of the early payments are allocated to interest. Even if the new loan has a lower interest, the total cost of the real property may ultimately go up if the amortization period is the same as the original loan because it will take longer to pay it off. However, if the amortization period on the new loan is the same as the remaining term on the original loan, the mortgagor may lower the cost of financing the property.

There are other types of amortization methods. For example, a loan may be interest only during the term of the loan with a "balloon payment" due at the end of the term. A construction loan, known as interim financing, is a type of loan with interest payable during the construction of improvements and a balloon payment or principal due the end of the loan term. The mortgagor usually will have a permanent lender already in place to "take out" the construction loan. The permanent loan is usually a long-term loan (e.g., 30 years).

3. Interest

The interest that a lender will charge on a loan is a significant factor in determining the best option to finance a real estate purchase. Today, interest rates are very low, and it is not uncommon for a purchaser to have an interest rate of 3% or 4%. In the 1980s it was not uncommon for loans to have interest rates around 17%. Undoubtedly, a loan with a higher interest rate affects its affordability.

Lenders will charge higher rates on more risky loans. Secondary lenders routinely charge higher interest rates because senior mortgages have priority. Lenders also charge a higher interest rate on loans for mortgagors with subpar credit histories. Lenders will apply underwriting standards not only to determine the viability of the loan but also loan terms, including the interest rate.

Generally, a mortgagor will receive a loan with a fixed rate or an adjustable rate. A fixed interest rate means that the rate is constant throughout the loan period. An adjustable rate mortgage is one where the interest rate is adjusted at stated intervals based on an index, such as the prime rate or LIBOR. An adjustable rate mortgage usually starts with a lower interest rate than fixed rate interest mortgages. However, over time the adjustable rate mortgage interest rate may end up higher than a fixed mortgage. Many mortgagors plan to refinance the adjustable rate mortgage before the interest rate gets too high. But, that is not always a possibility. During the subprime loan crisis, many homeowners took out adjustable rate loans with low or "teaser" rates at the outset but very high rates at scheduled resets. The homeowners had planned to refinance their loans before the teaser rates became effective, but the fair market value of homes plummeted during the crisis leaving many homeowners without sufficient equity in their homes to refinance their loans. Indeed, many homeowners were "underwater" or "upside down" which meant that the fair market value of their homes was lower than the outstanding balance of their mortgage loans.

VI. GOVERNMENT INVOLVEMENT

The government has always been involved in regulating real estate finance. However, after the subprime loan crisis and the Great Recession, many laws were enacted or modified. The most important legislation that Congress enacted was the Dodd-Frank Wall Street Reform and Consumer Protection Act of 2010, Title III, Pub. L. No. 111–203 (2010) (Dodd-Frank Act). The Dodd-Frank Act changed the landscape of real estate finance. It imposed regulations to reform the financial industry and established new governmental agencies responsible for overseeing lending to reduce the likelihood of future predatory lending that was a factor in causing the subprime loan crisis. Significantly, the future of the Dodd-Frank Act is unclear as one of President Donald Trump's campaign promises was to repeal major portions of it. Whether President Trump is successful in his efforts will unfold in the future. However, one thing that is certain is that the government will continue to enact laws to regulate the real estate financing process to deal with market conditions and specific problems.

CHAPTER 2

REAL ESTATE FINANCING DEVICES

I. MORTGAGE

A. IN GENERAL

The mortgage is the most common means of effectuating real estate financing. It is both relatively uncomplicated and flexible. The mortgage is between two individuals, the mortgagee/lender and the mortgagor. A mortgage can secure the mortgagor's debts or the debts of a third party if the mortgagor is willing to secure the debt with mortgagor's property. It can also secure an antecedent debt. Most states have a statutory mortgage form that may be expanded as the parties desire. In addition, because the mortgage is a time-tested financing device, the rights and obligations of the parties are generally well established within each state.

B. PURCHASE MONEY MORTGAGES

The purchase money mortgage is an important mortgage species. It has been traditionally defined as a mortgage taken by the seller of real estate to secure payment of part of the purchase price. For example, assume that an owner sells the owner's house to a purchaser for $100,000. The purchaser pays the owner $10,000 in cash and gives the owner a promissory note for $90,000 secured by a mortgage on the house. The mortgage is a traditional purchase money mortgage.

Today, in many jurisdictions, a purchase money mortgage arises whenever a mortgage is granted to secure a portion of the purchase price even if a third party is the mortgagee. *See, e.g.*, Idaho Code § 45–112 (2017) (defining a purchase money mortgage as any mortgage given for the price of real property); Wis. Stat. § 708.09 (2017) (providing that a purchase money mortgage is any mortgage given to a vendor or a 3rd party on the purchase of real estate). *Accord* Md. Code Ann., Real Property § 7–104 (2017); Miss. Code Ann. § 89–1–45 (2017).

> *Illustration*: Assume that a seller sells land to a purchaser for $80,000. The purchaser has only $20,000 cash, so the purchaser obtains a $60,000 loan from a mortgagee. The purchaser grants the mortgagee a mortgage on the land to secure repayment of the $60,000 loan. The mortgage is generally considered a purchase money mortgage.

It is necessary to identify the purchase money mortgage for two reasons: (1) it is the type of mortgage transaction with which the home-buying public is most familiar; and (2) it receives a preferred lien priority position.

C. TAX CONSIDERATIONS

There are significant federal income tax considerations related to mortgage loans. For example, as a general rule, an individual is prohibited from deducting personal interest. IRC § 163(h)(1) (2017). However, a mortgagor may take an income tax deduction for interest paid on the mortgage loan if the interest is "qualified residence interest." IRC § 163(h)(2)(D) (2017). Qualified residence interest includes mortgage loans on the acquisition or improvement of real property up to $1,000,000. IRC § 163(h)(3)(B) (2017). It also includes home equity loans and lines of credit secured by the residence up to $100,000. IRC § 163(h)(3)(C) (2017). A mortgagor is only able to deduct interest on mortgage loans as an itemized deduction on a Schedule A of the Form 1040 if the mortgaged property is used for personal purposes only. With respect to the mortgagee, the mortgagee must report the interest received as income and it is taxed at the ordinary income rates. *See* IRC § 61(a)(4).

In commercial situations, however, tax matters are often of paramount concern. Indeed, certain financing devices discussed in this chapter were developed in large part as vehicles for tax planning. Given these circumstances, it is imperative that one entering any real estate financing transaction ascertain its tax consequences at the outset. Many tax consequences will be discussed in this book, including this chapter. Chapter 13 is devoted to advanced tax issues.

II. DEED OF TRUST

The deed of trust is a kind of mortgage used in many jurisdictions. It is a tripartite arrangement in which a landowner-borrower (mortgagor) transfers an interest in land to a trustee as security for the repayment of a loan or the performance of another obligation owed a lender (mortgagee). The chief practical distinction between the deed of trust and the standard mortgage is the manner of enforcement available if the borrower fails to repay the underlying obligation. The deed of trust provides for foreclosure by power of sale; the standard mortgage may or may not do so. Indeed, the deed of trust is popular in most states in which out-of-court sale is the prevalent method of foreclosure.

The deed of trust is generally treated as a mortgage with a power-of-sale provision. The principles of mortgage law discussed in this book, therefore, generally govern the deed of trust.

III. EQUITABLE MORTGAGES

An equitable mortgage arises whenever a court finds that an apparent non-security transaction is in reality a security arrangement. It arises where an owner intends to grant a party a mortgage but actually transfers legal title to the party. Sutter v. U.S. Nat'l Bank, 665 F.3d 722, 728 (6th Cir. 2012) (recognizing equitable mortgages but not finding one because of the doctrine of unclean hands). In addition, an equitable mortgage may be created when an executed mortgage is invalid for some reason. In Cox v. Countrywide Home Loans, Inc., 408 B.R. 407 (D. Kan. 2009), the court determined that there was an equitable mortgage on a couple's homestead even though the wife's name was forged. Id. at 418–19. The court's conclusion was based on the fact that the lenders had performed part of the contract and were not aware of the forgery and the couple accepted the proceeds and used them to refinance a home mortgage. Id. at 419. Further, the couple would have benefitted from a windfall without the equitable mortgage. Id.

Many situations exist where an equitable mortgage will be created. Thus, the longstanding maxim: "If a transaction resolves itself into a security, whatever may be its form and whatever name the parties may choose to give it, it is, in equity, a mortgage." Capital Lumber Co. v. Saunders, 26 Idaho 408, 414 (1914). Those transactions that commonly spawn equitable mortgages are treated in this section.

A. ABSOLUTE DEED GIVEN AS SECURITY

A lender occasionally will require a borrower to convey property to the lender upon the understanding that the lender will hold title as security for the debt. This type of transaction is used by some lenders to eliminate the debtor's equity of redemption and thereby avoid foreclosure. If, however, the debtor can prove that a deed absolute on its face was intended as a security device, courts will find that an equitable mortgage was created and give the debtor an equity of redemption. Given the robust public policy against irredeemable mortgages, courts generally do not consider the parol evidence rule and the Statute of Frauds to be obstacles to this result.

The problem of proof is, however, a difficult matter. The key is the intention of the parties, a question upon which direct testimony is invariably at odds. The courts, therefore, apply a facts and circumstances test looking at the totality of facts. In applying this test, courts look at various objective factors that include: the parties' prior negotiations, their relative bargaining positions, the adequacy of consideration, and who is in possession of the property. *See, e.g.,* Patterson v. Grace, 661 N.E. 2d 580, 585 (Ind. App. 1996) (finding an equitable mortgage after applying factors); Thomas v. Gansen, 872 N.W. 2d 409 (Iowa 2015) (applying the factors but concluding that there was not an equitable mortgage). Courts usually require clear and convincing evidence of intent to create a security arrangement.

> *Illustration*: An owner who desperately needs money, asks a lender a mortgage loan. The lender offers to give the owner $30,000 if the owner will deed the owner's land worth $50,000 to the lender. The owner agrees upon the condition the owner can continue to occupy the property without paying rent. The transaction is consummated. One year later the owner tenders $30,000 plus interest to the lender and requests a deed to the property. The lender refuses, claiming complete ownership. The owner's financial difficulty, the owner's request for a loan, the amount the owner received compared to the value of the property, and the owner's continued possession indicate that the parties intended the absolute deed as security for a loan. The transaction, therefore, constitutes an equitable mortgage, and the owner can redeem the land by paying the debt.

B. CONDITIONAL SALE

The conditional sale consists of an absolute deed coupled with an option or contract to repurchase. Again, the issue is whether the transaction was intended as a security device. The same evidentiary factors considered in conjunction with the absolute deed are relevant here, but certain courts are more receptive to claims that a conditional sale arrangement was crafted for security purposes.

> *Illustration*: An owner of a house worth \$100,000, asks a lender for a mortgage loan. The lender requires and receives a deed to the house. The lender gives the owner \$60,000, and the parties enter a contract in which the owner agrees to repurchase the house for \$70,000 within one year. The character of the negotiations between the owner and the lender, the inadequacy of consideration, and the owner's obligation to repurchase indicate that this conditional sale was intended as a security transaction. Even if the owner fails to repurchase within the time period specified, courts will view the arrangement as an equitable mortgage and grant the owner an equity of redemption that the lender can cutoff only by foreclosure.

C. NEGATIVE PLEDGE

A lender may require a borrower to agree not to encumber or convey certain of the borrower's realty until a specified loan is repaid. This type of transaction is called a negative pledge. It has been employed when the property in question is already encumbered and the lender either legally cannot take a second mortgage or chooses not to do so as a matter of customer relations. A negative pledge also has been utilized by lenders who, for local procedural reasons, wish to have the alternative of selecting between secured and unsecured creditor status depending upon which position is more advantageous from a debt collection standpoint.

The generally accepted view is that a negative pledge does not create an equitable mortgage. The affirmative intent to create a security interest cannot reasonably be inferred from a negative promise. There is, however, some authority to the contrary.

> *Illustration*: An owner owns a house. The owner obtains a loan from a bank. The bank does not take a mortgage on the owner's house, but wants the owner to retain the house free from other liens so that the owner's general financial position is not weakened. Consequently, the bank makes the loan upon the condition that the owner not convey or further encumber the house until the loan is repaid. If the owner conveys or further encumbers the house, the bank may have the right to declare its entire loan due, but it has no lien to foreclose. Courts generally refuse to impose an equitable mortgage in the bank's favor on the ground there was no intent to create a security device. *But see* Coast Bank v. Minderhout, 38 Cal.Rptr. 505 (Cal.1964) (holding that under existing circumstances equitable mortgage arose from negative pledge).

D. VENDOR'S AND VENDEE'S LIENS

Breach of a real estate contract may give rise to a lien in favor of either the vendor or the vendee as equity requires. An equitable lien generally may be imposed for the benefit of a vendor who passed legal title to the vendee, but did not receive the entire purchase price. In some states, however, the vendor's lien is not recognized unless it was expressly reserved. An equitable lien also may be imposed in favor of a vendee who paid part of the purchase price, but did not receive title because the vendor breached the contract. In either case, the lien is unlike the other types of equitable mortgages discussed in this section in that it arises by operation of law to prevent injustice, not by virtue of the judicially determined intent of the parties.

Illustration: A seller owns a parcel of land. The seller enters a binding real estate contract to convey the land to a purchaser for consideration of $10,000 in cash and a $5,000 promissory note payable thirty day after closing. The purchaser gives the seller the cash and the note; the seller deeds the land to the purchaser. At the end of thirty days, the purchaser fails to pay the note. In most states, the seller receives a $5,000 equitable vendor's lien on the land. In some jurisdictions, however, the seller does not receive a lien unless it was expressly reserved.

Illustration: A seller owns a parcel of land. The seller enters a binding real estate contract to convey the land to a purchaser. The purchaser makes a $3,000 down payment. The seller breaches the contract by not having a marketable title as agreed. The purchaser has a $3,000 equitable vendee's lien on the property.

IV. INSTALLMENT LAND CONTRACT

A. TRADITIONAL CONTRACT APPROACH

In a country where buying on credit is a way of life, it is to be expected that a financing device providing for the long-term installment purchase of land would be developed. The installment land contract, referred to in some states as a contract for deed, fits the bill. It gives the purchaser possession of the land immediately, but allows the purchaser to pay the sale price in monthly installments over a number of years. The seller, on the other hand, is not obligated to convey legal title until all payments have been made. Moreover, the installment land contract features a forfeiture provision to the effect that upon default the seller may recover possession, keep payments received as liquidated damages, and retain title free from any rights the purchaser had under the contract. Note that this type of agreement for the sale of land differs markedly from purchase money mortgages, which immediately convey title to the mortgagor.

Because the parties to an installment land contract are in essentially the same situation as a mortgagor and a mortgagee, one might logically conclude that the forfeiture provision is really an illegal attempt to clog the purchaser's equity of redemption. This conclusion would be correct if courts applied mortgage law to this financing device. The installment land contract, however, developed under contract law, where freedom of contract was the guiding principle. For this reason, the installment land contract was enforced as written, forfeiture provision and all.

Treatment of the installment land contract as a contract, not a mortgage, caused it to become a popular means of real estate financing. It remains a viable arrangement in many areas of the country. Most jurisdictions still recognize the traditional contract approach, at least in limited circumstances.

Under the traditional view, the installment land contract seller enjoys the right of forfeiture—the authority to repossess the land upon default and to keep all payments made. Foreclosure of the purchaser's interest is not required. Purchasers, undeterred by the possibility of forfeiture, enter installment land contracts primarily because a low down-payment is required and many costs associated with mortgage financing are avoided.

> *Illustration*: A seller owns land that a purchaser desires to purchase. Because mortgage-financing funds are scarce and the purchaser cannot make a large down payment, the purchaser is unable to obtain a purchase money mortgage loan from an institutional lender. The seller and purchaser, therefore, enter an installment land contract that provides for a twenty-year term with equal monthly payments of $100. The purchaser takes possession and makes payments for fifteen

years. Because the purchaser is ill and out of work, the purchaser misses the first two payments in the sixteenth year. The seller declares forfeiture. Under the traditional contract approach, the seller can terminate the purchaser's interest, regain possession, and keep the payments that the purchaser made ($18,000 out of the total $24,000 contract price).

B. PROTECTING PURCHASER

There is a strong judicial and legislative trend to devise methods of protecting the purchaser from the potential severity of the traditional contract approach to installment land contracts. Protection afforded purchasers has taken a variety of forms. In some jurisdictions, more than one protective method is employed.

1. Period-of-Grace Statutes

In certain states, statutes give the purchaser a specified amount of time to cure default before forfeiture can occur. Under these period-of-grace statutes, the seller typically is required to follow specific procedures for notifying the purchaser and terminating the purchaser's interest.

2. Compelling Equities View

Courts in a substantial number of states have demonstrated a willingness to examine individual installment land contracts to determine whether forfeiture is appropriate under the circumstances. This approach has been labeled the compelling equities view because forfeiture will be enforced unless the purchaser can establish reasons why it would be unjust to do so. In order to decide the appropriateness of the forfeiture in question, courts following the compelling equities view inquire into such matters as the extent of the default, the reason for default, and particularly the forfeiture involved in comparison to the contract price.

> *Illustration*: Assume the same facts as in the immediately preceding illustration. The default was slight, of recent origin, and not willful. Further, the amount to be forfeited was the lion's share (3/4s) of the contract price. Courts in states following the compelling equities view, therefore, would not enforce the forfeiture as written. The form of relief might vary; reinstating the contract upon the payment of the overdue installments, imposing a period of grace before forfeiture, or requiring foreclosure of the purchaser's interest are three likely possibilities.

3. Equitable Mortgage View

A few states recognize the installment land contract as a disguised mortgage and give purchasers an equity of redemption after default. *See, e.g.*, Mich. Comp. Laws § 600.5744(3) (2017) (providing a 90-day redemption period where vendee has paid less than 50% of purchase price and 6 months if vendee has paid 50% or more); *In re* Kingsmore, 295 B.R. 812, 818 (D. S.D. 2001) (stating that court of equity relieves vendee from forfeiture and providing redemption rights based on equitable considerations); Wis. Stat. Ann. § 846.30 (2017) (allowing a redemption period of seven days after the court determines that the vendor is entitled to a judgment of strict foreclosure).

This equitable mortgage view is significantly different from the compelling equities approach. All defaulting purchasers, not just those with substantial equities, are entitled to a foreclosure sale of their interest in the property. *See, e.g.,* Porter v. Bolen, 169 S.W. 3d 59, 64 (Ky. 2005) (stating that the vendor's remedy upon vendee's breach was foreclosure because there was no practical difference between a land contract and a purchase money mortgage).

4. Restitution

In some jurisdictions, the courts give defaulting purchasers restitution, the right to recover payments made under the installment land contract to the extent the payments exceed the seller's actual damages.

5. Waiver

Courts everywhere may employ the doctrine of waiver to grant relief to an installment land contract purchaser. A seller who has accepted late payments may be estopped to declare a forfeiture unless the seller gives reasonable notice of the intent to assert the seller's contract rights in future cases of default. *See, e.g.,* Freedman v. Cont'l Serv. Corp., 127 Ariz. 540, 622 P.2d 487, 490 (Ariz. Ct. App. 1980) (stating that Arizona's well-settled law requires the vendor to notify the buyer of the vendor's intention to declare forfeiture after the vendor previously waived strict performance of installment payments and must give the vendee reasonable time to make the late payments).

C. ENCUMBERING PURCHASER'S INTEREST

The purchaser under an installment land contract holds an interest in the land that may be encumbered. If the installment land contract purchaser mortgages the purchaser's interest and then defaults on the underlying installment land contract, controversy often arises between the seller and the mortgagee. Conflict centers on two issues. First, must the seller notify the mortgagee before terminating the purchaser's interest? Second, what are the mortgagee's rights after the purchaser's default?

With respect to the first issue, the general rule is that the mortgagee is entitled to notice of the impending termination of the purchaser's interest only if the seller has received notice of the mortgagee's encumbrance. Authority is split, however, as to when the seller is on notice of the mortgagee's interest. Some courts hold that the seller must have actual notice of the mortgage. These courts reason that recordation of the mortgage is not sufficient notice to the seller because recording statutes are designed to impart notice to subsequent purchasers, not prior interest holders. Other courts find that the seller need only have constructive notice of the mortgage. These courts conclude that recordation of the mortgage imparts such notice to the seller because the seller should check the records before extinguishing another's interest. This latter approach is closely analogous to the requirements imposed on a senior mortgagee who seeks to foreclose junior interest holders.

Assuming that the mortgagee is entitled to notice of the impending termination of the purchaser's interest, a question arises concerning the mortgagee's rights in the land. In a few states, the mortgagee apparently is permitted to pay the seller the balance of the contract price and take title to the property. This approach, however, unjustly enriches the mortgagee to the extent the value of the land exceeds the total amount remaining unpaid on the installment land contract and the mortgage. Courts in other jurisdictions treat the mortgagee as a second lienor of the fee and the seller as a first lienor. In these states, the mortgagee, therefore, may either: (1) pay off the seller and be subrogated to the seller's rights, thus becoming the holder of both the first and second liens on the property, or (2) force a sale of the property and satisfy the mortgage lien out of the sale proceeds that remain after the vendor's lien is satisfied. Under either alternative, the mortgagee is entitled to recover the value of its lien, but no more. This treatment of the seller and mortgagee as first and second lienors is consistent with the overall movement toward treating installment land contracts as mortgages and, hence, can be expected to gain support.

D. ENCUMBERING SELLER'S INTEREST

The installment land contract seller also holds an interest in the property that may be encumbered. This is commonly accomplished by the seller executing, as security for a loan, both an assignment of the right to receive payments under the contract and a mortgage on, or a conveyance of, the legal title that the seller retains. Sometimes the seller in an installment land contract only pledges as security the mere right to payments. Holders of these various kinds of security interests may insure priority over the seller's future lien creditors and bankruptcy trustee by filing a financing statement under Article 9 of the Uniform Commercial Code (UCC). Recording in the land records is neither required nor adequate to achieve this purpose.

V. GROUND LEASES AND OTHER FORMS OF LEASES

A. GROUND LEASE IN GENERAL

The lease plays an important part in real estate finance, particularly in the area of commercial development. Leases may be used in a variety of ways, frequently in conjunction with another financing device.

1. Fundamentals of Ground Leases

A ground lease is a long-term lease employed to acquire raw land for commercial development. One of the principal advantages to the lessee of a ground lease over the outright purchase is that no "up-front" capital is needed to acquire the land. The ground lessee may construct improvements on the property and take out a mortgage to finance the development.

The tenant under a typical ground lease is responsible for taxes, insurance, and maintenance. When a lease contains a provision of this type it is said to be a "net" lease because the rental income to the lessor is not reduced by payment of operating expenses. The landowner/ground lessor essentially becomes a passive investor. To illustrate a ground lease, assume that a developer desires to develop a shopping center on an owner's unimproved land. The developer and owner enter a ground lease for a sixty-year term. Other lease provisions are as follows: the developer will complete the shopping center within a certain time period; ground rent is not payable until the center is completed; the developer must pay all taxes, utilities, insurance, and maintenance on the property; hence, the developer has a net lease. If the developer breaches the lease, the owner may terminate the lease after properly evicting the ground lessee and take possession and ownership of the improvements.

Generally, a ground lease extends for many years. There are several reasons why the ground lease is long term. It is likely that the ground lessee is operating a business on the land. It is not financially prudent for the ground lessee to construct a building on someone else's land and run a business under a short-term lease. The lessee would not be able to recoup the lessee's construction costs. In addition, the lessee would need to find another place to operate the business. While the ground lessee owns the improvements on the land during the ground lease, at the end of the lease term all improvements belong to the owner of the land. Frequently, the ground lease includes an option to renew at the end of the lease and an option to buy the land.

2. Tax Considerations

Ordinarily, an owner is entitled to claim depreciation deductions to recover the cost of certain property over a period of time to account for wear, tear and exhaustion. *See* IRC § 167 (2017); IRC § 168 (2017). However, the owner is prohibited from claiming depreciation on unimproved land because land is not subject to wear and tear. Conversely, the Internal Revenue Code permits a person to claim a deduction for rental expenses provided that the property is used in a trade or business or for the production of income. *See* IRC § 162(a)(3) (2017); IRC § 212 (2017). Therefore, by structuring the transaction as a lease of the land rather than a sale of it, a ground lessee can convert a nondepreciable asset to one that generates a tax deduction. Chapter 13 provides a detailed discussion of depreciation rules.

The ground lessee is also able to claim depreciation on the improvements (the building) even though the lessee is only leasing the land. Finally, the landowner/ground lessor is required to include the rental income from the land in gross income. *See* IRC § 61(a)(5) (2017).

B. OTHER TYPES OF LEASES

1. Space Lease

The financial success of many developments depends upon the developer's ability to rent the store, apartment, or office space in the project. Space leases play such a significant role in the success of shopping centers and office buildings that permanent mortgage lenders generally require the developer to obtain space lease commitments from a number of substantial tenants before construction begins.

2. Acquisition Lease

In many instances, a business will utilize a long-term lease to acquire improved commercial property for expansion of its operations. Because this type of lease is employed as an alternative to the purchase or construction of new facilities, it is called an acquisition lease in these materials.

The attractions of an acquisition lease to the lessee are much the same as that of a ground lease: small front-end cash outlay and tax-deductible rental payments. These attractions, however, are somewhat stronger in the case of an acquisition lease because of the generally higher value of the leasehold being acquired.

An acquisition lease is usually a net lease and often contains an escalator clause that adjusts the amount of rent to keep pace with inflation. The Consumer Price Index maintained by the Department of Labor is an economic indicator frequently used to accomplish this result. An acquisition lease, of course, is not the only type of lease in which escalator clauses are found.

C. LEASEHOLD MORTGAGE

Typically, a ground lessee obtains mortgage financing to construct the improvements. The mortgage on this leasehold estate is known as a leasehold mortgage. Although the discussion of mortgage law in this book concerns fee mortgages, it is generally applicable to leasehold mortgages. However, additional issues arise when a mortgagee accepts a leasehold as security.

1. Nature of Security

Leasehold mortgage financing involves an inherent drawback; the mortgagee's security interest is subject to the rights of the lessor/owner. Consequently, many mortgagees will not make a leasehold mortgage loan unless the ground lessor allows the land to be encumbered by the mortgage in case the ground lessee defaults on the leasehold mortgage. The ground lessor may be hesitant to do so because this encumbrance impairs the lessor's ability to borrow on the reversion and subjects the fee to sale upon the lessee's default. Nevertheless, important financial factors may cause the lessor to take this step. Encumbering the fee usually enables the lessee to obtain financing that is otherwise unavailable. Hence, the lessor may demand higher rent and receive property of greater value at the end of the lease term.

2. Lease Provisions

When the lease and leasehold mortgage are successive steps in one financing package, the lease is drafted to meet the requirements of the proposed mortgagee. If, however, the lease predates the mortgage negotiations, it usually is amended as specified by the mortgagee. In either case, leasehold mortgage financing presents unique problems. The areas of greatest concern to the mortgagee are treated in the following subsections of this chapter. Discussion of many other matters important to the mortgagee is outside the purview of this work.

a. Term

The lease term should be at least as long as the mortgage term; otherwise the security will cease to exist before the mortgage debt is paid. In other words, if the lease ends before the mortgage term, the leasehold mortgagee relinquishes the right to foreclose on the leasehold estate and can only pursue a deficiency action, if allowed.

b. Transfer

As a general rule, the lessee may encumber, assign, and sublet the leasehold unless the lease or a statute provides otherwise. The lessee's ability to encumber the estate is obviously essential to the creation of a leasehold mortgage. The lease, therefore, should not limit the lessee's rights in this regard and preferably should specifically permit the lessee to mortgage the leasehold. Also, because the mortgagee may acquire the leasehold upon foreclosure, the lease should not impose restrictions on assignment or subleasing, at least as against the mortgagee.

c. *Default*

Termination of the lease extinguishes the leasehold mortgage. Thus, the mortgagee usually requires that it receive notice of and the right to cure the tenant's defaults under the lease. Conversely, if the ground lessee defaults on the leasehold mortgage (presuming that the leasehold mortgagee does not have a mortgage on the land), the leasehold mortgagee steps into the shoes of the ground lessee and must pay rent to the landowner/ground lessor. At the end of the lease term, the leasehold mortgagee has no rights to the improvements and relinquishes all rights to the property. To avoid this result, the leasehold mortgagee frequently requires its mortgage to encumber the land as well. If so, the leasehold mortgagee has the right to foreclose the improvements and land.

D. SALE AND LEASEBACK

The lease also constitutes part of an important financing vehicle known as the sale and leaseback. The seller/lessee conveys its ownership interest in the property but can continue to possess or lease the property under the leaseback. This financing technique is enormously complex in its many variations. This book discusses some of the fundamental concepts related to sale and leaseback transactions.

A typical sale and leaseback is structured as follows: the owner of improved commercial property sells it to an investor who leases the property right back to the seller on a long-term, net basis. The reasons behind this rather puzzling transaction lie in the intricacies of business finance and federal income tax law.

The essential business finance factors are not difficult to comprehend. The owner of the property can obtain more capital from the sale and leaseback arrangement than from mortgage financing. Although mortgage loans usually are subject to loan-to-value limits, the sale aspect of the sale and leaseback may produce almost 100% of current fair market value. Investors are willing to provide such financing because they generally receive a higher rate of return from a sale and leaseback than from a mortgage loan. Furthermore, the return is not limited by usury statutes, which apply only to loan transactions.

The form of the sale and leaseback may not be given legal effect if factors indicate that the transaction is actually a disguised mortgage. Factors that tend to indicate that the transaction is really a disguised mortgage are similar to those noted in the section of this chapter on equitable mortgages. They include the following: the parties have not dealt at arm's length; the sale price is inadequate; the transaction, if a mortgage loan, would be usurious; and the seller/lessee is given an option to purchase for a nominal amount.

If the true substance of the sale and leaseback transaction is a disguised mortgage, disastrous consequences may result. For example, a question of usury may arise. In addition, upon default the investor must terminate the "lessee's" interest in the property by utilizing foreclosure procedures, rather than by declaring forfeiture under the lease and seeking summary eviction.

Chapter 13 discusses the tax consequences of a sale and leaseback transaction, including the principles to determine whether it is a disguised mortgage and tax consequences if it is indeed a disguised mortgage.

VI. MEZZANINE LOAN

Although not a mortgage arrangement itself, a mezzanine loan may be linked with mortgage financing. A lending institution may make a loan secured by equity in an entity that is the remote owner of mortgaged realty via its ownership of the mortgagor. Such a mezzanine loan, situated higher than the equity and lower than the mortgage in general terms of priority, has the potential of producing more financing than is possible through a second mortgage loan.

CHAPTER 3
MORTGAGED PROPERTY

I. MORTGAGEABLE INTERESTS

A. GENERAL

Any transferable interest in realty may be mortgaged. Thus, a fee simple, joint tenancy interest, leasehold, life estate, reversion, and remainder are all mortgageable interests. It is important to note that the mortgage is to the extent of the mortgagor's interest in the mortgaged property. For example, if the mortgagor possesses a life estate interest in real estate and grants a mortgage to a bank, the security is on the life estate only. Hence, if the bank forecloses and is the highest bidder at the foreclosure sale, the bank has a life estate for the life of the mortgagor (pur autre vie). Upon the mortgagor's death, the bank's interest passes to the holder of the future interest by operation of law.

With respect to joint tenancy interests, joint tenants are entitled to survivorship rights. This means that once a joint tenant dies, that tenant's interest passes to the surviving joint tenants by operation of law. If a mortgagor owns a joint tenancy interest in real property and grants a mortgage to a bank, there is a question of whether the mortgage severs the joint tenancy and converts it to a tenancy in common. A tenancy in common interest is devisable, descendible and inheritable. In a title theory jurisdiction, the joint tenancy is severed when a mortgage is granted by a joint tenant to a mortgagee. This means that the mortgaging joint tenant no longer has survivorship rights. To illustrate this concept, assume that a mortgagor owns an apartment building as a joint tenant with a brother and sister. The mortgagor grants a mortgage to a bank. In a title theory jurisdiction, the mortgagor's joint tenancy interest is severed; therefore, the mortgagor is a tenant in common with the brother and sister who continue to hold their interests in the building as joint tenants. If the brother dies, his interest passes automatically to the sister. The sister now owns a 2/3 interest in the building and is a tenant in common with the mortgagor who continues to have a 1/3 interest in the building. If the mortgagor defaults on the mortgage and there is a foreclosure sale, the purchaser at the sale receives a 1/3 interest in the building as a tenant in common with the sister.

In a lien theory jurisdiction, the joint tenancy is not severed when the mortgagor grants a mortgage to the bank. This is the majority approach. Severance occurs when the mortgagor's interest is conveyed to the highest bidder at the foreclosure sale. However, if the mortgagor dies before foreclosure and satisfaction of the mortgage loan, there is a question whether the mortgage continues to encumber the apartment building. Most jurisdictions that have addressed the issue have concluded that the mortgage does not survive the mortgagor's death. *See, e.g.*, People v. Nogarr, 164 Cal. App. 2d 591, 594 (1958) (concluding that the mortgage was a lien that did not sever the joint tenancy but when the mortgagor/joint tenant died, the surviving tenant did not take the property subject to the mortgage); Harms v. Sprague, 105 Ill. 2d 215, 224–225 (1984) (holding that the mortgage neither severed the joint tenancy nor survived the mortgagor's death); Smith v. Bank of Am., N.A., 103 A.D. 3d 21, 27 (N.Y. App. Div. 2012) (finding that a mortgage was a lien that didn't survive the death of the mortgaging joint tenant); CitiMortgage, Inc. v. Brown, 45 N.E. 3d 258, 261 (Ohio Ct. App. 2015) (concluding that there wasn't a severance, but the mortgage was extinguished upon the death of the mortgaging joint tenant). *But see* Wis. Stat. Ann. § 700.24 (West 2017) (providing that the joint tenancy is not severed but the surviving joint tenants take the property subject to the mortgage).

If the bank forecloses on the mortgage and the mortgagor's interest is sold at a foreclosure sale while the mortgagor is still alive, it is irrelevant whether the jurisdiction follows the lien theory or the title theory. In both jurisdictions, the purchaser becomes a tenant in common with the brother and sister who continue to own their interests as joint tenants.

The discussion in this book presumes a fee mortgage unless otherwise indicated.

B. MORTGAGING SEPARATE INTERESTS IN SAME LAND

Two or more interests in the same real property may be mortgaged independently. For example, if real property is own concurrently by two co-tenants, they can both encumber their individual interest with a mortgage. If one of them defaults and the mortgage is foreclosed, the purchaser of that co-tenant's interest at the foreclosure sale will become a co-tenant of the real property. The same principle applies in other situations.

> *Illustration*: A landlord leases a farm to a tenant for a twenty-year term. The landlord mortgages the reversion in the fee to a bank. The tenant mortgages the leasehold to a credit union. Each mortgage is a valid lien on a separate interest in the farm. A tenant frequently grants a mortgagee a leasehold mortgage when the tenant leases the land and takes out a mortgage to construct improvements on the land.

C. DESCRIPTION

The mortgagee usually does not take possession of the mortgaged property, at least not before default. Thus, the mortgagee generally may impart notice of its lien only by recording the mortgage. It is, therefore, imperative that the mortgaged realty be described accurately in the mortgage. The description of the mortgaged property in a mortgage is consistent with the description required in deeds. *In re* 1025 Assoc., Inc., 106 B.R. 805, 809 (Del. 1989).

The validity of a mortgage is determined under state law. For example, under Ohio law, the validity and extent of a mortgage is determined under contract law in which the intent of the parties is effectuated. Field v. Wells Fargo Home Mortgage (*In re* Jared), 474 B.R. 521, 525 (Ohio 2011). If the language is ambiguous, the court will consider extrinsic evidence, and it is considered unambiguous if the contract has a "definite legal meaning." Id. According to *Field*, under Ohio law, a complete legal description of the mortgaged property in the mortgage is not required. Id. at 526. In the case, the mortgage was ambiguous because it incorrectly identified the lot number of the mortgaged property but properly identified its address and parcel number. Id. at 523. Hence, extrinsic evidence needed to be considered to determine the parties' intent. Id. at 525. The court reasoned that if Ohio law required only a correct non-legal description, then the Bankruptcy Court did not believe that the legal description with an incorrect lot number rendered the mortgage defective. Id. at 526.

II. EXTENT OF MORTGAGE COVERAGE

The mortgage lien may attach to certain property not specifically described in the mortgage.

A. AFTER-ACQUIRED PROPERTY

The mortgagee may seek to extend the mortgage lien to land the mortgagor subsequently obtains. The mortgagee usually may achieve this result by inserting an after-acquired property clause in the mortgage. The Restatement defines an after-acquired property clause as "any language in a mortgage that purports to be effective against any other parcel of real estate that mortgagor subsequently acquires." Restatement (Third) of Property, Mortgages § 7.5(a) (1997). As a general rule, the clause creates an equitable lien on all real estate the mortgagor acquires after the execution of the mortgage.

> *Illustration*: A mortgagor owns Blackacre. The mortgagor borrows funds from a mortgagee. The mortgagor executes a note and a mortgage on Blackacre to the mortgagee. The mortgage contains an after-acquired property clause. The mortgagor purchases Whiteacre. An equitable lien in favor of the mortgagee generally attaches to Whiteacre upon its acquisition by the mortgagor.

The predominant theory underlying the enforcement of after-acquired property clauses is that the mortgagee is entitled to specific performance of the parties' contractual arrangement. Some states, however, apparently restrict the application of after-acquired property clauses to property functionally related to that initially encumbered.

After-acquired property clauses may be included in corporate mortgages to make all the company's ever-changing real and personal property collateral for the loan. Subject to certain qualifications, personal property as well as realty is covered by an after-acquired property clause. However, the coverage of personalty under such a clause, and related personal property issues, are beyond the scope of this work.

A mortgage containing an after-acquired property clause is outside the chain of title of real estate subsequently obtained by the mortgagor. Hence, purchasers or lienors of such real estate from the mortgagor generally will not be on record notice of the mortgagee's equitable lien. The mortgagee, therefore, must take further action to preserve the priority of its lien. It may by mortgage provision require the mortgagor to execute recordable mortgage amendments specifically describing after-acquired land as it is obtained.

B. EASEMENTS

An easement is a nonpossessory interest in another person's real property and permits the holder of the easement to use that person's property. The benefit of an easement is either appurtenant or in gross. An in gross easement benefits a person. Common examples of in gross easements include easements granted to utility companies and railroads. If the easement is appurtenant, it benefits land, known as the dominant estate. An appurtenant easement follows the land or runs with the land. It is a part of the title to the land, and automatically passes to the new owners of the land even if they don't have notice of it.

If the dominant estate is encumbered with a mortgage, appurtenant easements become a part of the mortgaged property. Thus, they are automatically subject to the mortgage lien irrespective of whether they arise before or after the execution of the mortgage. If the mortgagor has a right of way easement across a neighbor's property and a mortgagee forecloses its mortgage, the purchaser of the property at the foreclosure sale is automatically entitled to use the right of way easement.

The land burdened by the easement is known as the servient estate. For the burden to run with the land and be binding on a subsequent purchaser for value, it must be determined that it was intended for the easement to run with the land and that the purchaser had notice of the easement. If the purchaser of the property at the foreclosure sale is a bona fide purchaser without notice of the easement, the purchaser does not take the property subject to the mortgage. Hence, the easement is extinguished.

An easement is also extinguished under the merger doctrine. Merger is where the owner of the dominant estate acquires the servient estate. However, in WT Props., LLC, v. Leganieds, LLC, 195 Wash. App. 344 (2016), the court determined that the merger doctrine was inapplicable because it would prejudice the lender, an innocent third party. Id. at 349. In the case, the debtor reserved a right of way and utilities easement across property known as "Access Strip." Id at 347. Subsequently, the debtor granted a deed of trust to the lender. Id. at 348. The deed of trust expressly granted the lender a security interest in all easements related to the property subject to the deed of trust. Id. at 350–351. The debtor then acquired Access Strip; hence, the debtor owned both the dominant and servient estate. Id. The debtor defaulted on the deed of trust, and there was a nonjudicial foreclosure sale in which the purchaser acquired the property at the foreclosure sale. Id. at 348.

Under the general merger rule, the easement would have been extinguished upon the debtor's ownership of both the servient and dominant estates. However, because the lender was an "innocent person," the court determined that it would have prejudiced the lender. Id. at 351. The court noted that it was irrelevant that the lender rather than the purchaser was the innocent person and that the lender wasn't a party to the action. Id. at 352. Finally, the court noted that the innocent third person exception was recognized by other courts in the state of Washington and other "respected authorities." Id. at 352. Therefore, the easement did not terminate under the merger doctrine.

C. FIXTURES

A fixture is an item of tangible personal property that becomes realty by its attachment to land with the intent it remains permanently affixed. The fixture concept presents several real estate finance problems.

The first issue is whether the item in controversy is a fixture. If it is a fixture, the item constitutes part of the mortgaged land and is subject to the mortgage lien without additional description, regardless of whether it became part of the realty before or after the execution of the mortgage. If the item is not a fixture, it is not part of the mortgaged land and hence, is not subject to the mortgage lien unless specifically covered in the mortgage. Most mortgage transactions involve no controversy with respect to identifying fixtures. For example, the parties generally agree that a building on the property is covered by the mortgage. Moveable articles, however, present troublesome questions that should be resolved by the parties at the time the mortgage is negotiated.

Even if the item in question is found to be a fixture subject to the mortgage, a second problem arises. The mortgagee must insure that the mortgage constitutes a first lien on the fixture. This issue is treated in Chapter 10 which deals with lien priorities.

Another issue is the mortgagor's liability for removal of fixtures. During the Great Recession, it was widely recognized that countless mortgagors removed fixtures from their homes during the foreclosure process. This included the removal of countertops, toilets, cabinets, faucets and light fixtures. In People v. March, 499 Mich. 389 (2016), the Supreme Court of Michigan considered whether a mortgagor committed criminal larceny by removing fixtures from the home after the foreclosure sale but before the statutory redemption period had ended. Id. at 392. The mortgagor removed several fixtures, including kitchen cabinets and countertops, doors, a furnace, a hot water tank and duct work. Id. at 394–395. Because the mortgagor was considered the owner of the home and had rightful possession during the redemption period, the court determined that the mortgagor did not commit larceny which required the mortgagor to take property belonging to another. Id. at 421–422. However, the court determined that the purchaser could pursue a civil action for damages resulting from the mortgagor's removal of the fixtures during the redemption period. Id. at 417.

D. CONDEMNATION AWARDS

Under the 5th Amendment to the Constitution, the government must pay just compensation to an owner if the government condemns or takes property for a public purpose. For example, if the government wants to build a highway on private property, the government is entitled to take the property through eminent domain. If all or part of the mortgaged property is taken by eminent domain, the mortgagee's lien attaches to the condemnation award (just compensation) on the theory that the award is a substitute for the realty. City of Orange Township v. Empire Mortgage Services, Inc., 341 N.J. Super. 216, 221 (2001). When all the mortgaged property is taken, the mortgagee is immediately entitled to satisfy the underlying obligation out of the award. Id. When only part of the mortgaged property is taken, authorities differ regarding how much of the award the mortgagee should receive. Thus, the issue of condemnation is often the subject of extensive negotiation and mortgage provision.

Even with a condemnation provision in the mortgage loan documents, issues still arise. In construing these provisions, courts will apply their plain meaning. For example, in *City of Orange Township*, the loan documents contained a condemnation clause that condemnation proceeds would be paid to satisfy the mortgage loan, "whether or not then due" and any excess payments would be paid to the mortgagor. Id. at 224. A city declared a taking of the mortgagor's property that was subject to a $50,000 mortgage loan at a 13.5% interest rate.

Id. at 219. After the city estimated the appraised value of the property, it deposited \$50,000 in condemnation proceeds with the court that paid only 5.5% interest while commissioners examined and appraised the property. Id. at 219–220. The mortgagor did not make any additional mortgage payments after the city deposited the proceeds. Id. After it was determined that the property was appraised at \$75,000, the city deposited an additional \$25,000; but, the mortgagee did not immediately file an order seeking the proceeds. Id. at 220. Under the loan documents, the mortgagee was entitled to withdraw the condemnation proceeds before final judgment. Id. at 228. The mortgagor argued that the mortgagee would have been unjustly enriched by not withdrawing the proceeds and collecting 13.5% interest and fees from the mortgagor. Id. at 223. In deciding in favor of the mortgagor, the court looked at the clear and unambiguous condemnation provision in the loan documents that allowed the mortgagee to withdraw the proceeds. The court concluded that it would be "inequitable and unfair" to allow the mortgagee to fail to withdraw the proceeds and keep receiving an extra 8% in interest payments from the mortgagor. Id. at 227–228.

E. INSURANCE PROCEEDS

A casualty insurance policy is a personal indemnification contract. Insurance proceeds generally are not considered to be a substitute for the destroyed property. The mortgagee, therefore, has no interest in the proceeds of a policy obtained by the mortgagor unless the policy specifically insures the interests of both parties.

Mortgages commonly provide that the mortgagor must insure the mortgaged property for the benefit of both the mortgagor and the mortgagee. The mortgagee's interest may be covered by the addition of a clause to the mortgagor's policy. Two types of clauses are used to accomplish this result—the standard mortgage clause and the loss payable or open mortgage clause. The standard mortgagee clause is preferred by lenders because the mortgagee thereby receives an independent right of recovery against the insurer. This right continues even if the mortgagor voids the mortgagor's coverage by violating the terms of the policy. On the other hand, the mortgagee's rights under a loss payable clause are derived from the mortgagor and are lost if the mortgagor negates the mortgagor's coverage by breaching the policy.

When the parties are both insured as required by the mortgage and loss occurs, controversy may arise regarding whether the insurance proceeds should be applied to reconstruction of the premises or to payment of the mortgage debt. When the mortgage is silent on this issue, the generally accepted view is that the mortgagee may choose between these alternatives. There is, however, some authority to the contrary, which holds that under certain circumstances insurance proceeds must be used to rebuild. *See* Starkman v. Sigmond, 446 A.2d 1249 (N.J.Super.Ch.1982).

The application of insurance proceeds often is specifically covered in the mortgage. Sometimes the mortgage provides for rebuilding if certain conditions are met. On other occasions, the mortgage gives the mortgagee the option to use the proceeds for rebuilding or for payment of the debt. Courts generally enforce these clauses as written. However, one court refused to recognize a lender's right to apply proceeds to the debt under an "option" clause where the security was not impaired and the loan payments were current. It found that "good faith" and "fair dealing" required use of the funds for reconstruction. Schoolcraft v. Ross, 146 Cal.Rptr. 57 (Cal.App.1978).

III. WASTE OF MORTGAGED PROPERTY

A. DOCTRINE OF WASTE

Once the mortgagee has accepted the real estate as adequate security for the debt, it is concerned, of course, that the mortgagor maintains the mortgaged premises so that the property does not decrease in value. The mortgagor's duties in this regard are generally governed by the doctrine of waste, the principle that prohibits a lawful possessor from physically damaging or destroying the property occupied.

B. MORTGAGEE'S REMEDIES FOR WASTE

When the mortgagor commits waste, the mortgagee generally may pursue one or more of the following courses of action: seek damages, request an injunction, commence foreclosure proceedings.

1. Damages

In title theory states, the mortgagor is treated as a tenant liable for common law waste and the mortgagee is viewed as fictional legal titleholder who can recover actual damages to the realty either before or at foreclosure. In lien theory states, the mortgagor, as owner of the mortgaged property, cannot commit common law waste. That doctrine applies only to acts committed by rightful possessors such as life tenants, lessees, and concurrent owners. Although in lien theory jurisdictions the mortgagee may not recover damages to the real estate, it may recover damages for the impairment of its security interest. Authorities, however, differ as to what constitutes impairment and whether an action for damages may be brought before foreclosure.

2. Injunction

In all jurisdictions, a mortgagee may obtain an injunction against waste when the mortgagor causes the mortgaged realty to diminish in value to the extent that the mortgagee's security is impaired. It is generally agreed that impairment in this case occurs when the property depreciates in value to a point at which the margin between the value of the real estate and the amount of the mortgage debt is less than prudent lenders normally require.

> *Illustration*: A mortgagor owns land worth \$11,000. The mortgagor mortgages the property

to a mortgagee to secure an $8,000 promissory note. The mortgagor cuts timber on the land that reduces it in value to $10,000. Assuming that mortgage lenders generally will not make loans in excess of 80% of the value of the mortgaged property, the mortgagee may enjoin the mortgagor from cutting more timber.

3. Foreclosure

Mortgages commonly provide that waste is an event of default and therefore, a basis for acceleration and foreclosure.

CHAPTER 4
UNDERLYING OBLIGATION

I. NECESSITY FOR UNDERLYING OBLIGATION

A mortgage is only security. It cannot exist without an underlying obligation. For example, in Koster v. Wingard, 50 Wash.2d 855 (1957), the appellant had previously been in the fish business but did not have the financial resources to return to the industry. Id. at 856. He informed the respondents about four partially completed fishing boats and proposed that if they bought and completed then, he would purchase them when he was financially able to do so. Id. The appellants purchased and completed the boats. Id. Three years later, the appellant claimed to have an equitable mortgage in the fishing boats. Id. at 855. The court held that there was no mortgage on the boats because there wasn't a debt, and a mortgage could not exist without a debt. Id. at 857.

The Appellate Court of Connecticut in Amresco New England II, L.P. v. Colossale, 774 A.2d 1083 (Conn. App. 2001), set forth two widely recognized rules pertaining to the relationship between the mortgage and underlying obligation. First, a mortgage cannot survive the discharge of the debt. Id. at 1087. Second, the mortgage follows the debt or underlying obligation. Id. These principles apply whether the jurisdiction follows the lien, intermediate or title theory of mortgages.

There is no requirement that the mortgagor or anyone else be personally liable on the underlying obligation or debt. *See, e.g.*, Bedian v. Cohn, 10 Ill.App.2d 116, 118 (1956) (stating that a mortgage cannot exist without a debt but it is enforceable even if the mortgagor is not personally liability on the note). A mortgage transaction in which no person or institution has liability is known as a "nonrecourse" or "in rem" mortgage loan. If a mortgagor takes out a nonrecourse loan and grants a mortgage to the mortgagee, the mortgagee's only remedy in the event of default is to foreclose. However, the mortgage is valid because a "real" obligation supports it.

> *Illustration*: A mortgagor executes a promissory note and a mortgage to a mortgagee. The mortgagor conveys the mortgaged property to a purchaser "subject to" the mortgage. The purchaser does not assume personal responsibility to pay the note. The mortgagee then releases the mortgagor from liability, but retains its rights under the mortgage. The mortgage continues unaffected by this transaction even though no one is personally liable on the note.

II. FORM OF OBLIGATION

A mortgage may secure any obligation that has an ascertainable monetary value. Borsheim v. Owan, 467 N.W.2d 95, 97 (N.D. 1991). Upon foreclosure, a court must be able to determine the amount of the lien to distribute the sale proceeds properly. As a result, the obligation must be reduced to a monetary equivalent. In Pawtucket Inst. for Sav. v. Gagnon, 475 A.2d 1028 (R.I. 1984), Gagnon contracted R. & R. Construction Company (R&R) to build a nine-unit apartment building. Id. at 1029. Gagnon agreed to pay $82,000 upon the building's completion and immediately advanced $25,000 to R&R in exchange for a mortgage on the property, which was properly recorded. Id. at 1030. However, R&R failed to complete construction. Id. As the court stated, "[t]he issue presented before us is whether the obligation described in the Gagnon mortgage is capable of reduction to a definitely ascertainable amount so as to render the mortgage valid." Id. Here, the court first noted that a mortgage must secure an underlying obligation. Id. The underlying obligation secured in this case was the construction of a nine-unit apartment building. *See id.* at 1031. Additionally, according to the court, a mortgage may only secure obligations that are identified in the parties' agreement, and the mortgage identified the parties' construction agreement, which articulated the obligation to construct the apartment building. Id. The court held the amount secured by the mortgage was reasonably ascertainable because, at the point of foreclosure, the mortgage secured the $25,000 payment made to R&R under the contract along with R&R's obligation to construct the building. Id. Accordingly, the court held this mortgage valid. Id.

The underlying debt can be absolute or contingent, liquidated or unliquidated and can secure an antecedent debt or a future advance. Devlin v. Wiener, 232 Conn. 550, 555 (1995). Moreover, a mortgage can secure a nondebt obligation. In Jeffrey

Towers, Inc. v. Straus, 31 A.D.2d 319 (N.Y.App.Div.1969), a purchase money mortgagee sold a mortgagor several acres from a larger tract of land that the mortgagee owned. Id. at 320. The mortgage secured a mortgage debt of $500,000 and several promises by the mortgagor, including the obligation to build a sewer connection and a driveway to service the entire original tract. Id. at 320–321. Subsequently, the mortgagor sold the land to a purchaser who took it subject to the mortgage. The mortgagor eventually paid off the $500,000 mortgage debt and demanded satisfaction of the mortgage, but the mortgagee refused to grant it because the purchaser had not built the sewer connection and driveway. Id. at 322. In reaching a decision in favor of the mortgagee, the court noted that a mortgage could secure unliquidated obligations such as the obligations to build the sewer connection and driveway. Id. at 322. The court determined that the mortgagee's refusal of mortgage satisfaction was proper because the purchaser had not satisfied its obligation under the mortgage to build the driveway and sewer. Id. at 325.

The underlying obligation may be embodied in the mortgage itself, but is usually evidenced by a separate promissory note. The promissory note may be negotiable. *See* U.C.C. § 3–104(a). A statement in the instrument that it is secured by a mortgage does not destroy its negotiability. *See* U.C.C. § 3–106(a). The note's negotiability is likewise unimpaired by its reference to the mortgage for rights as to prepayment or acceleration. *See* U.C.C. § 3–106(b). If, however, the note incorporates terms of the mortgage for other purposes, it becomes a conditional promise and is thereby rendered nonnegotiable.

III. DESCRIPTION OF OBLIGATION

As between the mortgagor and the mortgagee, it is prudent, but not necessary, to describe the underlying obligation in the mortgage. A description of the obligation, however, is necessary to protect the mortgagee against subsequent purchasers and lienors. State law determines the extent to which the underlying obligation must be described in a mortgage. In Indiana, the description of the underlying obligation in a mortgage does not need to be literally correct but must contain enough information to avoid misleading or deceiving someone about the nature or amount of the obligation. Kraft, LLC v. Greiner, 29 B.R. 637, 651 (Bankr. Ind. 2010). According to the *Kraft* court, the reason for this requirement is to prevent the parties from substituting the obligation with another one. Id.

Authorities disagree regarding what information is required to impart adequate notice of the obligation to third parties; however, the description should specify the obligation's form, amount, interest rate, execution date, and maturity date. If essential information is not included in the mortgage, it is invalid. In SPCP Group, L.L.C. v. Dolson, Inc., 934 N.E.2d 771 (Ind. Ct. App. 2010), the court considered whether a mortgage was valid and unenforceable. Under statutory law in Indiana, the mortgage must include the date of repayment and at least one of the following: (1) the mortgage's principal amount; (2)

the notes or other evidences of debt; or (3) a description of the debt secured. Id. at 775–776. The court noted that the description must be correct and full enough to prevent parties from erroneously or fraudulently substituting other debts. Id. at 776. In *Dolson*, the mortgage correctly identified the promissory note's date but incorrectly identified the identities of one of its co-makers. Id. The court held such misidentification in this case was material and could mislead or deceive because it placed the parties in different positions and affected their risks of loss. Id. Accordingly, this court held the mortgage invalid because its description of the obligation was inaccurate and materially misleading. Id. at 779.

Similarly, in *In re* Willows II, LLC, 485 B.R. 528 (Bankr. E.D.N.C. 2013), the court delineated the following reasons why a mortgage must identify the obligation secured: (1) proper identification is important to place subsequent purchasers on notice and ensures that they are not misled or deceived of an obligation's nature or amount; (2) proper identification limits a mortgage to the obligations the parties intended to be secured; and (3) proper identification prevents "fraudulent substitution" of "fictitious debts." *Id.* at 536–37 (internal quotations omitted). The court in *Willows* considered a deed of trust and ultimately determined that it was valid. Although the deed of trust incorrectly referenced the note's date of execution, it properly identified the obligation and put inquiring parties on notice of the obligation's nature and amount. Id. at 537. It also noted that the obligation contained a variable interest rate, identified all involved parties, and specified the property that served as collateral. Id. Accordingly, the deed of trust was valid because its description of the obligation was sufficient and accurate as required. Id.

The mortgagee, of course, must also record the mortgage to preserve its priority.

IV. FUTURE ADVANCES

A. THE BASIC CONCEPT

A mortgage may secure the repayment of funds that the mortgagee advances to the mortgagor in the future. In fact, many commonly used mortgage forms contain a future advances clause. Home equity loans, for example, sometimes include such a provision. The future advances clause also is an integral part of construction loan mortgages under which the lender advances funds as construction on the mortgaged property progresses.

A mortgage that covers future advances constitutes an executory agreement by the mortgagor that the mortgaged property stands as security for all funds advanced by the mortgagee. The arrangement is essentially one transaction, not a series of independent loans. It is specifically so designed for the convenience and economic advantage of the parties. Thus, the lien of a mortgage for future advances arises as at the date of the execution of the mortgage, not when advances are made.

B. METHODS OF SECURING FUTURE ADVANCES

The parties generally provide for coverage of future advances by drafting the mortgage in either of two ways. One technique is to specify a present loan amount in excess of funds actually advanced. A second approach is to state the amount of the current debt and then provide that the mortgage secures future advances, with or without limit on the total amount secured. Both methods have been upheld by the courts, but the second alternative is more common.

C. DRAGNET CLAUSE

The dragnet clause is related to the future advances clause, but is broader in scope. The typical dragnet clause, sometimes referred to as an anaconda, cross-security, or omnibus clause, provides that the mortgage secures all indebtedness owed by the mortgagor to the mortgagee. Every obligation is included, regardless of whether it arose before or after the execution of the mortgage or whether it was originated or acquired by the mortgagee. The impact of a dragnet clause can be illustrated by the following example. A mortgagor receives a $2000 loan from a lender and gives the lender an unsecured promissory note. The following month, the mortgagor borrows $5,000 from a mortgagee and grants a mortgage in favor of the mortgagee on land. The mortgage contains a dragnet clause. The mortgagee then purchases the unsecured note from the lender at a discount for $1,500. The outstanding balance of that loan remained $2000. The mortgagee now has a $7,000 mortgage on the land because both notes are fully secured by the mortgage.

Because a dragnet clause can be used to expand the amount of a mortgage far beyond the mortgagor's expectations, its scope has been limited by both judicial decision and state legislative action. Numerous forms of limitation exist. Judicially crafted restrictions confine application of the dragnet clause to certain obligations, such as those created directly between the original parties to the mortgage, those arising after execution of the mortgage, or those consistent with the objective of the initial loan. The extent to which courts employ any of these restrictions varies among the states. In Capocasa v. First Nat'l Bank of Stevens Point, 36 Wis.2d 714 (1967), a married couple owned an interest in a house as joint tenants, and a mortgage on the house contained a dragnet clause which provided that the house served as security for $10,600 and "any further sums of money which may be or become owing to the bank." Id. at 718–19. The question presented in the case was whether the dragnet clause could be used to secure a subsequent personal note by the husband that was unrelated to the mortgage and where the wife did not have knowledge of the note and did not consent to it. Id. at 719–20. Indeed, the wife did not know about the note until she tried to sell the house. Id. at 721. The mortgagee claimed that any debt by either the husband or wife would have been secured by the mortgage pursuant to the dragnet clause irrespective of how the debt was incurred. Id. at 720. The court determined that when a dragnet clause in a mortgage is executed by joint tenants, each joint tenant pledges his or her undivided interest in the mortgaged property to secure any existing or future joint debts to the mortgagee. Id. at 726. A co-tenant's interest in the mortgaged property will also secure any existing or future debt of the other joint tenant if it enhances the value of the mortgaged property or if the co-tenant has knowledge of the debt and consents to securing the debt on the co-tenant's interest in the mortgaged property. Id. at 726–27. In this case, the dragnet clause was not effective to encumber the wife's interest in the house because she did not provide consent nor did the debt enhance the value of the house. Id. at 727. Consequently, only the husband's undivided one-half interest in the house was subject to a mortgage on his individual debt.

V. INTEREST ON LOANS

A. FIXED RATE INTEREST

The underlying obligation normally bears interest at a fixed percentage rate per annum. The precise interest rate charged is usually dictated by money market conditions existing at the time the mortgage loan is made. But regardless of what the rate may be, it remains constant over the entire term of the loan.

A lender may increase its yield beyond the stated fixed interest rate by requiring the borrower to pay discount points at the time the loan is made. One discount point equals one percent of the loan amount.

Illustration: The mortgagee agrees to make a $100,000 thirty-year mortgage loan to a mortgagor at a 10% fixed interest rate plus two points. The mortgagor must pay $2,000 to the mortgagee at the time the loan is made. This payment increases the loan's effective yield to above 10%. The amount of the increase depends upon when the loan is paid off. The earlier the payoff, the greater the increase.

B. ALTERNATIVE MORTGAGE INSTRUMENTS

During periods of rampant inflation, a fixed rate of interest provides the lender with less yield than originally projected. Consequently, mortgagees have devised other methods to insure a satisfactory return on their investments. Lenders who employ these variations from the norm also may charge discount points for making the loan.

In the 1970s and early 1980s, the Comptroller of the Currency, the Federal Home Loan Bank Board (today the Office of Thrift Supervision), and the National Credit Union Administration authorized the federally-chartered lending institutions under their control to develop alternatives to the traditional mortgage. Moreover, the Alternative Mortgage Transaction Parity Act of 1982, 12 U.S.C.A. § 3801 *et seq.*, preempted state law on the subject and enabled nonfederally-chartered institutions to compete effectively in the residential real estate financing marketplace by authorizing them to offer the same alternative residential mortgage instruments available from similar federally-chartered institutions. The states had three years from the passage of the Act to override this preemption. Some states reinstituted local law by doing so.

As a consequence of these regulatory and legislative measures, several significant alternatives to the traditional mortgage have been developed by institutional lenders. Those innovative instruments that alter the standard fixed-interest-rate approach are discussed in this section. Newly developed mortgage formats that provide payment alternatives are treated later in this chapter. Neither analysis is intended to be exhaustive. Some existing alternative mortgage instruments are not mentioned, and additional variations constantly are being introduced.

1. Adjustable Rate Mortgage

Mortgage lenders offer adjustable rate mortgages (ARMs) in which the interest rate rises and falls over the term of the loan in accordance with prevailing market conditions. Important features of ARMs are caps/ceilings, indexes and frequency of the adjustments. A cap or ceiling is the maximum amount that the ARM can increase, both during the adjustment period and the life of the loan. The index is some recognized predetermined economic indicator, such as LIBOR or the prime rate, that is used to determine whether the rate in the ARM will increase or decrease. Hence, if the prime rate is the index and it goes up, there will be an increase in the ARM interest rate. The ARM rate will not equal the prime rate, but the prime rate will simply determine whether the rate in the ARM will adjust. This guards against extreme interest rate fluctuations by establishing floor and ceiling limits. The frequency of adjustments or adjustment period determines when the rates may be adjusted. Hence, if the frequency is six months, the lender will look at the agreed upon index to determine whether the ARM rate should adjust during that six-month period.

ARMs, sometimes referred to as variable rate mortgages (VRMs), may be structured in an almost infinite number of ways. Variations exist not only with respect to the index and the use of ceilings, but also as to the frequency and amount of each interest rate adjustment and the way in which interest increases are paid. Moreover, an ARM may be drafted to include other flexibility features such as a graduated payment provision.

Many predatory loans during the subprime loan crisis were ARMs or VRMs with the teaser rates followed by substantial increases in the rates upon adjustment. Today, certain restrictions apply to these types of loans and states must make disclosures to borrowers when making them in the residential setting. For example, in Wisconsin, variable rate contracts on a first mortgage secured by owner-occupied residential property containing no more than four units must meet several criteria, including: 1) the term can't be more than 40 years; 2) an increase in the interest rate can't be for more than one percent and the increase can't be more than once every six months; 3) decreases can be made at any time; 4) the borrower must have the right to prepay the loan, and the lender cannot impose a prepayment penalty five years after the date of the loan; 5) the lender must make variable rate loans without prepayment penalties and must provide a borrower with written notice of this requirement; and 6) if the rate will increase, the lender must provide the borrower with the amount and date of the interest rate increase, the changes in the index that resulted in the increase, the new principal and interest and the borrower's prepayment rights. Wis. Stat. § 138.056 (2017). In addition, before a lender makes a variable interest loan, the lender must disclose the following: 1) the loan contains a variable rate clause; 2) the index; 3) the borrower's prepayment rights after the lender notifies the debtor of an increase; and 4) a statement that the lender must provide notice of any increase. Wis. Stat. § 138.056(6) (2017).

Some ARMs include another noteworthy feature. If increases in the interest rate are added to the principal obligation rather than reflected in increased monthly payments or extended maturity, the phenomenon of negative amortization may occur. That is, over time the principal balance of the loan may increase instead of decrease.

A study conducted by Freddie Mac revealed that ARMs had achieved a prominent position in the mortgage-financing marketplace by the early 1980s. The ARM's share of the residential mortgage market has varied over the years depending upon inflation and the volatility of interest rates. During periods of moderate inflation and relative interest rate stability, ARMs tend to become less popular with borrowers.

For a time, an unsettling development in the case law made ARMs less attractive to purchasers of mortgage loans on the secondary mortgage market. Several courts concluded that ARM notes were nonnegotiable on the ground the notes did not contain an obligation to pay a "sum certain." *See* UCC §§ 3–104(1)(b), 3–106 (pre-1990). Assignees of such nonnegotiable instruments are not eligible to receive the favorable treatment available under Article 3 of the UCC for assignees of negotiable instruments. Experts in the field, therefore, called for amendment of the UCC to include ARM notes within the definition of negotiable instruments. In 1990, the UCC was revised to so provide. *See* UCC § 3–112(b). Consequently, the ARM-negotiability issue has been resolved.

2. Price Level Adjusted Mortgage

A mortgage format often used in other parts of the world to insulate lenders against inflation is the price level adjusted mortgage (PLAM), also known as an indexed mortgage (IM). This instrument deals with the problem of inflation by tying the outstanding principal to an economic index. Thus, the interest rate remains constant over the term of the loan, but the loan principal varies. In this sense, a PLAM is the opposite of an ARM.

An advantage of the PLAM to the mortgagor is that it bears a low interest rate because inflation need not be factored into the rate of return required by the lender. On the other hand, the PLAM's primary drawback for the borrower is that it produces negative amortization which is usually covered by increased monthly payments.

3. Shared Appreciation Mortgage

Shared appreciation mortgages (SAMs) are designed to insure mortgagees of an adequate return during inflationary times and to provide an alternative form of financing for individuals who otherwise might be unable to obtain a mortgage loan. SAMs combine aspects of the standard fixed-interest-rate mortgage with a novel type of return to the lender. Typically, SAMs bear a fixed-interest-rate well below current market rates thereby enabling a greater number of individuals to qualify for this form of financing than for standard fixed-interest-rate mortgages or ARMs. The SAM instrument also provides that the mortgagee will receive a portion (e.g., one-third) of the amount the mortgaged property appreciates in value. The lender's fractional share of the appreciation is paid when the property is sold or at the end of a certain period (e.g., ten years), whichever comes first. This share is often called contingent interest.

Although the SAM has appeal to both mortgagees and mortgagors, its use raises a myriad of issues: How does one determine the amount of appreciation? How are improvements made by the mortgagor factored into the calculation of appreciation? If the mortgagor does not sell the property before the lender's share of appreciation must be paid, will satisfactory refinancing be available? These and other questions cloud the SAM picture and lead authorities to draw differing conclusions regarding its future in the residential mortgage marketplace.

C. REVENUE/EQUITY PARTICIPATION

As a hedge against inflation, mortgage lenders sometimes demand a portion of the revenue generated by the project being financed. When this occurs, the lender is said to receive contingent interest or an "equity kicker." Under such an arrangement, the lender typically is entitled to a percentage of gross income or net profits in addition to the specified interest.

Mortgagees may go even further and obtain an ownership interest in the project. Several types of such equity participations exist. The lender may become directly involved by entering a joint venture with the developer or by taking an ownership interest in the entity that controls the project. Equity participation should be distinguished from loan participation discussed earlier.

D. BUY-DOWN MORTGAGE

Mortgagees generally are willing to make below-market interest rate loans if they receive sufficient upfront money to offset the reduced interest rate of return. A mortgage loan made on this basis is called a "buy-down." Real estate developers and other sellers may use the buy-down technique to make their residential properties more marketable by paying an institutional lender to offer low-interest-rate financing to purchasers. In such case, the interest buy-down is typically for only a short term, such as a year or two; thereafter the interest rate returns to the market level.

VI. THE IMPACT OF USURY ON THE UNDERLYING OBLIGATION

A. IN GENERAL

The amount of interest a lender may receive is limited by state usury statutes. The provisions of these measures differ considerably with regard to: (1) the maximum legal interest rate (2) statutory exemptions, and (3) penalties for violation.

The maximum allowable interest rate on loans varies dramatically among the states. In many jurisdictions, different maximum rates exist for different types of borrowers. For example, there may be one rate for individuals and another higher rate for corporations.

There is an issue of whether a prepayment penalty is interest. Most cases that have addressed this question have determined that a prepayment penalty is not interest for purposes of usury. *See* French v. Mortgage Guarantee Co., 16 Cal. 2d 26, 31 (1940). In Bearden v. Tarrant Sav. Ass'n, 643 S.W. 2d 247 (Tex. App. 1982), the court stated that the prepayment penalty was not interest subject to usury; rather, the court reasoned that it was a payment for the privilege of paying off a loan and avoiding high interest payments. Id. at 249.

B. EXEMPTIONS

1. Borrowers

Most usury statutes exempt certain borrowers, lenders, transactions, or a combination of the three.

a. Corporate Borrowers

Corporate borrowers are commonly exempt from usury statutes. *See, e.g.*, Ala. Code § 11–97–19 (2017). Some states go beyond the corporate exemption and exempts partnerships, limited partnerships and limited liability companies as well. *See, e.g.*, N.C. Gen. Stat. § 24–9(a)(3)(a) (2017) (exempting any borrower other than a natural person), W. Va. Code § 47–6–10 (2017).

Moreover, as previously indicated, where corporate borrowers are not exempt, they are usually permitted to pay a higher rate of interest than other borrowers. Authority is divided on the issue of whether the lender may avoid usury laws by requiring the borrower to incorporate.

Courts have considered whether an individual who guarantees a corporate debt is able to claim the defense. The prevailing view is that where an individual guarantees the corporate debt, that individual is unable to claim the usury defense. *See, e.g.*, Feller v. Architects Display Bldgs. Inc., 54 N.J. 205, 212 (Super. App. Div. 1959); Associated East Corp. v. Highland Park, Inc., 172 Conn. 395, 406 (1977).

b. Lenders

Banks and savings and loan associations are exempt from usury statutes in several states.

c. Transactions

FHA insured loans and VA loans are often excluded from the application of usury laws. *See, e.g.*, La. Rev. Stat. Ann. § 9:3504(A) (West 2017); N.J. Stat. Ann. § 31:1–1 (West 2017). In addition, a purchase money mortgage loan taken by a seller of real estate is exempt in many jurisdictions on the theory that a buyer and seller are in substantially equal bargaining positions. Various other transactions, such as loans for business purposes, are sometimes given exempt status.

C. PENALTIES

In some states, the penalty for usury is merely forfeiture of interest in excess of the legal rate. In many jurisdictions, the lender forfeits all interest. In Washington, if the borrower has paid usurious interest, the lender is entitled to recover principal only less twice the amount of interest paid. Wash. Rev. Code § 19:3504(A) (West 2017). West Virginia has a similar statute, but the borrower is entitled to four times the interest agreed to be paid. W. Va. Code § 47–6–6 (2017). In other states, the lender not only forfeits all interest, but also loses the right to recover the principal.

Significantly, in some jurisdictions, usury is punishable as a crime. *See, e.g.*, Or. Rev. Stat.

§ 2502.22 (2017). In Massachusetts, if a lender makes a loan with interest and charges exceeding 20%, the lender is guilty of criminal usury punishable by imprisonment up to 10 years and/or a fine no more than $10,000. Mass. Gen. Laws Ann. ch. 271, § 49 (West 2017). In *In re* Loucheschi, LLC, 471 B.R. 777 (Bankr. D. Mass. 2012), a case dealing with the mortgagor's bankruptcy petition, the lender filed a proof of claim asserting a claim on the secured property. Id. at 778. The contract interest rate under the loan was 16%, the default rate charge was 20% and the late charge was 10% Id. at 779. The Bankruptcy Court determined that a construction loan where a lender "contracted for" a rate that was usurious even if the amounts were never actually charged; hence, the loan was usurious under the statute. Id. at 782. Instead of declaring the construction loan void, as was allowed under the Massachusetts criminal usury statute, the Bankruptcy Code found that the appropriate remedy was to disallow the interest portion of the lender's claim. Id. at 783.

D. FEDERAL PREEMPTION

The Depository Institutions Deregulation and Monetary Control Act of 1980 preempted several aspects of state usury law. The most significant provision for real estate financing purposes is that portion of the Act which exempts most residential first mortgage loans from state interest rate limits. 12 U.S.C.A. § 1735f–7a. The Act gave the states the option to override this federal preemption within a three-year time frame. Several states did so. Thus, although the Act provides some uniformity in this area of usury law, considerable diversity still exists among the states.

VII. MODIFICATION OF OBLIGATION

A mortgage secures an obligation, not the instrument that evidences it. A change in the form of the obligation by substitution, extension, or renewal, therefore, generally does not affect the mortgage lien. For example, in Lennar Northeast Partners v. Buice, 49 Cal. App. 4th 1576 (1996), the court stated that if a senior debt was extended in a manner that merely changed the date of payments, this extension would not adversely impact the junior interests. Id. at 1585. If, however, either the obligation's principal or its interest rate is increased by modification, the mortgage lien may lose priority to junior encumbrances for the amount of the increase. The court in *Lennar* noted that an increase in the rate of interest could negatively affect the property's income. Id. The court reasoned that an increase in expenses would decrease the rate of return of the property which would materially affect the value of the junior liens. Id.

VIII. DISCHARGE OF OBLIGATION AND MORTGAGE

A. PAYMENT

As discussed previously, a mortgage merely secures an underlying obligation. It is automatically extinguished when, usually by payment, the underlying obligation is satisfied. *See* Northwest Carpets, Inc. v. First Nat'l Bank of Chatsworth, 630 S.E.2d 407, 409 (2006); NattyMac Capital LLC v. Pesek, 784 N.W.2d 156, 159 (S.D. 2010).

The typical modern mortgage loan is amortized over fifteen to thirty years with provision for repayment in monthly installments of principal and interest. The amount of the mortgage lien is reduced proportionately as each monthly payment is made. When the debt is paid in full, the mortgage is discharged.

> *Illustration*: A mortgagor executes a $25,000 promissory note and a mortgage to a mortgagee. The mortgagor pays the mortgagee $15,000 on the principal of the note. The amount of the mortgage lien is reduced automatically to $10,000 notwithstanding the fact the mortgage states that it secures a $25,000 debt.

1. Payment Alternatives

Lending institutions have been authorized to offer alternatives to the traditional payment format.

a. Graduated Payment Mortgage

Under the graduated payment mortgage (GPM), the interest rate usually remains constant throughout the life of the loan, but monthly mortgage payments increase over several years to a specified level. Initial payments are lower than normally required, whereas later payments are abnormally high. Thus, younger homebuyers may make smaller mortgage payments in their early years of employment and larger ones as their income presumably increases. This graduated payment feature may be coupled with an adjustable interest rate.

b. Reverse Mortgage

The reverse mortgage allows older homeowners to borrow money on the equity in their homes. Reverse mortgages may take various forms. Under one approach, the loan proceeds are advanced to the mortgagor in monthly installments and are repaid in a lump sum at the end of a set term, when the home is sold, or at the homeowner's death.

c. Growing Equity Mortgage

One alternative mortgage instrument includes a fixed interest rate, but provides for increasing monthly principal payments so that the loan is repaid in fifteen years or so. It is from this feature that the instrument takes its name—growing equity mortgage (GEM).

Initial payments under a GEM are based on a twenty-five or thirty year amortization. The rate of increased principal payments is specified in the document and may be fixed at a certain percentage or tied to an economic index.

2. Balloon Loans

Many residential mortgage loans executed before the Depression were short-term "balloon" loans upon which the borrower paid only interest until maturity.

If the borrower lacked sufficient funds to satisfy the debt when it fell due, the borrower was forced to refinance. This arrangement worked well as long as mortgage loans were readily available. During the Depression, however, money was in short supply, and many borrowers were unable to refinance. Consequently, numerous mortgagors lost their land through foreclosure. This situation caused the federal government to develop programs, notably FHA mortgage insurance, to encourage the use of long-term, fully-amortized mortgages.

Today, a balloon mortgage loan may be defined as one that requires a substantial payment at the end of the term to cover the unamortized loan principal. Disclosure and other aspects of balloon payment terms may be governed by regulation or statute.

3. Escrow Accounts

The mortgagor frequently is required to make monthly payments that cover not only principal and interest, but also build an escrow account from which the mortgagee may pay real estate taxes and insurance on the mortgaged property as they come due. The escrow account system originated during the Depression when many mortgagors were unable to pay real estate taxes or insurance premiums, and lenders were forced to pay these obligations in order to protect their security.

The handling of escrow account funds traditionally has been left to the mortgagee's discretion. Mortgagees commonly invest escrowed monies with their other funds and keep the resulting returns.

Mortgagors in numerous jurisdictions have instituted lawsuits, often class actions, contesting the legality of a mortgagee's decision not to pay interest on funds held in escrow. Mortgagors have sought relief on various grounds, including express trust and constructive trust theories. These suits generally have been unsuccessful, although mortgagors occasionally have prevailed. *See, e.g.,* Buchanan v. Century Federal Savings and Loan Association of Pittsburgh, 542 A.2d 117 (Pa. Super. 1988). However, courts usually have been unwilling to require mortgagees to account for earnings received from the investment of escrowed funds.

The mortgagors' attack on interest-free escrow accounts has achieved greater success outside the courtroom. Controversy fueled by their lawsuits has precipitated federal and state legislative action. The federal Real Estate Settlement Procedures Act limits the amount of funds that may be placed in escrow, and statutes in some states require the payment of interest on these accounts.

4. Late Charges

The mortgagor is often required to pay a late charge when tardy in making monthly payments. Considerable division of opinion exists regarding whether to treat late charges as liquidated damages or as additional interest. Nonetheless, as a general proposition, courts uphold late charges calculated on a reasonable basis as nonusurious compensation for the cost of handling overdue payments. Some courts have refused to permit lenders to recover late charges on top of default interest. In many states, late charges are limited in amount or otherwise regulated by statute.

5. Default Interest

Mortgage loan documents sometimes call for an increased rate of interest post-default. Courts typically uphold provisions for default interest, either as contractual arrangements regarding interest or as establishing liquidated damages. Nevertheless, default interest has been invalidated in certain cases as unconscionable or unreasonable. In this regard, some courts have prohibited lenders from receiving default interest along with late charges. Default interest also may be restricted by usury statutes.

B. PREPAYMENT

The mortgagee contracts to receive interest over the agreed term of the loan. The mortgagor, therefore, has no right to pay the underlying obligation prior to maturity unless the mortgage, the note, a local statute, or a court opinion specifically authorizes the mortgagor to do so.

> *Illustration*: A mortgagor borrows $5,000 from a mortgagee and executes a $5,000 promissory note and a mortgage to the mortgagee. The note is due five years from the date of execution and bears interest at 12% per annum. The instruments are silent regarding prepayment. The next day the mortgagor's parents give the mortgagor $5,000. The mortgagor immediately

tenders the mortgagee $5,000 to satisfy the loan. In most jurisdictions, the mortgagee may reject the mortgagor's tender and collect interest as specified in the mortgage note. In a few states, however, a statute or a court opinion gives the mortgagor a right to prepay even though the mortgagor does not have a contractual right to do so.

Residential mortgage loan documents frequently authorize prepayment without charge. Commercial mortgage documents commonly contain a provision giving the mortgagor the privilege to prepay for a fee. The fee, often called a prepayment penalty, may be calculated in various ways. Prepayment penalties usually are not included in residential mortgage loans.

Prepayment penalties generally are enforceable as reasonable compensation for lost interest and other costs. One of the leading cases on whether a prepayment charge is enforceable is Lazzareschi Inv. Co. v. San Francisco Fed. Sav. & Loan Ass'n, 22 Cal. App. 3d 303 (1971). In *Lazzareschi*, the borrower argued that the prepayment penalty was excessive because the lender could lend the repaid loan to other borrowers at a higher interest rate and hence no had relationship to any damage that the lender could have sustained. Id. The court rejected the borrower's argument but recognized that a court could invalidate a prepayment penalty if it was "palpably exorbitant" so as "to shock the judicial conscience." Id. at 308–309. The borrower also unsuccessfully argued that the prepayment penalty was a restraint on alienation. Id. at 311.

The broad proposition that prepayment penalties are enforceable, however, is subject to several caveats. First, statutes in many states limit the use of prepayment penalties in residential mortgage financing. Second, Truth in Lending regulates prepayment penalties in certain residential mortgage loans. Third, some bankruptcy decisions have curtailed or invalidated prepayment penalty provisions. Fourth, courts are reluctant to permit the lender to collect a prepayment penalty when the mortgagor is forced to pay off the loan because the lender accelerated under a general default provision or a due-on-sale clause. Involuntary payment required under such circumstances generally is not viewed as *pre*payment triggering a penalty unless the mortgage specifically so provides. In this regard, Office of Thrift Supervision regulations issued under the Garn-St. Germain Depository Institutions Act of 1982 prohibit mortgagees from charging a prepayment penalty in connection with the enforcement of a due-on-sale clause in a mortgage on a borrower-occupied residence. 12 C.F.R. § 591.5(b)(2) (2008).

C. RELEASE OF MORTGAGE

Although the mortgage lien is automatically extinguished when the underlying obligation is satisfied, the recorded mortgage continues to cloud the mortgagor's title. The mortgagor, therefore, is entitled to a recordable mortgage release upon final payment. A mortgagee releases a mortgage by executing and recording a signed written document.

The majority of jurisdictions have statutes that impose penalties, including attorneys' fees and costs, if mortgagees neglect or refuse to execute a release upon request. The statutory penalties vary widely in these statutes. *See, e.g.*, N.H. Rev. Stat. Ann. § 479:8 (2016) ($2500 maximum fine); Okla. Stat. Ann. tit. 46 § 15 (West 2016) (maximum penalty is $100 each day mortgage is not released with a maximum penalty equal to the amount of the debt); Va. Code Ann. § 55–66.3 (2016) ($500 fine). Significantly, some of these statutes allow the mortgagor to recover additional damages for actual damages under common law principles. Nelson, Whitman, Burkhart, Real Estate Finance Law, § 6.6, at 517 (6th ed. West 2015). *See, e.g.*, Cal. Civ. Code § 2941 (West 2016) (imposing forfeiture of $500 and all damages sustained by the mortgagor); Ga. Code Ann. § 44–14–3(c) (2016) (allowing $500 as liquidated damages and additional amounts for loss caused to the mortgagor); Idaho Code § 45–915 (2016) (imposing forfeiture of $100 and actual damages sustained); Nev. Rev. Stat. § 106.290 (2016) (providing that mortgagee is liable for a fine of $1000 and actual damages caused by the mortgagee's failure to comply).

D. STATUTE OF LIMITATIONS

In some states, the statute of limitations on the obligation is shorter than the statute of limitations on the mortgage. When the statute runs on the obligation but not the mortgage, controversy arises regarding the enforceability of the mortgage. The generally accepted view is that the mortgage is still enforceable and may be foreclosed if the obligation is not paid. The running of the statute of limitations renders the obligation unenforceable, but does not discharge it. Because the obligation continues to exist, so does its security. A second view is that the remedy on the mortgage is barred with the remedy on the obligation because the mortgage is dependent on the obligation for its existence and thus, also for its enforceability.

CHAPTER 5

MORTGAGE MARKET

The principles of real estate finance law discussed in this book are meaningful only when considered in light of the practical aspects of mortgage lending. This chapter, therefore, deals with the structure and operation of the mortgage market.

I. PURPOSE OF FINANCING

A. GENERAL

The purpose of the mortgage loan is the initial point of inquiry. Distinctions in two categories are important: (1) Is the mortgage loan money to be used for construction or permanent financing? (2) Is the mortgage loan to be secured by residential or commercial property? The answers to these questions determine to a large extent the source of the loan and the terms of the mortgage agreement.

B. CONSTRUCTION/PERMANENT FINANCING

1. Descriptions and Distinction

Real estate construction projects are typically financed in two stages: construction financing and permanent financing. Construction lenders are generally commercial banks while permanent lenders are oftentimes investment institutions or insurance companies. First Nat'l State Bank of New Jersey v. Commonwealth Fed. Sav. & Loan Ass'n of Norristown, 610 F.2d 164, 167 (3rd Cir. 1979).

A construction mortgage loan, sometimes referred to as an interim loan, is a short-term loan to an owner-developer for the construction of improvements on the real estate that secures the loan. A take-out provision intends to ensure construction lenders are paid once construction is completed.

Illustration: A mortgagor is a real estate developer who wishes to build an apartment building on land the mortgagor already owns. A mortgagee loans the mortgagor money to construct the project, to be disbursed as construction progresses. The loan, secured by a mortgage on the land and improvements, is due in eighteen months. The mortgagee collects only interest during the eighteen months. This is a simplified construction mortgage loan.

A permanent mortgage loan, sometimes referred to as a final loan, is a long-term loan to the owner of the real estate that secures the loan. A typical permanent loan is used where a mortgagor secures a loan to purchase a house and grants the lender a mortgage using the house as security for the loan. It is common for a residential mortgage loan to extend for a thirty-year term.

Illustration: A mortgagor obtains a loan from a mortgagee to purchase a house and gives the mortgagee a mortgage on the house as security. The loan, extending for a thirty-year term, is payable in equal monthly installments of principal and interest.

2. Relationship Between Construction Lenders and Permanent Lenders

A construction loan finances the project's actual construction, which typically makes it a short-term loan. Upon completion of construction, the construction lender is usually paid by funds obtained from a permanent lender. As a result, the permanent loan replaces the construction loan and, therefore, exists for a much longer period. A permanent lender's obligation to replace a construction loan is called a "take-out" provision. Before construction funds are advanced, the lenders enter into a buy-sell agreement whereby the permanent lender agrees to takeout the construction loan upon completion of construction. In accordance with these provisions, the construction lender either assigns its mortgage to the permanent lender or releases the construction loan mortgage so that the permanent lender's mortgage has first lien priority.

Because a permanent loan's takeout provision obligates the permanent lender to pay off a construction loan upon the construction's completion, construction lenders often will not extend a loan until developers first secure a permanent loan. The permanent loan commitment may take the form of a standby commitment that enables the mortgagor to secure construction financing but allows the mortgagor to consider alternative sources of permanent financing. First Nat'l State Bank of New Jersey, 610 F.2d at 167.

If a permanent lender breaches its commitment to provide the permanent loan, the permanent lender may be liable to the mortgagor for damages for its breach. *See, e.g.*, Pipkin v. Thomas & Hill, Inc., 298 N.C. 278, 291 (N.C. 1979) (stating that the damages are the difference "between the cost of obtaining new financing and the interest payments specified in the contract").

3. Construction Lender's Special Risks

a. Nature of Construction Lender's Risk

A construction mortgage loan involves greater risk than a permanent mortgage loan. The mortgage usually secures a partially completed building. The developer may never complete the construction project because the developer becomes insolvent or files for bankruptcy. There may be cost overruns resulting from inflation in the cost of material or labor. As a result, the developer may need to find additional financing to cover these additional expenses.

As compensation for assuming these risks, the construction lender charges a higher rate of interest than does the permanent lender. The construction lender's investment is fully secured only when the project is completed in accordance with the plans and specifications under the terms that the parties originally agreed. Thus, the construction lender closely supervises construction and advances funds under the construction loan agreement as the project properly progresses.

b. Mortgagor's Failure to Meet Conditions of Take-Out Commitment

In the takeout or buy-sell agreement, a permanent lender requires that certain conditions be met. For example, the buy-sell agreement may condition its take-out commitment on the solvency of the mortgagor. *See, e.g.*, Mellon Bank, N.A. v. Aetna Business Credit, Inc., 619 F.2d 1001 (3rd Cir. 1980). For loan commitments on the construction of an office or a retail building, the permanent lender may require that tenant leases be executed for a stated portion of the property. *See, e.g.*, Johnson v. Am. Nat'l Ins. Co., 126 Ariz. 219, 221 (Ariz. Ct. App. 1980) (loan commitment required leases of at least 13,200 square feet on terms approved by the lender).

Courts have addressed whether the doctrine of strict compliance or substantial compliance applies to conditions in the buy-sell agreement where a permanent lender refuses to take out the construction lender's loan. The general rule is that substantial compliance will suffice. Nelson, Whitman, Burkhart & Freyermuth, Real Estate Finance Law 1051, n. 90 (West 2015). However, in Analytical Design & Constr. Group, Inc. v. Murray, 690 P.2d 269 (Co. Ct. App. 1984), the court concluded that the doctrine of substantial performance was not applicable to a unilateral loan commitment and required strict compliance. Id. at 272. In *Murray*, the permanent lender required that its mortgage be a first mortgage, but a mechanic's lien had not been released. Id. The court rejected the mortgagors' argument that they had substantially complied with that condition by giving the permanent lender an irrevocable letter of credit for the estimated mechanic's lien claims against the property. Id.

In Whalen v. Ford Motor Credit Co., 475 F. Supp. 537 (D. Md. 1979), the permanent lender refused to take out the construction loan as agreed upon because it asserted the project's construction was incomplete. The permanent lender argued that its commitment to take out the construction loan required that the building be 100% completed. Id. at 540. The court noted that a mortgagor would seldom be able to rely on a permanent lender's take-out commitment if 100% completion were a condition precedent. Id. at 542. Unless the 100% completion was expressly required in the permanent lender's commitment, the lender must take out the loan if the building was substantially completed. Id. at 543. In *Whalen*, the commitment simply stated that the building "shall be completed in accordance with plans and specifications." Id. at 540. *See also* First Nat'l State Bank of New Jersey v. Commonwealth Fed. Sav. & Loan Ass'n of Norristown, 610 F.2d 164 (3rd Cir. 1979) (rejecting the permanent lender's argument that its obligation to take out the construction loan did not arise because the developer failed to strictly comply with construction plans).

There are several things the construction lender can do to minimize its risk of loss in the event the project should encounter construction difficulties. A construction lender's security interest is typically the land and building under construction. As noted, one of the construction lender's greatest risks is that the mortgagor will file for bankruptcy, stopping progress on the building and restricting the project's value. In order to minimize this risk, construction lenders may require the mortgagor to spend its cash investment before relying on any loan proceeds in order to protect the construction lender against losses if the project fails. BB Syndication Services, Inc. v. First Am. Title Ins. Co., 780 F.3d 825, 827 (7th Cir. 2015). Based on this approach, after the cash investment is spent, loan proceeds are advanced as work on the building is completed to fund invoices from contractors and providers of materials Id. In addition, construction lenders often carry title insurance. *See id.* at 826. Construction lenders also take steps to ensure that its mortgage has first lien priority. They may require the mortgagor to personally guaranty completion of construction. Finally, construction lenders may require the mortgagor to obtain performance and payment bonds in their joint names.

c. *Performance and Payment Bonds*

In order to be protected by performance and payment bonds, the construction lender must be named as an obligee together with the mortgagor. When this is done the bond is called a dual obligee bond.

The dual obligee performance bond assures the construction lender that the project will be completed in accordance with the construction contract. However, the coverage afforded a construction lender by a dual obligee bond is commonly limited by a savings clause, often called a Los Angeles clause, that releases the bonding company from liability if the mortgagor breaches the construction contract. Consequently, the savings clause may operate at a critical time to eliminate the construction lender's protection under the dual obligee performance bond.

The dual obligee payment bond assures the construction lender that all charges for labor or material used in construction will be paid. This prevents loss resulting from the attachment of any mechanics' liens that might gain priority over the construction loan mortgage, but at the same time raises the possibility that the bonding company may seek to be subrogated to the rights of mechanics' lienors. Moreover, the bond may contain a savings/Los Angeles clause. Hence, as a practical matter, the dual obligee payment bond may afford the lender no protection at all.

d. Liability for Construction Defects

Construction lenders have faced an unexpected additional risk—liability for faulty construction. Generally, construction lenders have not been found liable for construction defects. One exception is where the construction lender takes on some role as the developer or builder. For example, in Central Bank, N.A. v. Baldwin, 94 Nev. 581 (Nev. 1978), the Supreme Court of Nevada determined that a lender was liable for construction defects because the lender engaged in a joint venture with the mortgagor. Id. at 584. *See also* Chotka v. Fidelco Growth Investors, 383 So.2d 1169, 1170 (Fla. 2d Dist. Ct. App. 1980) (lender held liable where it "became more than just a lender when [it] took title to the condominium project, completed construction, and, [held itself] out to be the developer and owner of the project, advertised and sold units to purchasers"). However, the Supreme Court of California in a landmark decision prior to *Central Bank* found a construction lender liable notwithstanding the lack of a joint venture. In Connor v. Great Western Sav. & Loan Ass'n, 73 Cal.Rptr. 369 (1968), the court found the construction lender liable for construction defects under an independent negligence theory because the lender went beyond the domain of the usual lender by acting as a buyer and seller of land, too. Id. 376–377. The *Connor* court imposed a duty based on the following public policy considerations:

> (1) the extent to which the transaction was intended to affect the plaintiff, (2) the foreseeability of harm to him, (3) the degree of certainty that the plaintiff suffered injury, (4) the closeness of the connection between the defendant's conduct and the injury suffered, (5) the moral blame attached to the defendant's conduct, and (6) the policy of preventing future harm.

Id. at 377 (citing Biakanja v. Irving, 49 Cal.2d 647, 650 (Cal. 1958)). The lender in *Connor* argued that the court should defer to the legislature because the question of the lender's liability was based on policy. Id. at 379.

Significantly, almost immediately after the Supreme Court of California decision in *Connor*, the state legislature enacted a statute purporting to limit construction lenders' liability to third parties for construction defects unless the alleged damage resulted from a lender acting outside the scope of lending. Cal. Civ. Code § 3434 (West 2016). A few other states have enacted similar legislation or adopted the same approach under common law. *See, e.g.*, Mo. Rev. Stat. § 369.264 (2017) (permitting a lender's liability where the lender has knowingly been a party to misrepresentations); Nev. Rev. Stat. Ann. § 41.590 (2017) (limiting a lender's liability to loss or damage resulting from some other action or activity other than the loan transaction); Tex. Fin. Code § 59.011 (2015) (prohibiting lender's liability to a subsequent purchaser of property that the lender had acquired in foreclosure for any construction defects where the lender had no knowledge prior to acquisition of property); Rudolph v. First Southern Fed. Sav. & Loan Ass'n, 414 So.2d 64, 71 (Alabama 1982) (holding a lender may be held liable where a borrower "prove[s] the lender's voluntary assumptions of activities beyond those traditionally associated with the normal role of a money lender" but incurs no liability for an independent, negligent inspection); Stempler v. Frankford Trust Co., 365 Pa. Super. 305, 310–311 (1987) (holding that construction lender was not liable to the mortgagor for negligence because it had no obligation to inspect property to determine its condition and any inspection was solely for its own benefit).

C. RESIDENTIAL/COMMERCIAL PROPERTY

The distinction between residential and commercial mortgage loans is important because some lenders specialize in making loans secured by a particular kind of property. Residential mortgage loans are loans secured by any form of residential property—for example: single-family dwellings, duplexes, apartments, or condominiums. Sometimes residential mortgage loans are further broken down into loans on one-to-four-family properties called home loans and loans on larger multi-family projects. Commercial mortgage loans are loans made on non-residential property—for example: shopping centers, hotels, office buildings, warehouses, or manufacturing plants.

II. ORIGINATING/SERVICING/HOLDING

In order to fully understand the mortgage market, one must appreciate the differences among originating, servicing, and holding mortgage loans. The institution that initially advances funds "originates" the mortgage loan. The organization that collects the mortgage payment from and otherwise deals directly with the borrower "services" the loan. The lender that owns the mortgage loan at any one time "holds" the loan. Sometimes the same entity originates, holds, and services the loan. On many other occasions, the originator sells the mortgage loan to a new holder who hires someone, frequently the originator, to service the loan.

The right to service a mortgage loan is a valuable asset because of the fee involved and the possibility of earning interest on escrowed funds. Accordingly, a vigorous market for mortgage servicing rights exists. Indeed, several different entities may service a particular mortgage loan over its lifetime, perhaps to the consternation of the mortgagor.

III. SOURCES OF REAL ESTATE FINANCING

The institutions that make mortgage loan funds available form the core infrastructure of the mortgage market. The most significant sources of real estate financing are described in general terms in this section.

The following treatment of real estate financing sources includes discussion of periods when several mortgage lenders were experiencing financial difficulty and what then transpired. Part VII discusses lenders' role in creating the subprime loan crisis and the Great Recession that began in 2007.

A. COMMERCIAL BANKS

Commercial banks are depository institutions chartered by either a state or the federal government. Although commercial banks make a substantial number of permanent mortgage loans, traditionally they have limited such long-term investments in order to maintain liquidity to meet demand deposits. Construction lending is usually a more significant part of their mortgage loan operation; the yields are higher, and the bank's funds are not tied up for prolonged periods.

By 1990, numerous commercial banks were in financial difficulty. Many of their mortgage loans were in jeopardy because of overbuilding and a sluggish real estate market. Bankers and regulators took various steps to avert further trouble. By the mid-1990s, the mortgage lending situation for commercial banks had improved.

B. SAVINGS AND LOAN ASSOCIATIONS

Savings and loan associations (S&Ls) are also either state or federally chartered. They are specialists in housing finance and heavily invest in both construction and permanent residential mortgages.

In the late 1980s, the savings and loan system entered a state of crisis (the so-called S&L crisis). Many of the savings and loan associations became insolvent, and numerous others teetered on the brink of collapse. Several factors contributed to the S&L crisis, including mismanagement, fraud and investments with low returns combined with high interest rates on liabilities. Three of the most important causes were deregulation, the insurance deposit system and changes in the tax law. First, there was substantial deregulation of S&Ls that contributed to the crisis. As originally established during the 1930s, S&Ls were established to promote homeownership, and they were limited to making home loans. However, under the Garn-St. Germain Depository Institutions Act of 1982, S&Ls were permitted to make other types of loans to help make them more profitable and competitive. S&Ls also began offering other types of investment options, such as mutual funds. Prior to that time, depositors had been moving their money from S&Ls to other investment opportunities, like mutual funds, that had higher rates of return. One problem with this new investment offering was that S&Ls had limited expertise in this area. Second, the Tax Reform Act of 1986 (TRA of 1986) contributed to the S&L crisis. Prior to the enactment of the TRA of 1986, investors were investing in ventures for their tax benefits rather than investment returns. Many of these investors had taken out nonrecourse mortgage loans; therefore, mortgagees were limited to foreclosure if the investors defaulted on the loans. In 1981, Congress enacted the accelerated cost recovery system that increased investors' depreciation deductions during the earlier years. Unfortunately for the investors, things changed when Congress enacted the TRA of 1986, which limited the investors' ability to claim the deductions related to owning unprofitable depreciable property. As a result, investors began abandoning these properties, resulting in the investors defaulting on their loans. Because the investors lacked personal liability, the S&Ls were unable to pursue deficiency judgments against them. Finally, the federal government insured the deposits under the Federal Deposit Insurance Corporation. As a result, when S&Ls began making more risky loans, the government was required to cover the S&Ls' liabilities, the investors' deposits. The S&Ls had little financial concern about the riskier loans because if their investment was successful, they retained the profits; however, if the investment failed, the government would repay the depositors because of the insurance system. Indeed, many of these loans failed leading to the government bailout of the S&Ls.

As part of the Financial Institutions Reform, Recovery and Enforcement Act of 1989, Congress created the Resolution Trust Corporation (RTC) to depose of the assets of failed savings and loan associations. These assets included construction loan mortgages, permanent mortgages, and a significant amount of real estate obtained from defaulting mortgagors. The RTC completed its work in late 1995 and discontinued business the last day of that year.

C. MUTUAL SAVINGS BANKS

Mutual savings banks, or savings banks, are state or federally chartered institutions located primarily in the northeast. They operate in the same general sphere as savings and loan associations, but tend to concentrate their mortgage investments in permanent residential mortgages acquired from other institutional lenders.

D. LIFE INSURANCE COMPANIES

Life insurance companies are state chartered and subject to local insurance law. Because of a relatively predictable flow of funds, life insurance companies are heavily involved in permanent financing of both commercial and multi-unit residential projects. This predictability is based on insurance companies' use of mortality tables. This enables them to use the premiums on policies to fund their long-term loans. While many insured individuals die prematurely, many others live beyond their expected life spans and others eventually cancel their policies without recouping the cost of their premiums.

The long-term nature of their mortgage investments, however, puts life insurance companies in a difficult position during periods of rapid inflation. As a consequence, they may require the right to participate in income from the project being financed.

E. RETIREMENT/PENSION FUNDS

Public and private employee pension funds are an increasing source of capital for real estate financing, particularly in the area of permanent commercial mortgages and mortgage-backed securities. Like insurance policies, individuals invest in various forms of retirement accounts for a lengthy period of time. Indeed, individuals are generally subject to a 10% additional tax on early distributions from certain retirement plans. *See* IRC § 72(t) (2017). One key exception to the additional tax is that first-time homeowners can withdraw up to a lifetime maximum of $10,000 to purchase a principal residence without being subject to the early withdrawal tax. IRC § 72(t)(8) (2017). Generally, the term "first-time homebuyer" means an individual who has not owned a principal residence for the two years prior to the acquisition of the principal residence. IRC § 72(t)(8)(D) (2017).

F. REAL ESTATE INVESTMENT TRUSTS

Real estate investment trusts (REITs) are a product of federal tax legislation of the early 1960s designed to give the small investor an opportunity to participate in sophisticated and diverse real estate investments. If a REIT meets a number of tax requirements, it will not be taxed on income and capital gains distributed to its shareholders.

The first qualified REITs were "equity" trusts that developed or purchased income producing commercial property. They were not generally successful. In the late 1960s, however, REITs that engaged solely in mortgage lending became popular. Although mortgage REITs made permanent loans, they achieved importance primarily as suppliers of construction financing. Consequently, the building slump of the middle 1970s hit mortgage REITs hard. Some went bankrupt, and many others barely survived.

REITs made a comeback in the 1980s and 1990s. Equity REITs led the resurgence, and by the mid-1990s, mortgage REITs had regained a solid position in the world of mortgage lending.

G. MORTGAGE BANKING COMPANIES

Mortgage banking companies are incorporated and operated under state law. Although mortgage bankers are a source of some real estate financing funds, they are more important as intermediaries between borrowers and other lenders.

Mortgage bankers perform their intermediary function in two major ways. First, they originate home mortgage loans for sale to institutional investors and then service the loan for the investor who holds it. Second, they put commercial borrowers, construction lenders, and permanent lenders in contact with one another.

In performing the latter role, mortgage bankers often facilitate the overall operation of a transaction by financing the project for a short time between the completion of construction and the sale of the loan to the permanent investor. They frequently obtain funds for such interim financing from a commercial bank under a line of credit secured by an assignment of the mortgage loans involved. This arrangement is known as mortgage warehousing. Mortgage bankers also utilize this financing technique to enable them to serve as construction lenders in their own right. In either case the mortgage banker realizes a profit from mortgage warehousing by borrowing money, often at the commercial bank's prime interest rate, and then lending it to the developer at a higher rate of return.

H. OTHER SOURCES

Credit unions, individuals, syndications, service corporations, state development agencies, and community housing authorities are other less significant sources of real estate investment capital.

1. Credit Unions

State and federal credit unions offer residential mortgage loans. Moreover, certain federal credit unions have made substantial mortgaged-based investments.

2. Sellers

As discussed in Chapter 2, sellers finance acquisitions with purchase money mortgages or installment land contracts. With purchase money mortgages, sellers immediately convey title to the purchasers, and the purchasers grant them purchase money mortgages on the property that is sold. Installment land contracts are similar to purchase money mortgages, but the key difference is that vendees (purchasers) do not receive title until the final payment is made. These transactions, however, constitute only a small percentage of the total mortgage loans outstanding at any one time.

3. Syndications

Syndications are groups of individual real estate investors often formed as limited partnerships. They, however, commonly invest by purchasing realty rather than by making mortgage loans.

4. State Development Agencies

State development agencies have been created by many state legislatures to deal with intrastate housing problems by financing the construction of low-and-moderate-income housing. These development agencies generally have the power to raise funds by issuing tax-exempt bonds.

5. Community Housing Authorities

Many cities have established a housing authority that finances the construction of low-and-moderate-income housing from the sale of tax-exempt bonds.

I. MORTGAGE BROKERS

Mortgage brokers deserve consideration in this section even though they typically do not serve as a source of funds for real estate financing. Instead, the primary business of mortgage brokers is to arrange loan transactions between borrowers and mortgage lenders. Mortgage brokers thus contribute to mortgage market efficiency, particularly in the residential area, by performing a significant coordination/administrative function. Mortgage brokers have been involved in an increasing number of mortgages over the years and frequently receive a controversial type of remuneration—a portion of loan interest called the yield spread premium.

IV. OBTAINING REAL ESTATE FINANCING

A. APPLICATION AND COMMITMENT

Once a potential source of funds is identified, the borrower secures the mortgage loan through the process of application and commitment. The borrower initiates the process by making a formal or informal mortgage loan application to the lender who evaluates it in light of the risk involved.

The risk in mortgage financing is a two-tier one. The lender initially must assess the borrower's financial position with a view to predicting the likelihood that the underlying obligation will be repaid. Next, the lender must anticipate default and decide whether the mortgaged property will produce a sufficient amount at a foreclosure sale to pay the mortgage debt.

If the lender determines that the overall risk is acceptable, it will issue a mortgage loan commitment detailing the amount, duration, interest rate, and other pertinent items. Loans to financially weaker borrowers on less favorable terms are categorized as subprime. The length, formality, and specificity of the commitment vary from lender to lender and loan to loan. Commercial loan commitments naturally are rather complex and commonly include a provision for a nonrefundable commitment fee.

A loan commitment contains numerous terms and conditions not found in the application. Consequently, the typical commitment constitutes a counteroffer to make a loan. When the borrower accepts the commitment, a binding contract for a mortgage loan is created.

B. MORTGAGE LOAN CONTRACT

Mortgage loan contracts have been a source of litigation. Two areas are particularly controversial: nonrefundable commitment fees and the borrower's remedy for breach.

1. Nonrefundable Commitment Fees

The commitment fee issue arises when a borrower decides not to go through with the loan and then demands return of the "nonrefundable" commitment fee on the ground the lender has done nothing to earn it. Courts have consistently rejected this contention and held that the lender is entitled to the commitment fee either as liquidated damages for breach of contract or as compensation for keeping money available for loan to the borrower.

2. Borrower's Remedy for Lender's Breach

On the other hand, when the lender refuses to complete the loan in accordance with the commitment, questions arise regarding the borrower's remedy for breach of contract. Although the transfer of a security interest in real property is an aspect of the contemplated loan, the borrower ordinarily is not entitled to specific performance. Damages at law are normally considered adequate to compensate the borrower for any loss the borrower may have suffered by reason of the lender's failure to advance the promised funds. Nevertheless, the borrower should be entitled to specific performance of the mortgage loan contract when the borrower is unable to obtain a similar loan elsewhere.

V. LOAN PARTICIPATION AND MORTGAGE-BACKED SECURITIES

A. LOAN PARTICIPATION

A lender is sometimes presented with the opportunity to make an attractive loan, but does not have the entire loan amount conveniently available. Instead of losing the loan, the lender may ask other lenders to provide a share of the funds. An arrangement of this kind is known as a loan participation. A loan participation can also take place where the lender has already made the loan to a borrower, contracts with loan participants, recoups a portion of the loan made to the borrower and uses the loan participation funds to make additional loans. Bayer Corp. v. Masco Tech, Inc., 269 F.3d 726, 736 (6th Cir. 2001) (citations omitted). The originating mortgagee is the "lead" lender; the others are participants. The participants' interests in the loan are usually evidenced by participation certificates issued by the lead lender who holds the loan documents, collects payments, and disburses the appropriate share of the payments to each investor.

Loan participation allows a lender to share the risk of the loan with the loan participants, and the participants gain the benefit of the lender's mortgage and its priority. Id. Courts look at four factors in defining a loan participation agreement: 1) The lead lender makes a loan to a borrower; 2) loan participants are only entitled to repayment when the borrower pays the lead lender; 3) the lead lender is the only party that can file an action against the borrower; and 4) the contractual agreement between the lead lender and the loan participants is evidence of their true intentions. Id. at 736–737.

B. MORTGAGE-BACKED SECURITIES

A special type of participation involves the sale of undivided interests in a large pool of mortgage loans. The Government National Mortgage Association (GNMA or popularly Ginnie Mae), Fannie Mae (previously the Federal National Mortgage Association or FNMA), and Freddie Mac (previously the Federal Home Loan Mortgage Corporation or

FHLMC) utilize such mortgage-backed securities to stimulate private investment in housing.

GNMA's "pass-through" program is an early and well-known example of this type of participation. In that program, a mortgagee issues securities backed by a pool of mortgages. The pool is comprised of mortgages insured by FHA or guaranteed by VA. The periodic mortgage payments made by mortgagors in the pool are distributed among the investors (participants) in proportion to their investments. GNMA guarantees that the investors will be paid even if mortgagors in the pool fail to make their mortgage payments.

Mortgage securitization has blossomed over time. Fannie Mae and Freddie Mac became active in the field by issuing mortgage-backed securities and guaranteeing these securities themselves. Private issuers also entered the marketplace with a range of offerings. Various forms of mortgage-backed securities have evolved, commonly involving conventional mortgages. In sum, mortgage-backed securities have achieved a substantial and increasingly important position in the mortgage market. However, as discussed in Part VII, the increased in the use of mortgaged-backed securities contributed to the financial crisis during the Great Recession.

VI. SECONDARY FINANCING

Several lenders may independently acquire separate security interests in the same property by utilizing the mortgage market technique known as secondary financing.

A. THE BASICS

1. Creation of Junior Mortgages

Because the modern mortgage is just a security interest in real property, a mortgagor is free to mortgage the same property to as many lenders as are willing to make mortgage loans to the mortgagor. The placing of a second, third, or even fourth mortgage on the property is termed secondary financing. The second and subsequent mortgages are categorized as junior mortgages.

> *Illustration*: A mortgagor executes a mortgage to a first mortgagee. The mortgagor then executes a second mortgage to a second mortgagee and finally a third mortgage to a third mortgagee. All mortgages are valid. The mortgagor gave the first mortgagee only a security interest in the land, not ownership. The second and third mortgages held by the second mortgagee and the third mortgagee are referred to as junior mortgages.

> *Illustration*: An owner owns a house subject to a $40,000 mortgage held by a bank. The owner desires to sell the house for $70,000. A purchaser agrees to purchase it at that price, but has no ready cash and is unable to obtain a first mortgage loan for the full amount of the purchase price. The parties, therefore, agree to the following arrangement in order to ensure

that the sale is consummated. The owner conveys the house to the purchaser subject to the existing $40,000 mortgage that the purchaser assumes and agrees to pay. The purchaser gives the owner a $30,000 promissory note for the balance of the purchase price and a second mortgage on the house as security for payment of that note. The bank's $40,000 first mortgage and the owner's $30,000 second mortgage are both valid liens on the property.

2. Importance of Mortgagor's "Equity"

Lenders should make junior mortgage loans only if the fair market value of the mortgaged property exceeds the unpaid balance of prior mortgages. The difference is known as the mortgagor's equity. The use of the term "equity" in this context is really a convenient way of stating the value of the mortgagor's equity of redemption.

A mortgagor's equity may accumulate in two ways: (1) the principal balance due on existing mortgage loans may be reduced by partial payment; and (2) the mortgaged property may appreciate in value.

Illustration: A mortgagor owns a house worth $100,000. The mortgagor obtains a $100,000 loan from a first mortgagee secured by a mortgage on the house. (A mortgagor may be unable to obtain 100% financing, but it is assumed to be available here for purposes of illustration.) The mortgagor has $0 equity in the house, but still has an equity of redemption. Five years later the house has appreciated to a market value of $110,000, and the mortgagor has paid the principal on the mortgage note down to $90,000. The mortgagor, therefore, has $20,000 equity in the house. Needing cash, the mortgagor obtains a $15,000 loan from a second mortgagee secured by a second mortgage on the house. After this transaction, the mortgagor has $5,000 equity in the house.

The preceding illustration demonstrates the general circumstances upon which the home equity loan market has developed. A home equity loan may consist of just one advance of a certain amount, as in the illustration, or involve a line of credit contemplating a series of advances over time. Tax considerations, i.e., the deductibility of interest paid, have fueled the popularity of home equity loans.

3. Second Mortgages vs. Refinancing

If a mortgagor wants to pull out equity from the property, the mortgagor can take out a second mortgage loan or refinance a mortgage loan with a cash out. There are several factors that a mortgagor must consider before deciding which option is appropriate. Refinancing simply means the substitution of a new loan for an existing loan. A mortgagor should be apprehensive of refinancing when the current interest rates are higher than the rate on an existing mortgage loan. In such a case, it may be better to take out a second mortgage and keep the favorable existing mortgage loan. This is true even if the mortgagee requires a slight increase over the current interest rate because of the additional risk of secondary financing. Refinancing may be a better option when the current interest rate is lower than the existing mortgage loan rate. However, there are other factors that must be considered. A mortgagor must account for the closing costs. In addition, if the existing mortgage loan contains a prepayment penalty, the benefits from the lower interest rate may be offset by the prepayment penalty.

For example, assume that the mortgagor's property is worth \$400,000, but there is a \$150,000 mortgage that encumbers the property with a 5% interest rate. The current interest rate is 3%. The mortgagor wants to pull out \$50,000 of equity. The existing mortgage loan contains a prepayment penalty of 2% based on the outstanding balance of the mortgage loan. Hence, if the loan is prepaid, there will be a prepayment penalty of \$3,000. When closing costs are considered, this may be a costly way to pull out equity. Secondary financing may be a more viable option even though the interest rate is higher. The mortgagor can take out a second mortgage on the property without incurring a penalty. Without the prepayment penalty, refinancing may be the better way to pull out equity in this situation. The important point is that the mortgagor must balance numerous factors before deciding whether refinancing or taking out a secondary mortgage is the best way to pull out equity from the property.

4. Risk and Rate

Junior mortgage loans involve a relatively high risk because the secondary lender's security interest extends only to the value of the land in excess of prior liens. Hence, lenders generally make junior mortgage loans for a shorter term and at a higher interest rate than first mortgage loans.

> *Illustration*: A mortgagor owns a house worth $100,000. The mortgagor obtains a $100,000 loan from a first mortgagee secured by a mortgage on the house. Five years later the house has appreciated to a market value of $110,000, and the mortgagor has paid the principal on the mortgage note down to $90,000. Needing cash, the mortgagor obtains a $15,000 loan from a second mortgagee secured by a second mortgage on the house. Assume that the mortgagor fails to pay the loans to the first mortgagee and the second mortgagee. Both mortgagees foreclose, and sale of the house produces $100,000 after expenses. The first mortgagee receives $90,000, the unpaid balance on the first mortgage loan. The second mortgagee receives $10,000. In reality, the second mortgagee's $15,000 second mortgage loan was only partially secured. It is important to note, however, that the second mortgagee may be able to file a deficiency action against the mortgagor for the unpaid outstanding balance.

B. BEYOND THE BASICS/ WRAPAROUND MORTGAGES

The wraparound mortgage is an innovation in secondary financing. This financing device can be used either to derive additional funds from mortgaged real estate or to finance the purchase of such property. In either case, the wraparound mortgage is like a typical second mortgage in that it attaches to realty already encumbered by a mortgage. Its unique feature is that the face amount of the wraparound mortgage is equal to the amount actually disbursed to the mortgagor plus the unpaid balance of the prior encumbrance. The mortgagor's payments on the wraparound mortgage, therefore, cover both the money advanced under the wraparound mortgage and the amount due on the first mortgage. The wraparound mortgagee takes a portion of the payment it receives and makes the necessary payment on the original mortgage.

The interest rate on the face amount of the wraparound mortgage is generally higher than the rate on the existing mortgage. The result is that the wraparound mortgagee receives a higher than stated interest rate on the money actually advanced. This is because it collects an interest differential on the first mortgage payments as they pass through its hands, in addition to interest on the funds it disbursed. At the same time, the wraparound mortgagor pays less interest than would have accrued on alternative forms of financing.

Illustration: A mortgagor has a 30-year mortgage with Lender A. The outstanding balance is $100,000 and the fair market value of the mortgaged property is $320,000. The original mortgage was $150,000, and the mortgagor has been paying the mortgage for 15 years. The interest rate on the loan is 6%, and the monthly payment for interest and principal is $900. The mortgagor wants to pull out $150,000 in equity for the mortgaged property but is reluctant to refinance because of the prepayment penalty of 3% computed on the outstanding balance of the mortgaged property, and the current interest rate is 9%. Lender B agrees to provide a wraparound mortgage in the amount of $250,000, at an interest rate of 8%. The amount of cash that Lender B will advance to the mortgagor is $150,000. The balance of $100,000 represents the outstanding balance of the existing mortgage. The term of the wraparound mortgage is 15 years. Lender B's rate of return is slightly higher than 9% because Lender B earns interest on money that it did not actually advance, in this example $100,000. At the same time, the mortgagor pays only 8% on the $250,000, 1% below the current interest rate.

Illustration: A owner owns a farm subject to a first mortgage in favor of the first mortgagee. The mortgagor purchases the farm from an owner. The mortgagee assumes the first mortgage and executes a wraparound mortgage to the owner in the amount of the purchase price less the down payment. This transaction is a purchase money wraparound mortgage. It is structured and administered the same as the wraparound mortgage described in the immediately preceding illustration.

VII. THE SUBPRIME LOAN CRISIS

The real estate market suffered a terrible collapse from 2007–2011 that was known as the Great Recession. The Great Recession was caused by many factors. It affected the real estate market, stock market, investment banks and credit market. Several investment banks such as Bear Stearns and powerhouse Lehman Brothers failed. An extremely roiled mortgage environment, particularly its subprime sector, marked by a spate of foreclosures severely weakened the financial well-being of some mortgage lenders. This section focuses on four significant causes of the financial crisis.

A. INCREASE IN RISKY LOANS AND LOANS WITH ADJUSTABLE RATES

Prior to the collapse in the real estate market, there was a substantial growth in home financing resulting from low interest loans, lenient credit conditions, high risk loans and low-documentation loans. *In re* Fannie Mae 2008 Securities Litigation, 742 F. Supp. 2d 382 (2010). There was an increased demand for homes and an increase in new construction leading to housing prices soaring 125% from January 2000 to May 2006. Fed. Hous. Fin. Agency v. Nomura Holding Am., Inc. 104 F. Supp. 3d 441, 538 (2015). Many homeowners took out adjustable rate mortgages (ARMs). These loans, the so-called subprime loans, contributed to the collapse of the real estate market and the economy as a whole. Subprime loans grew from 1.1 million to 1.9 million from 2003 to 2005, and 20% of mortgage loans provided in 2005 were subprime loans. Fed. Hous. Fin. Agency v. Nomura Holding Am., Inc. 104 F. Supp. 3d 441, 538 (2015). Originations of subprime and Alt-A loans (e.g., loans with little or no documentation and loans made without regard to the mortgagor's ability to repay) doubled from $400 billion in 2003 to $830 billion in 2006. Bureau of Consumer Fin. Protection, Ability-to-Repay and Qualified Mortgage Standards Under the Truth in Lending Act (Regulation Z), 78 Fed. Reg. 113, at 35431 (June 12, 2013) [hereinafter Regulation Z]. Many of the homeowners took out these high-risk mortgage loans on the assumption that they would be able to refinance them in the future. *In re* Fannie Mae 2008 Securities Litigation, 742 F. Supp. 2d at 391. The ARMs were more expensive for the mortgagor even though the introductory interest rate was generally low. Id. The expectation was that the mortgagor would refinance the mortgage loan before interest rates reset. However, in 2006, the housing market contracted, homes lost value and mortgagors were unable to refinance their loans and to repay their loans. Fannie Mae, 742 F. Supp. at 391. The housing market contraction was caused by the following factors:

> The factors contributing to the contraction of the housing market and the decline in house prices were numerous and mutually reinforcing: Higher prices and higher interest rates led to a

softening of demand for homes; falling demand, coupled with oversupply, put downward pressure on house prices; and falling prices led to negative equity, which together with newly tightened underwriting standards limited the ability of homeowners to refinance existing loans. As the economy soured and unemployment soared, defaults and foreclosures increased; with the increase in defaults, investor demand for securitized mortgages collapsed.

Shoddy underwriting practices (as opposed to relaxed underwriting standards) like those at issue here contributed to both the spectacular expansion of the subprime mortgage and securitization markets and their contraction. The ability of originators to quickly sell and shift the risk of subprime loans off their books reduced their incentive to carefully screen borrowers. They approved loans that did not comply with stated underwriting guidelines and they misrepresented the quality of those loans to purchasers. Appraised values were overstated, owner occupancy was misreported, credit risk was hidden, and second liens were undisclosed. In short, these shoddy practices contributed to the housing price boom.

* * *

By the end of 2009, approximately 24% of all mortgaged residential properties in the U.S. had negative equity. Defaults on mortgage obligations became more rampant. This was particularly true for subprime mortgages, where

> serious delinquencies increased by more than five times from mid-2005 to late-2009. At the end of that period, about 30% of subprime mortgages were delinquent.

Fed. Hous. Fin. Agency v. Nomura Holding Am., Inc. 104 F. Supp. 3d 441, 539 (2015).

By 2010, 40% of subprime and Alt-A loans were 90 days past due or in foreclosure. Regulation Z, at 35431.

B. INCREASE IN MORTGAGED-BACKED SECURITIES

The collapse in the real estate market expanded beyond that industry to the stock market, investment banks and credit market because of the securitized mortgages. While the 2007–2009 financial crisis had many interrelated and reciprocal causes, certainly one of the greatest causes was the plummeting values of asset-backed securities, which included mortgage-backed securities (MBSs) and collateralized-debt obligations (CDOs). Many of the subprime loans were bundled as MBSs on the secondary market. An MBS is created when a mortgage originator, such as Countrywide Home Loans, combines or bundles a portfolio of mortgages into a trust. Fed. Hous. Fin. Agency v. JPMorgan Chase & Co., 902 F.Supp.2d 476, 482 (S.D.N.Y. 2012). Trust certificates, which entitled their owners to income from the mortgage loan repayments, were then transferred to an underwriter who sold the certificates to investors, including Fannie Mae, Freddie Mac, and major Wall Street investment institutions. Id. Underwriters sold rights to both the MBS's equity and cash flows—the interest in cash flows resulting from dividing the underlying mortgages into different classes, or "tranches." Loreley Financing (Jersey) No. 3 Ltd. v. Wells Fargo Securities, LLC, 797 F.3d 160, 164 (2nd Cir. 2015). Each tranche contained mortgages of a different risk. Id. Interests in less risky tranches were priced lower and received more moderate returns that were paid out before other tranches while investing in the riskier tranches was cheaper but paid out higher returns only after low-risk tranches' returns were paid. Id. This repayment system may be referred to as a "waterfall," whereby mortgage payments first "water" a low-risk tranche before flowing down to tranches of increasing risk and eventually reaching the equity interests—if any water remains. Id. at 164–65. Accordingly, the equity interest holders were first affected by mortgage defaults because they were the last to be paid. Id. Just as an MBS was comprised of a bundle of mortgages, a CDO was comprised of a bundle of MBSs. Id. at 165. Like an MBS, a CDO paid out in the same way that was likened to a waterfall. Id.

In 2001, about half of the subprime mortgage loans had been securitized; however, by 2005, more than 80% of these mortgages had been securitized. Fed. Hous. Fin. Agency v. Nomura Holding Am., Inc. 104 F. Supp. 3d 441, 538 (2015). One of the greatest causes of the Great Recession was the plummeting values of these MBSs.

C. LOSSES SUSTAINED IN MAJOR INSTITUTIONS

Major American institutions experienced huge losses resulting from the falling values of MBSs. For example, Citibank held billions of dollars of MBSs. During 2007, it announced that it planned a $1.4 billion write-down or reduction in the book value on its highly leveraged finance commitments and later announced an additional $8 billion to $11 billion write-down related to its subprime exposure. *In re* Citigroup Inc. Shareholder Derivative Litigation, 964 A.2d 106, 113 (Del. Ch. 2009). Around the same time, Citigroup announced a 57% decline in net income from the prior year's income and that it would lay off 2,000 employees in March of 2008, which brought Citigroup's total layoffs to 6,000 since the subprime meltdown began. Id. at 114.

Citigroup's struggles were emblematic of trouble throughout the national economy. In April of 2007, Freddie Mac announced it would refinance $20 billion of subprime mortgages because borrowers could not afford payments once their ARMs reset to a higher rate. Id. at 115. The ratings agencies downgraded bonds backed by subprime mortgages in July of 2007, and two Bear Stearns-managed hedge funds that were heavily invested in subprime mortgages declared bankruptcy a month later. Id. Moreover, American International Group (AIG) noted that mortgage defaults were spreading and becoming increasingly common among borrowers outside the subprime sector. Id.

Fannie Mae and Freddie Mac were some of the largest purchasers of mortgages and MBSs leading up to the Great Recession, purchasing more than $33 billion worth of MBSs between September 2005 and September 2007 alone. Id. The roiled mortgage environment of 2007–2008 eroded the financial underpinnings of Fannie Mae and Freddie Mac. Recognizing the worsening housing market, Congress passed the Housing and Economic Recovery Act of 2008 (HERA), which allowed the Federal Housing Finance Agency (FHFA) to place Government-Sponsored Enterprises (GSEs) in conservatorship. Fed. Hous. Fin. Agency v. UBS Americas, Inc., 858 F.Supp.2d 306, 311 (S.D.N.Y. 2012). Fannie Mae and Freddie Mac were GSEs and put in conservatorship under the FHFA's authority after HERA was passed. Id. This allowed the FHFA to oversee Fannie Mae and Freddie Mac's " 'reorganizing, rehabilitating, or winding up [of their] affairs.' " Id. (quoting Pub. L. No. 110–289, 122 Stat. 2654, § 1367(a)(3) (2008) (codified at 12 U.S.C. § 4617)). By placing Fannie Mae and Freddie Mac under FHFA conservatorship, the FHFA could also assert claims on their behalf. Id. This arrangement was part of a revitalization scheme for Fannie Mae and Freddie Mac predicated on extensive federal government involvement including loans, preferred stock acquisition, mortgage-backed securities purchases, and common stock acquisition rights. These steps were designed to fortify Fannie Mae and Freddie Mac through various means such as enhanced regulation, increased credit, and authorization for the federal government to purchase their stock.

The FHFA brought at least sixteen unique actions against the nation's major financial institutions, alleging their misconduct in creating, underwriting, or selling asset-backed securities that caused huge losses and institutional failures during 2007 through 2009. JPMorgan Chase, 902 F.Supp.2d at 480–81. Defendants involved in the FHFA cases resulting from their role in the securitization process included JPMorgan Chase, Bear Stearns, Washington Mutual (WaMu), and Long Beach Securities (a WaMu subsidiary), among others. Id. at 481 Defendants involved based on their role as underwriters included Citigroup, Goldman Sachs, Credit Suisse, and RBS Securities, among others. Id.

D. MISREPRESENTED STANDARDS APPLIED TO MBSs

In *JPMorgan Chase*, the FHFA contended that Fannie Mae and Freddie Mac suffered billions of dollars in damages due to their justifiable reliance on the defendants' representations that the securities' underlying mortgages comported with stated underwriting guidelines. Id. at 482–83. For example, an appraiser who conducted business with WaMu described the bank's origination practices during the early 2000s: "It was the Wild West . . . If you were alive, they would give you a loan. Actually, I think if you were dead, they would still give you a loan." Id. at 486. However, deviation from underwriting guidelines was not limited to WaMu. In the FHFA examination of thousands of loan files, it found over 90% of loans underwritten by Bear Stearns were not underwritten according to underwriting guidelines while 79% of loans underwritten by JPMorgan likewise breached underwriting guidelines. Id. at 487.

One type of breach that frequently occurred was underwriters' unwillingness to verify borrowers' stated incomes. Id. For example, it was alleged in the case that a $368,000 mortgage was issued in 2007 to a borrower who claimed he earned $13,500 per month working as a fire systems company inspector/ foreman. Id. The Bureau of Labor Statistics reported an average salary for an inspector in the 90th percentile in the same geographic region was only $7,675, however. Id. Additionally, the borrower previously reported monthly income of only $6,835 for 2006 and 2007 in a Statement of Financial Affairs that was filed as part of his Chapter 13 proceedings. Id. The borrower's debt-to-income ratio was 88.37% when recalculated according to his actual income while the guideline maximum was 50%. Id. That particular borrower subsequently defaulted—like so many other borrowers—and his loan was liquidated for a $248,583.81 loss. Id.

The evidence in the case indicated that loan originators were blatantly candid in intentionally disregarding their own underwriting standards with shocking candor at times. For example, at JPMorgan's subprime lending arm in Oregon, supervisors issued a memorandum to loan officers that contained "cheats & tricks" to use in order to qualify borrowers for low-documentation loans. Id. at 492. The memorandum instructed loan officers to attempt to override the bank's automated underwriting software: "[T]ry resubmitting with a slightly higher income. Inch it up $500 to see if you can get the findings you want." Id.

Similarly, additional evidence in the case showed that at a Bear Stearns affiliate, an Assistant Manager for Quality Control-Underwriting emailed employees instructing them to not retrieve borrowers' credit reports or make phone calls to verify borrowers' employment. Id. at 494. WaMu employees were likewise discouraged from questioning borrowers' salary representations or collecting much loan documentation. Id. at 495. A WaMu loan sales associate reported that, to get new loan approval, "his colleagues would cut-and-paste the name and address of the applicant into bank statements taken from the file of an entirely different borrower." Id.

VIII. POST-SUBPRIME LOAN CRISIS

The Great Recession lasted for about two years. As discussed above, it weakened housing and financial markets. It resulted in massive losses for investors in the stock market. In addition, their retirement accounts also suffered massive losses because many of these funds were invested in securities. However, in the years since the crisis ended, the economy has rebounded, the housing market is stable and the stock market is setting all-time highs.

CHAPTER 6

FEDERAL GOVERNMENT INVOLVEMENT IN FINANCING PROCESS

Long before the Great Recession, Congress frequently addressed housing concerns and other matters related to mortgage law and real estate finance. Its activity in these areas has had a considerable impact on the mortgage market. This chapter discusses the federal government's involvement in the real estate financing process via housing subsidies, mortgage insurance, secondary mortgage market support institutions, and various legislative measures, particularly those intended to address predatory lending and the other causes of the Great Recession and the subprime loan crisis.

I. HOUSING SUBSIDIES

Some Congressional action in the real estate finance area is designed to produce more and better housing for low-and-moderate-income families through housing subsidies administered by the Department of Housing and Urban Development. The form of the subsidy varies greatly from program to program.

Congress has also enacted tax benefits under the Internal Revenue Code to incentivize owners to establish and maintain rental housing for low income individuals. For example, the Low-Income Housing Credit (LIHC) provides a tax credit to taxpayers for the construction or rehabilitation of residential rental housing for low income individuals. *See* IRC § 42 (2017). The owner is entitled to claim the credit over a 10-year period beginning with the tax year that the owner placed the building in service or, if the owner elects, the following tax year. IRC § 42(f) (2017). The credit is based on 70% of the adjusted basis (e.g., the owner's cost) of a new building where the owner has not received any federal subsidies and 30% of the adjusted basis of all other buildings. IRC § 42(b)(1)(B) (2017). An owner must meet one of two tests elected by the owner to claim the credit. Under the first test for eligibility, at least 20% of units available in the rental building must be affordable housing and occupied by residents with income 50% or less of the median income in the community. IRC § 42(g)(1)(A) (2017). The second eligibility test requires at least 40% of the units available in the rental building to be affordable housing occupied by tenants with income that is 60% or less of the median income in the community. IRC § 42(g)(1)(B) (2017). Before the owner can claim the LIHC, the owner must receive a housing credit allocation from the state or a local housing agency delegated by the state to allocate the credit. Treas. Reg. § 1.42–1T(a)(2) (2017).

II. GUARANTY PROGRAMS

A less direct but highly significant form of government involvement in the real estate financing process is found in the federal mortgage insurance and guaranty programs administered by the Federal Housing Administration (FHA) and the Department of Veterans Affairs (VA). These programs do not make new loans but encourage private institutional lenders to make residential mortgage loans to borrowers who otherwise might not qualify. This is accomplished by insuring or guarantying mortgagees against loss on certain residential loans. In essence, the insurance or guaranty takes the place of a large down payment. Mortgage loans that are insured or guaranteed by FHA or VA are termed "FHA mortgages" or "VA mortgages," respectively.

With respect to FHA mortgages, there are maximum loan amounts for mortgagors to qualify for these mortgages. The limits are based on the cost of local housing and whether the residence is a single-family home or a multi-unit dwelling, such as a duplex. All mortgagors with FHA mortgages are required to pay mortgage insurance premiums (MIP) to reduce the risks as FHA mortgages permit low down payments. The MIP is payable upfront and with monthly payments based on the loan-to-value ratio. It is cancelled after a mortgagor has paid the mortgage loan for 11 years unless the loan-to-value ratio was greater than 90% at the time the loan was made.

Any loan to a veteran is automatically guaranteed if it is made to purchase, construct or improve a home that the veteran will occupy or to refinance an existing mortgage loan that is secured by the veteran's owner-occupied home. 38 U.S.C.A. § 3710(a) (2017).

Although FHA and VA mortgages are similar, they differ in the following generally described ways. First, FHA mortgage loans may be obtained by members of the general public. VA mortgage loans are available only to veterans, servicemembers and some surviving spouses. Second, FHA primarily insures eligible mortgage loans. VA issues a guaranty of partial repayment. VA borrowers, therefore, do not pay mortgage insurance premiums, as do FHA borrowers. However, VA borrowers must pay a funding fee.

Mortgage loans that are ineligible under these programs are referred to as "conventional mortgages."

III. SECONDARY MORTGAGE MARKET SUPPORT INSTITUTIONS

Congress also has created several institutions designed to maintain a national secondary market for residential mortgages. The policy underlying this secondary mortgage market approach is that the support institutions can promote the even distribution of real estate investment capital throughout the country by buying mortgages from originators and selling them to investors. Distinguish the secondary mortgage market which involves the sale of first mortgages from the separate concept of secondary financing, addressed earlier this chapter, which involves the creation of junior mortgages on already encumbered real estate.

The institutions charged with responsibility for maintaining a viable secondary mortgage market are Fannie Mae (previously the Federal National Mortgage Association or FNMA), the Government National Mortgage Association (GNMA or popularly

Ginnie Mae), and Freddie Mac (previously the Federal Home Loan Mortgage Corporation or FHLMC.) Each organization plays a major role in this loosely constructed system.

Created near the end of the Depression, Fannie Mae is the oldest element of the secondary mortgage market. Originally part of FHA, it became privately owned, but subject to considerable governmental regulation and control. Fannie Mae buys and sells FHA, VA, and conventional mortgages in order to improve the nationwide distribution of investment capital available for mortgage financing. Fannie Mae is active in issuing mortgage-backed securities.

Ginnie Mae, a 1968 spin-off from Fannie Mae, is a government owned entity within the Department of Housing and Urban Development. Ginnie Mae engages in a variety of special assistance activities. It also is involved in the secondary mortgage market via special mortgage investment programs such as the "pass-through" mortgage-backed securities program.

Freddie Mac has operated as a privately owned corporation heavily regulated by the federal government. It was created in 1970 to establish a viable secondary mortgage market for conventional mortgages. Freddie Mac performs this function in good part by assembling pools of conventional mortgages and selling securities backed by these pooled mortgages. It also may acquire FHA and VA mortgages.

As noted during the discussion of the subprime loan crisis, Fannie Mae and Freddie Mac went into a federal-agency administered conservatorship.

IV. OTHER GOVERNMENT INVOLVEMENT

Over the years Congress has enacted laws on a variety of other real estate finance subjects. The following legislative measures have had an impact on the mortgage market.

A. TRUTH IN LENDING

The Truth in Lending Act of 1968 (15 U.S.C.A. § 1601 *et seq.*), implemented by the Board of Governors of the Federal Reserve System via Regulation Z, requires lenders to disclose financing costs and terms to prospective borrowers. As a general rule, Truth in Lending Act applies only to consumer credit transactions involving $25,000 or less. Business or commercial loans for any amount are not covered.

Many real estate credit transactions are governed by Truth in Lending. Although business or commercial real estate loans are, of course, exempt, the Act applies to consumer real estate loans regardless of amount. The $25,000 ceiling was removed from this type of transaction so that the average homebuyer is protected when embarking upon the only large-scale financing arrangement that person may ever enter.

As a general matter, the creditor in a standard real estate credit transaction must make the usual disclosure for closed-end transactions including a statement of the amount financed, the finance charge, and the annual percentage rate. Significant differences exist, however, between its disclosure obligations and those of a creditor in a non-real estate transaction. For example, the items to be included in computing the finance charge differ. Moreover, the real estate creditor must state whether the mortgage loan may be assumed. Further, in certain real estate credit transactions the borrower has a right to rescind that must be disclosed. If the transaction creates a lien on the debtor's principal dwelling that secures a non-acquisition or non-construction loan, the consumer may rescind the transaction within three business days after closing or after the rescission right and other material matters are disclosed, whichever is later.

Specialized disclosure requirements have been tailored for certain types of mortgage loans. Such is the case with respect to adjustable rate mortgages, reverse mortgages, closed-end home equity loans that bear a high interest/fee rate, and open-end home equity loans.

In addition to disclosure standards, Truth in Lending establishes substantive limitations on closed-end home equity loans that bear a high interest/fee rate. For example, prepayment penalties are curtailed for loans in this category. 'Higher-priced mortgage loans," which constitute a recently created separate classification, are subject to prepayment penalty constraints as well.

Certain dubious, rapacious, or misleading mortgage lending activities are prohibited under Truth in Lending. Closed-end home equity loans that bear a high interest/fee rate and "higher-priced mortgage loans" are the primary targets of the bulk of these protective mandates.

The Truth in Lending Act was amended by the Mortgage Disclosure Improvement Act of 2008 (Pub. L. No. 110–289, §§ 2501–2503). Among other things, this measure strengthens the disclosure scheme for adjustable rate mortgages. More importantly, as will be discussed later in this chapter, the Dodd-Frank Wall Street Reform and Consumer Protection Act of 2010 made significant changes to the Truth in Lending Act's disclosure standards. Briefly, the Real Estate Settlement Procedures Act of 1974 requires certain disclosures as well. The Dodd-Frank Act integrated the disclosures on two new forms under these two Acts, the Loan Estimate and the Closing Disclosure.

B. INTERSTATE LAND SALES FULL DISCLOSURE ACT OF 1968

Congress enacted the Interstate Land Sales Full Disclosure Act of 1968 (15 U.S.C.A. § 1701 *et seq.*) to eliminate the use of fraudulent or misleading practices in the marketing of certain types of raw land. The Act applies to developers who sell or lease unimproved subdivision lots as part of a common promotional plan in interstate commerce or through the mail. Numerous exemptions, both full and partial, are available. For example, developers of subdivisions that include less than twenty-five lots are totally exempt from the Act. Developers of subdivisions containing less than one hundred lots are exempt from the Act's registration and disclosure provisions described below, but are still subject to the Act's antifraud provisions.

Nonexempt subdivision developers must disclose the material facts about the land being offered for sale. Disclosure is accomplished by filing a statement of record with the Office of Interstate Land Sales Registration in the Department of Housing and Urban Development and by delivering a property report to prospective purchasers. The statement of record must include certain specific information about the subdivision, the surrounding area, and the developer. The property report is a condensed more readable version of the statement of record.

The Act gives the purchaser certain remedies for the developer's failure to make proper disclosure. Rescission is available in two general instances. First, if the developer fails to give the purchaser a property report prior to the execution of a sales contract, the purchaser may rescind the contract within two years of its execution. Second, even if the purchaser is furnished a property report before signing a sales contract, the purchaser may rescind the contract within seven days of its execution. Frequently, the contract is an installment land contract. If so, additional disclosure and rescission provisions of the Act apply.

The purchaser also has the right to obtain specific performance, damages, or other appropriate relief from the developer for violations of the Act. Although the Act does not apply to lending institutions engaging in the normal course of their real estate financing activities, a lender may be liable for damages if it actively participates in a plan to sell or lease property covered by the Act.

C. REAL ESTATE SETTLEMENT PROCEDURES ACT OF 1974

The Real Estate Settlement Procedures Act of 1974 (12 U.S.C.A. § 2601 *et seq.*), known as RESPA, is basically a disclosure statute designed to protect homebuyers or homeowners from the imposition of unanticipated, unwarranted, or excessive loan closing costs. RESPA covers all "federally related mortgage loans." Most residential mortgage loans fall within this category. As a general rule, RESPA applies when an institutional lender makes a loan that is secured by a mortgage, first or junior, on one-to-four-family residential real estate.

Congress has amended RESPA numerous times since its enactment. In accordance with the Dodd-Frank Wall Street Reform and Consumer Protection Act, Pub. L. 111–203 (July 10, 2010) (Dodd-Frank Act), Congress delegated rule-making responsibilities under RESPA to the Consumer Financial Protection Bureau (CFPB). The CFPB was required to publish rules related to the required integrated disclosures required under the Truth in Lending Act and RESPA. The CFPB issued a final rule on the integrated disclosure requirements on July 7, 2017. *See* Amendments to Federal Mortgage

Disclosure Requirements under the Truth in Lending Act (Regulation Z), 12 CFR Part 1026 (2017). The purpose of the final rule was to provide clarity for compliance purposes. In general, the CFPB issued the final rule to memorialize its informal guidance.

Lenders must provide loan applicants with two forms—Loan Estimate and Closing Disclosure. The Loan Estimate is a three-page document that replaced both the Good Faith Estimate (GFE) and Truth-in-Lending Disclosure. The Loan Estimate contains details such as the loan's estimated interest rate, monthly payments, and total closing costs. Additionally, the Loan Estimate contains important information on possible interest rate and payment adjustments, prepayment penalties, and negative amortization. It is intended to help borrowers understand the costs and risks of the loan. A lender must provide a Loan Estimate to borrowers within three business days of receiving their loan applications, and the Loan Estimate should be distributed to borrowers before a lender has decided whether to approve the loan application. A lender cannot charge a fee for the loan until the borrower receives the Loan Estimate and communicates an intent to close on the transaction.

The Loan Estimate also includes detailed information on adjustable rate mortgages. This information includes whether the payments are interest only, the monthly principal and interest payments, index and margin, initial interest rate, frequency in interest rate changes and limits on interest rate changes. Generally, the Loan Estimate must be delivered to the applicant no later than seven days before the loan is consummated. The lender must exercise good faith in completing the Loan Estimate. But, the lender may charge more than the amounts set forth in the Loan Estimate for certain situations such as changed circumstances or when the new charges fall within a tolerance limitation. If the applicant pays an amount in excess of the tolerance limitation, the lender must refund this excess within 60 days after consummation of the loan.

Effective October 3, 2015, CFPB replaced the standard lending form, Settlement Statement (HUD-1), which was the standard lending form, with the Closing Disclosure. The Closing Disclosure is intended to help a borrower understand the costs of the transaction. A noticeable physical difference is the Closing Disclosure's stylistic emphasis on particular information such as whether costs may increase. Likewise, the Closing Disclosure appears to include over a page of disclosures that the Settlement Statement did not contain. Also included on the Closing Disclosure but not the Settlement Statement is nearly half a page of contact information for involved lending institutions, brokers, and agents. Both the Loan Estimate and Closing Document are intended to provide information about whether the borrower can afford the loan.

Finally, the Closing Disclosure requires lenders to give borrowers at least three days to review the document before closing the loan while the Settlement Statement required lenders to give borrowers only one day to review the document before closing. The Closing Disclosure's three-day window is intended to give lenders time to compare the loan's final terms and costs to those contained in the Loan Estimate, which borrowers previously received from their lender, and clear up any questions or misunderstandings with the lenders. Within three days of the application, the lender must also provide the applicant a copy of a "special information booklet" that is published by the CFPB to help the borrower understand the transaction. If the borrower has applied for a home equity line of credit (HELOC), the lender is able to provide the "What You Should Know About Home Equity Lines of Credit" brochure in lieu of the special information booklet. In addition, the lender is not required to provide the booklet if the borrower is not using the loan to purchase a one-to-four unit residential property or is taking out a junior mortgage loan or a reverse mortgage.

The old documents—namely the Settlement Statement (HUD-1) and Truth-in-Lending Disclosure—are still used in specific instances. They are used with a reverse mortgage, HELOC, manufactured housing loan not secured by real estate, or a loan through certain homebuyer assistance programs.

RESPA also requires that lenders disclose to applicants for federally related mortgage loans whether the servicing of the loan may be transferred. Further, the borrower must be notified of any transfer of servicing.

In addition to these disclosure requirements, RESPA includes significant substantive provisions. One portion of the RESPA is designed to eliminate kickbacks and unearned fees. Another section limits the amount that a lender may require a borrower to place in an escrow account for the payment of casualty insurance premiums and property taxes.

For further information on the integrated disclosure rules, see Consumer Financial Protection Bureau, TILA-RESPA Integrated Disclosure, Guide to the Loan Estimate and Closing Disclosure forms (Oct. 2016).

D. HOME MORTGAGE DISCLOSURE ACT OF 1975

As noted earlier in this chapter, one aspect of the mortgage lender's risk is whether the land offered as security is of sufficient market value to satisfy the debt in the event the borrower defaults. Some lending institutions may consider all property located in a designated area of the community they serve as inadequate or high-risk collateral and hence, unacceptable as security for a standard mortgage loan. This form of lending discrimination is known as "redlining" because of the manner in which the designated areas may have been identified on a map of the community. Typically, redlined areas are older, integrated, middle-class or lower middle-class neighborhoods.

The Home Mortgage Disclosure Act of 1975 (12 U.S.C.A. § 2801 *et seq.*) is designed to identify and help eliminate redlining. The Act requires many financial institutions to disclose detailed information about their residential mortgage loans by reference to census tract. Such lenders also must report data regarding their loan applications. Although the Act makes redlining more visible, it does not provide a penalty for such activity. Congress apparently decided to rely on community pressure to force lenders to act responsibly in this regard. However, the Community Reinvestment Act of 1977 (12 U.S.C.A. § 2901 *et seq.*) does place an obligation on regulatory agencies to determine whether a financial institution adequately serves its community and to take this factor into consideration when examining the institution or reviewing its application for a merger, a new branch, or other special action.

E. COMPREHENSIVE ENVIRONMENTAL RESPONSE, COMPENSATION, AND LIABILITY ACT OF 1980

Congress enacted the Comprehensive Environmental Response, Compensation, and Liability Act of 1980 (42 U.S.C.A. § 9601 *et seq.*) (CERCLA) in an attempt to remedy environmental damage caused by hazardous substance sites. CERCLA, commonly called "Superfund", makes owners and operators of hazardous substance facilities liable for cleanup costs. CERCLA expressly excludes from this obligation anyone "who, without participating in the management of a . . . facility, holds indicia of ownership primarily to protect his security interest in the . . . facility." 42 U.S.A. § 9601(20)(A). Notwithstanding this provision, mortgagees, particularly those who take possession of a hazardous substance site upon default or acquire such a site at foreclosure or by deed-in-lieu of foreclosure, face potential liability for cleanup costs as an owner or operator under CERCLA.

In 1996, Congress amended CERCLA to clarify and restrict the meaning of "participating in the management of a . . . facility" and to limit the risk of liability for foreclosing mortgagees. Moreover, Congress provided that an Environmental Protection Agency final rule circumscribing lender liability, previously invalidated by court decision, "shall be deemed to have been validly issued. . . . " Pub. L. No. 104–208 §§ 2502, 2504. Even with these measures in place, it is not uncommon for commercial mortgage lenders to arrange appropriate environmental insurance coverage.

F. DODD-FRANK WALL STREET REFORM AND CONSUMER PROTECTION ACT OF 2010

The Dodd-Frank Wall Street Reform and Consumer Protection Act of 2010, Title III, Pub. L. No. 111–203 (2010) (Dodd-Frank Act) was enacted to address predatory lending, the subprime loan crisis and the Great Recession. The Dodd-Frank Act is extremely comprehensive. It enacted regulatory requirements for large banks and changes related to the required amount of reserves for capital banks. This section will focus on some of the key provisions of the Dodd-Frank Act related to protecting consumers/mortgagors. However, a detailed analysis of the Dodd-Frank Act is beyond the scope of this book. In addition, it is important to note that

President Donald Trump wants to repeal the Dodd-Frank Act and dismantle many of its regulations.

One of the most significant aspects of the Dodd-Frank Act was the creation of the Consumer Financial Protection Bureau (CFPB) within the Federal Reserve. It has vast authority including regulating consumer financial products and services. It also has authority over mortgages and loan servicing. Under the Dodd-Frank Act, the CFPB has supervisory and rulemaking authority over nondepository institutions, including those that offer or provide loan origination, servicing and brokerage for secured real estate that is used for personal purposes (e.g., principal residences and vacation cottages) or loan modification or foreclosure relief services related to these types of loans. The CFPB has rulemaking authority and can issue orders and guidance. For depository institutions and credit unions with more than $10 million in assets, the CFPB has exclusive authority to require reports and examine them to assess compliance with federal consumer laws, obtain information about activities related to these laws and detect and assess consumer risks. 12 U.S.C. 5515(a) & (b) (2017). The CFPB has primary enforcement authority over depository institutions and credit unions with more than $10 million in assets. 12 U.S.C. 5515(c) (2017). However, for depository institutions and credit unions with less than $10 million in assets, the prudential regulator has primary enforcement authority, but the CFPB may require reports to support its role of implementing federal consumer financial law and its examining discretion in conjunction with the prudential regulator. 12 U.S.C. 5516 (2017).

Congress enacted the Dodd-Frank Act because it believed that economic stability would be enhanced by regulating residential mortgage terms and credit practices while ensuring that affordable mortgage loans were available to homebuyers. 15 U.S.C. § 1639b(a)(1) (2017). One significant cause of the subprime loan crisis was that mortgagors were taking out predatory mortgage loans, particularly adjustable rate mortgages with "teaser" rates. In addition, loan originators ignored underwriting standards and made loans to mortgagors who did not have the ability to repay them. As a result, one of the stated purposes of the Dodd-Frank Act is to ensure that mortgagors receive residential mortgage loans with terms that are fair and affordable and are not deceptive or abusive. 15 U.S.C. § 1639b(a)(2) (2017).

Under the Dodd-Frank Act, a lender must make a good faith effort to verify that the mortgagor has the ability to repay the loan, taxes, insurance and any assessments based on verified documentation in making a residential mortgage loan. 15 U.S.C. § 1639c(a)(1) (2017). In making this determination, the Dodd-Frank Act requires lenders to consider many factors including the mortgagor's income, credit history, debt-to-income ratio, debts and employment status. 15 U.S.C. § 1639c(a)(3) (2017). To verify a mortgagor's income, the lender must review several documents, including the mortgagor's tax returns, W-2, pay stubs and financial institution records. 15 U.S.C. § 1639c(a)(4) (2017). Residential loan originators are prohibited from receiving fees in varied amounts based on the loan terms. 15 U.S.C. § 1639b(c)(1) (2017). The Dodd-Frank Act's ability-to-repay rules apply to most closed-end mortgages, such as traditional mortgages and home equity loans.

During the subprime loan crisis, some mortgagors took out mortgage loans on their homes with negative amortization. Negative amortization arises where the loan payment does not cover the interest charged, and the excess interest is added to the principal resulting in an increase in the principal balance. Under the Dodd-Frank Act, unless the mortgage is a reverse mortgage, if the mortgage secures a loan on a dwelling, the lender must provide the mortgagor with a statement that explains that the transaction may result in negative amortization which increases the principal balance of the loan and that it will reduce the mortgagor's equity in the dwelling. 15 U.S.C. § 1639c(f)(1) (2017). If the mortgagor is a first-time borrower and there is negative amortization on a loan secured by the dwelling, the mortgagor must provide the lender with documentation establishing that the mortgagor received homeownership counseling by competent counselors as certified by the Department of Housing and Urban Development. Id.

G. 2013 HOME OWNERSHIP AND EQUITY PROTECTION ACT RULE

Congress enacted the Home Ownership and Equity Protection Act of 1994 (HOEPA) to contend with abusive practices related to loan refinancing and home equity loans that had high interest rates or high fees. *See* Consumer Financial Protection Bureau, 2013 Home Ownership and Equity Protection Act Rule Guide (March 2016) [hereinafter HOEPA Guide]. HOEPA was enacted as an amendment to the Truth in Lending Act. The 2013 HOEPA Rule is a component of the rulemaking authority under the Dodd-Frank Act.

The rules and restrictions set forth in the 2013 HOEPA Rule were created as a result of the subprime loan crisis because many homeowners were taking out unfavorable loans that qualified as high-cost mortgages, such as adjustable rate mortgages with teaser rates. It prohibits certain terms and requires disclosures related to certain home equity loans and second mortgages on a mortgagor's principal residence. HOEPA does not cover mortgages for construction loans on new residences, vacation or second homes, FHA loans and certain U.S. Department of Agriculture loans. Pursuant to a Dodd-Frank Act mandate, the CFPB issued a rule that expanded the scope of HOEPA in 2013 to include home equity lines of credit and purchase money mortgages. *See* HOEPA Guide, at 9. The 2013 HOEPA Rule applies to loan applications submitted on or after January 10, 2014.

One of the primary concerns under HOEPA is "high-cost mortgages." As outlined in the HOEPA Guide, there are several coverage tests under HOEPA to determine if there is a high-cost mortgage. First, a high-cost mortgage on a first mortgage on the homeowner's principal residence is where the annual percentage rate at the consummation of the transaction is more than 6.5% above the prime rate or 8.5% above the prime rate for mortgages on personal property (e.g., RVs and houseboats) if the loan was less than $50,000. *See* HOEPA Guide, at 19. For junior mortgages, a high-cost mortgage is one on a homeowner's principal residence that is more than 8.5% above the prime rate. Id.

Second, a transaction is a high-cost mortgage if the points and fees exceed 5% of the total loan amount that is at least $20,000. HOEPA Guide, at 21. If the loan is less than $20,000, a high-cost mortgage is where the fees exceed the lesser of 8% of the loan amount or $1,000. Id. These amounts are adjusted annually for inflation. Third, pursuant to the Dodd-Frank Act, the 2013 HOEPA Rule includes a prepayment penalty test to determine coverage under HOEPA. A transaction is covered under HOEPA if a lender charges a prepayment penalty that is more than 36 months after the transaction closing or the penalty is more than 2% of the loan amount that the mortgagor has prepaid. HOEPA Guide, at 27. If the transaction is a high-cost mortgage, HOEPA prevents the lender from charging a prepayment penalty. Id. In addition, if a transaction is a high-cost mortgage, HOEPA generally prevents balloon payments and limits acceleration to situations where the mortgagor commits fraud, defaults on the payment of the loan or acts in a manner that adversely affects the lender's security interest. HOEPA Guide, at 30–31.

HOEPA contains numerous restrictions on fees or practices if a transaction is a high-cost mortgage. A few of these restrictions include: 1) lenders cannot charge a fee to modify a loan; 2) negative amortization is prohibited; 3) the interest rate cannot be increased after a mortgagor defaults on a loan; 4) a lender cannot sell the mortgage in the secondary market without notifying the mortgagor; and 5) points and fees cannot be financed. HOEPA Guide, at 31–32.

Further, as noted in the previous section, the Dodd-Frank Act contains ability-to-repay rules. However, those rules do not apply to home equity lines of credit. Instead, home equity lines of credit, including high-cost mortgages, are covered under HOEPA. The HOEPA Rule requires a lender to consider a mortgagor's verified current and expected income from forms such as W-2s and pay stubs and current obligations, including property taxes and homeowners' association fees. HOEPA Guide, at 34. Unlike closed-end mortgages, there is a presumption of compliance if the criteria is satisfied. Id.

If a transaction is a high-cost mortgage, the lender must disclose the following within three days of the closing: the loan is not effective until closing, the consequences of default, the loan terms such as the annual percentage rate and monthly payment and the maximum monthly payment on a variable rate mortgage. HOEPA Guide, at 30.

If a mortgage is a high-cost mortgage, the mortgagor must receive homeownership counseling from a HUD-approved counselor or a state housing finance counselor before getting the mortgage loan. HOEPA Guide, at 35. The counseling session must cover key terms of the mortgage transaction, the mortgagor's finances, including income, expenses and liabilities and whether the mortgagor can afford the mortgage loan. Id. In addition, lenders are required to provide consumers with a list of homeownership counseling organizations within three days of applicants' mortgage loan applications. *See* HOEPA Guide, at 14.

This section outlined some of the important rules under HOEPA. But, lenders who provide home loans and those advising mortgagors need to have a good understanding of all of the rules and requirements under HOEPA.

H. THE NATIONAL FLOOD INSURANCE PROGRAM

Over the years, large amounts of federal disaster relief funds have been paid to flood victims. A substantial portion of this money has been used to rebuild structures in the same high-risk location. This situation, coupled with the general unavailability of private flood insurance, led Congress to establish the National Flood Insurance Program in 1968 (42 U.S.C.A. § 4001 *et seq.*). The Program made flood insurance available to property owners in communities that established approved land use ordinances limiting construction in flood-hazard areas.

Few communities responded voluntarily. Thus, the Flood Disaster Protection Act of 1973 was enacted. It made participation in the Program virtually mandatory by prohibiting federally regulated lending institutions from making loans secured by mortgages on structures in flood-prone areas unless the borrower obtained the mandatory flood insurance, the lender must notify the borrower that the borrower needs to acquire the insurance at his or her expense. If the borrower fails to acquire the flood insurance within 45 days of the notification, the lender is required to purchase it on behalf of the borrower and is entitled to charge the borrower for the premiums and fees. In addition, because such insurance is available only in communities participating in the Program, cities and towns began to enact the required land use regulation. Soon flood insurance became available to property owners in most communities with areas prone to flooding.

In the late 1970s, the Program was amended to eliminate the prohibition against making mortgage loans on flood-plain property in a nonparticipating community. But by that time, the Program had taken hold throughout the country. Moreover, federally regulated lending institutions still must require mortgagors to obtain flood insurance, when available, on mortgaged structures in flood-prone areas.

The Program, which is administered by the Federal Emergency Management Agency, has been revamped in various ways by Congress during the last decade in an ongoing effort to rectify structural and implemental programmatic deficiencies. Congress enacted the Biggert-Waters Flood

Insurance Reform Act of 2012 (Biggers-Waters Act) which reauthorized the Program through September 30, 2017 and made several reforms to it. On September 8, 2017, President Donald Trump extended the Program for three months. As a result, the Program will lapse on December 8, 2017 unless Congress adopts a long-term plan to reauthorize it. As of this writing, Congress is considering several bills to reauthorize the Program.

The Biggert-Waters Act increased premium rates to better reflect the true flood risk and to make the Program more financially stable. It also increased the cap on annual premium amounts from 10% to 20%. In addition, the Biggert-Waters Act made flood insurance available to cover residential dwellings containing five or more units. The Biggert-Waters Act imposed minimum deductibles that ranged from $1000 to $2000 depending on when the structure was constructed or substantially improved and the amount of the damage to the structure. In addition, if the lender purchased mandatory flood insurance on behalf of a borrower, the Biggers-Waters Act required the lender to terminate this insurance within 30 days of receiving confirmation from the borrower that the borrower had existing coverage. In such a case, the lender must refund all premiums and fees paid by the borrower for the flood insurance that the lender purchased.

In 2014, Congress overhauled the Program under The Homeowner Flood Insurance Affordability Act of 2014 (Public Law No: 113–89) (HFIAA). HFIAA repealed and amended portions of the Biggert-

Waters Act because of the high increase in flood insurance premiums. For example, HFIAA reduces some of the premium rate increases enacted under the Biggert-Waters Act. HFIAA also requires refunds of certain excess premiums made under the Biggert-Waters Act. In addition, HFIAA imposed new annual surcharges on all policies to address some of the goals under the Biggert-Waters Act. These surcharges will be placed in a Program reserve fund. Although it repealed or amended some aspects of the Biggert-Waters Act because of their high costs, several provisions will continue to be implemented.

I. EMERGENCY ECONOMIC STABILIZATION ACT OF 2008

To stabilize the mortgage market during the Great Recession, the federal government passed measures to stabilize homeownership and reduce the number of foreclosures. The Emergency Economic Stabilization Act of 2008 (Pub. L. No. 110–343, Div. A) (EESA) authorizes the federal government to become directly involved in the secondary mortgage market through purchasing "troubled" mortgages and mortgage-backed securities from "financial institution(s)." Seller-institutions are required to grant the federal government stock acquisition rights. The Department of the Treasury is responsible for administering this bailout venture. EESA directs the federal government to strive to avert foreclosure of the residential mortgages and mortgage-backed securities it purchases.

Soon after the enactment of EESA, the federal government adjusted its bailout tactics. It rapidly crafted a stock purchase scheme designed to supply financial institutions with capital straightaway. Additional forms of federal government financial support also are part of this revised bailout endeavor.

EESA, as amended in 2009, authorized the Treasury Department to use various techniques to support loan modifications to reduce the number of foreclosures. Bureau of Consumer Fin. Protection, Ability-to-Repay and Qualified Mortgage Standards Under the Truth in Lending Act (Regulation Z), 78 Fed. Reg. 113, at 35435 (June 12, 2013) [hereinafter Regulation Z]. Pursuant to its authorization, the Treasury Department created the Troubled Asset Relief Program (TARP). Id. One of the programs created under TARP was the Making Home Affordable program that was created to combat the high number of foreclosures by providing federal assistance to homeowners who were in jeopardy of default or foreclosure. Id. At least 10 programs were established under the Making Home Affordable program. Id. One of these programs was the Home Affordable Modification Program (HAMP). HAMP allowed eligible homeowners to modify loans that originated on or before January 1, 2009 to reduce mortgage payments and the likelihood of foreclosure. The types of modifications under HAMP included reducing the interest rate, extending the term of the mortgage loan, forbearing principal and forgiving a portion of the principal. *See* Making Home Affordable, Understanding the Terms of Your Modification, https://www.makinghomeaffordable.

gov/already/pages/already-mha-understand-terms-modification.aspx. Under HAMP, mortgagees usually placed homeowners on a temporary trial plan to ensure that they made all modified payments. If so, the mortgagees executed permanent modification agreements. Id. After several extensions of its original sunset date, new modifications under the program finally ended on December 31, 2016. Modifications under the program saved homeowners billions of dollars.

The government also established programs that facilitated refinancings for homeowners who were in default or at risk of defaulting. Under the Home Affordable Refinance Program (HARP), homeowners with adjustable rate mortgages or fixed rate mortgages on homes that had lost value were able to refinance their mortgages that were guaranteed or owned by Fannie Mae or Freddie Mac. More than 3.4 million homeowners refinanced their loans under HARP. Fed. Hous. Fin. Agency, News Release, FHFA Announces New Streamlined Refinance Offering for High LTV Borrowers: HARP Extended through September 2017 (Aug. 25, 2016), *available at* https://www.fhfa.gov/Media/PublicAffairs/Pages/FHFA-Announces-New-Streamlined-Refinance-Offering-for-High-LTV-Borrowers-HARP-Extended-through-September-2017.aspx. After several extensions to its sunset, HARP was extended through September 30, 2017. Id.

Beginning October 2017 (after the sunset of HARP), Fannie Mae and Freddie Mac implemented a new refinance opportunity for homeowners with high loan-to-value ratios who are unable to refinance under traditional programs. Id. To qualify for this offering, the homeowner must have a source of income and cannot have missed any mortgage payments during the last six months and more than one during the last 12 months. They must receive some sort of benefit from refinancing the mortgage loan, such as a reduction in the mortgage payments. Id. The new program is distinguishable from HARP refinancing because homeowners may refinance multiple times and there are no eligibility cut-off dates. Id. However, consistent with refinancing under HARP, there is neither a debt-to-income ratio nor a maximum loan-to-value ratio, homeowners are not required to meet a minimum credit score and an appraisal will generally not be required. Id.

CHAPTER 7

TRANSFER OF MORTGAGOR'S INTEREST

I. MORTGAGOR'S INTEREST

The precise nature of the mortgagor's interest in the mortgaged property varies among the states depending upon the prevailing mortgage theory. Nonetheless, the mortgagor is viewed everywhere as owner of the property for transfer purposes. This is true even in title theory states where the mortgagee holds legal "title" solely as security. As owner of the mortgaged premises, the mortgagor may transfer the property by deed or by will or further encumber it by mortgage. Moreover, the mortgaged property may be transferred by forced sale or at death by devise or intestate succession laws. This chapter deals primarily with issues that arise when the mortgagor transfers the mortgaged property by deed. Some of the significant issues related to the mortgagor's conveyance of the mortgaged property by deed are whether the mortgagor remains liable on the mortgage debt, whether the grantee is liable to the mortgagee upon a default and whether the mortgagee is able to accelerate the loan upon the conveyance.

II. CONVEYANCE OF MORTGAGED PROPERTY

A. MORTGAGOR'S POWER TO CONVEY

The mortgagor may freely convey the mortgaged property. A mortgage provision purporting to prevent conveyance is void as an illegal disabling restraint on alienation. However, as discussed later in this chapter, the mortgage may include a due-on-sale clause that authorizes the mortgagee to accelerate the debt if the mortgagor conveys the mortgaged property without the mortgagee's consent.

B. EFFECT OF CONVEYANCE ON MORTGAGE

When the mortgagor conveys the mortgaged property, it is important to determine whether the mortgage is discharged before title passes or survives the conveyance. The answer depends upon the contractual arrangement between the mortgagor-grantor and the grantee.

1. Mortgage Is Discharged

The parties frequently agree that the mortgagor will pay off the mortgage debt at closing and transfer the property free from the mortgage. (It is assumed that the mortgage documents permit prepayment.) In such case, the purchase price is set at an amount sufficient to pay the mortgagor for the mortgagor's equity in the property and satisfy the mortgage debt. If the grantee does not have enough money on hand to pay the purchase price, and the grantee usually does not, the grantee must obtain a new mortgage loan to make up the deficit. The existing mortgage on the property is then discharged and replaced by the new mortgage.

> *Illustration*: A mortgagor owns a house encumbered by a $30,000 mortgage held by a mortgagee. A purchaser agrees to purchase the property for $90,000. The purchaser has $20,000 cash and obtains a $70,000 loan from a bank. The purchaser pays $60,000 to the mortgagor for the mortgagor's equity and $30,000 to the mortgagee to satisfy the mortgage loan. The mortgagee releases its mortgage, and the mortgagor deeds the property to the purchaser. The purchaser executes a new $70,000 mortgage to the bank. As will be discussed in Chapter 13, the $30,000 mortgage relief is included in the mortgagor's amount realized for tax purposes, and the purchaser's adjusted basis includes the $70,000 mortgage loan.

2. Mortgage Survives

The parties may agree that the existing mortgage will survive the conveyance. In that event, the grantee pays the mortgagor the value of the mortgagor's equity and takes title subject to the mortgage lien. Even absent such an agreement, a properly recorded mortgage will survive unless it is satisfied at or before closing.

C. RIGHTS AND OBLIGATIONS OF PARTIES WHEN MORTGAGE SURVIVES CONVEYANCE

When the mortgage survives the conveyance, the legal relationship among the mortgagee, the mortgagor, and the grantee depends upon whether the grantee assumes personal responsibility for the underlying obligation.

1. "Subject to" Conveyance

a. Grantee's Rights and Obligations

If the grantee does not assume the mortgage debt, the conveyance is merely "subject to" the mortgage. Upon default, the mortgagee may foreclose and have the encumbered real estate sold, but as a general rule the mortgagee may not proceed against the "subject to" grantee personally.

> *Illustration*: A mortgagor conveys mortgaged property to a purchaser by deed that provides that the conveyance is "subject to" a prior recorded mortgage. This means that the purchaser takes the property subject to the mortgage but generally has no personal responsibility to pay the underlying obligation. The term "subject to" is not a promise from the purchaser to pay the mortgage loan.

As indicated in the immediately preceding illustration, the deed from the mortgagor to the "subject to" grantee usually provides that the grantee takes title subject to the mortgage. Although a provision of this type is not necessary for the survival of a properly recorded mortgage, it is utilized by the mortgagor to limit the mortgagor's liability on the deed's covenants of title by excluding the mortgage from their coverage.

> *Illustration*: A mortgagor conveys mortgaged property to a purchaser by general warranty deed that does not mention a prior recorded mortgage. The purchaser takes the property subject to the mortgage because the purchaser is on constructive notice of the recorded instrument. However, the purchaser may have a cause of action against the mortgagor for breach of the deed's present covenant against encumbrances.

Although the "subject to" grantee is not personally liable on the mortgage loan, the grantee commonly pays the obligation to avoid losing the property by foreclosure, particularly when the grantee has equity (the fair market value is greater than the mortgage loan) in the property. On the other hand, if the outstanding balance of the mortgage loan exceeds the fair market value of the mortgaged property, the grantee does not have a financial incentive to pay the loan because there is no equity in the property to protect.

b. *Mortgagor's Rights and Obligations*

The mortgagor remains personally liable on the debt following a "subject to" conveyance unless released by the mortgagee. When not released, the mortgagor becomes a surety, liable to the extent the land proves to be of insufficient value to satisfy the debt. As a surety, the mortgagor generally is still subject to suit by the mortgagee directly on the underlying obligation and is liable for any deficiency resulting from a foreclosure sale. If, however, the mortgagor is forced to pay the entire debt, the mortgagor typically is subrogated to the mortgagee's rights and can foreclose to be reimbursed to the extent of the value of the property. However, the grantee is not liable to the mortgagor for a deficiency because the grantee is not personally liable on the mortgage loan. The mortgagor's only recourse against the grantee, like the mortgagee, is to initiate foreclosure proceedings.

> *Illustration*: A mortgagor executes a $10,000 promissory note and a mortgage to a mortgagee. The mortgagor then conveys the mortgaged property to a grantee by deed which provides that title is "subject to" the mortgage. The parties make no agreement regarding payment of the note. The grantee fails to pay the note. The mortgagee generally may either (1) foreclose and seek a deficiency judgment against the mortgagor if the sale proceeds are insufficient to satisfy the debt; or (2) sue the mortgagor on the note without foreclosing. Assume that the mortgagee chooses the second alternative, which is normally available. The mortgagor pays the mortgagee $10,000 and is subrogated to the mortgagee's right to foreclose. The mortgagor then forecloses, and the property brings $8,000 at sale. The mortgagor is entitled to the $8,000, but the mortgagor ordinarily must absorb a

$2,000 loss because the grantee was not personally liable on the note.

2. "Assumption" Conveyance

a. *Grantee's Rights and Obligations*

A grantee taking real property encumbered by a mortgage may personally assume liability for the mortgage debt. When that occurs, the transaction is termed an "assumption" conveyance. Although the assumption may be accomplished outside the conveyance, it is usually based on a clause in the deed to the effect that the grantee "assumes and agrees to pay" the mortgage debt. When the grantee accepts a deed containing a clause of this type, the grantee also accepts personal responsibility for the debt.

The mortgagor, as one of the contracting parties, of course may enforce the assumption contract. The mortgagee also may enforce the contract against the grantee under either of two theories: (1) The generally accepted view is that the mortgagee is a third-party beneficiary of the assumption contract, and (2) some courts consider the mortgagee's rights against the grantee as "derived" under equitable principles from the mortgagor's rights in the assumption contract. In either case, the consequence of an "assumption" conveyance is that, upon default, the mortgagee may foreclose and obtain a deficiency judgment against the grantee. Furthermore, in most jurisdictions the mortgagee may obtain judgment against the grantee on the obligation without foreclosing the mortgage. Some derivative theory states, however, refuse the mortgagee this right on the ground that the grantee is not liable on the assumption contract until the mortgagor suffers actual loss.

The Supreme Court of Idaho in Adams v. George, 812 P.2d 280 (Idaho 1991), provides a good discussion of determining whether a grantee has assumed a mortgage or taken it subject to a mortgage. The court notes that the mere conveyance of property that is encumbered by a mortgage doesn't make the purchaser personally liable on the loan. Id. at 284. According to the court, in Idaho it must be proved by clear and convincing evidence that the grantee is personally obligated on the mortgage loan, and mere payment by the grantee is insufficient to establish that the grantee has expressly assumed the loan. Id. The court states that some courts have determined that there is an inference that a grantee has impliedly assumed a mortgage loan if the grantee takes the property subject to the mortgage and the outstanding balance of the loan is reduced from the purchase price. Id. The Third Restatement agrees with the *Adams* court that a few jurisdictions presume the assumption of liability in this situation, but under the Restatement it does not establish an assumption of liability. Restatement (Third) of Property, Mortgages § 5.1 cmt. a (1997). The Restatement states that appropriate assumption language includes "assume the mortgage," "assume the mortgage loan" or "assume the mortgage and note." Id. Under this type of language, the grantee is generally considered to have assumed all covenants and obligations included in both the note and mortgage. Id. In addition, the Restatement states that assumption language may be included in a deed, separate agreement or even an oral assumption agreement because the Statute of Frauds usually is not considered to apply to these types of agreements. Id.

b. Mortgagor's Rights and Obligations

Generally, the grantee's assumption of personal responsibility for the mortgage debt does not relieve the mortgagor of liability. However, if the grantee assumes the mortgage secured by residential property, the mortgagee will release the mortgagor from personal liability under the Garn-St. Germain Act. *See* 12 C.F.R. § 591.5(b)(4) (2006). If it's not residential property, the mortgagor becomes a surety, this time liable for any deficiency resulting from a foreclosure sale and in most jurisdictions, subject to direct suit on the debt. The mortgagor is, however, in a much better position in an "assumption" conveyance than in a "subject to" transfer. First, because the assuming grantee is personally liable on the underlying obligation, the grantee has greater incentive to pay than when the grantee only risks loss of the land on default. Second, if the mortgagor pays the debt, the mortgagor is subrogated to the mortgagee's rights and may look to both the land and the grantee personally for reimbursement. Third, it is commonly recognized that the mortgagor may sue the defaulting grantee for breach of the assumption contract without first having paid the mortgage debt and apply monies recovered toward satisfaction of the debt.

Illustration: A mortgagor executes a $30,000 promissory note and a mortgage to a mortgagee. The mortgagor then conveys the mortgaged property to a purchaser by deed that provides that the purchaser assumes and agrees to pay the mortgage debt. The purchaser fails to pay. In most states, the mortgagee may either (1) foreclose and seek a deficiency judgment against the mortgagor and the purchaser if the sale proceeds are insufficient to satisfy the note, (2) bring suit against the mortgagor on the note without foreclosing, or (3) bring suit against the purchaser on the note without foreclosing. The mortgagee chooses the second alternative, which is widely available. The mortgagor pays the mortgagee $30,000 and is subrogated to the mortgagee's rights against the purchaser. The mortgagor may now either (1) foreclose and recover any deficiency from the purchaser or (2) sue the purchaser directly on the note and the assumption contract without foreclosing.

c. *Successive "Assumption" Conveyances/Break in Chain of Assumptions*

When successive "assumption" conveyances are made, each grantee is personally liable on the mortgage debt. The last assuming grantee, however, bears primary responsibility.

Illustration: A mortgagor executes a $20,000 note and a mortgage to the mortgagee. The mortgagor makes an "assumption" conveyance to a purchaser who in turn makes an "assumption" conveyance to a second purchaser who defaults. The mortgagee forecloses and receives $18,000 from the foreclosure sale. The mortgagee obtains a $2,000 deficiency judgment against the first purchaser. If the first purchaser pays, that purchaser has the right to obtain reimbursement from the second purchaser.

If the chain of assumptions is broken by a "subject to" conveyance, authorities are divided on whether grantees who assume after the break are personally liable on the mortgage debt. In jurisdictions that view the mortgagee as a third-party beneficiary of the assumption contract, a subsequent assuming grantee generally is liable. Some courts, however, have found the grantee free from liability on the ground that the parties did not intend the mortgagee to benefit from the assumption. In derivative theory states, a grantee who assumes after a break is not liable because the mortgagee has no claim against the "subject to" grantee and therefore, cannot derive rights from that individual's assumption contract with a subsequent grantee.

d. Termination or Modification of Assumption Contract

Authorities also disagree as to whether the mortgagee's rights against an assuming grantee are affected when the grantee is released from the assumption contract by the grantor. In most third-party beneficiary theory states, the mortgagee's rights survive the release if the mortgagee accepted or relied on the assumption agreement prior to the release. In a few third-party beneficiary jurisdictions, the mortgagee's rights survive the release in all cases on the theory that the mortgagee's rights vested immediately upon the execution of the assumption contract. In derivative theory states, the mortgagee's rights are destroyed by the release unless the mortgagee has previously filed a foreclosure suit or it would be inequitable to enforce the release.

A similar diversity of opinion exists on the question of whether the mortgagee's rights are affected by modification of the assumption contract.

3. Extension Problem

The grantee normally pays the mortgage debt in both the "subject to" and the "assumption" conveyance situations. If the grantee has difficulty doing so, the mortgagee may extend the time for payment. Serious collateral consequences may result. The extension may operate to discharge the mortgagor in whole or in part on the theory that it impairs the mortgagor's right as a surety to pay the debt at maturity and to be subrogated to the mortgagee's position at that time.

An extension granted an assuming grantee typically operates to completely discharge the mortgagor. This is because the extension denies the mortgagor subrogation rights against the grantee for the entire debt. The rule, however, operates to discharge the mortgagor only if the mortgagee had knowledge of the assumption when it granted the extension.

Authorities differ as to the effect of an extension granted a "subject to" grantee. The generally accepted view is that the mortgagor is discharged to the extent of the value of the land at the time the extension was granted. This is because the extension costs the mortgagor the opportunity to be subrogated to the mortgagee's right to foreclose. Some states go further and completely discharge the mortgagor in this situation. Other jurisdictions consider the mortgagor's liability to be unaffected by the extension.

These rules on discharge are subject to two important qualifications. First, the mortgagor is discharged only by an extension agreement that is legally binding on the mortgagee. Mere inaction by the mortgagee after default does not constitute such an extension. Second, even when the grantee obtains a binding extension, the mortgagor is not discharged if the mortgagor consents to the arrangement. Consequently, mortgages commonly provide that the mortgagee may grant extensions to subsequent grantees without affecting the mortgagor's liability.

D. ACQUISITION BY MORTGAGEE

A mortgagee may acquire the mortgaged realty from the mortgagor by a transaction separate and distinct from the mortgage agreement. Acquisitions of this type do not violate the rule that prohibits contemporaneous clogs of the mortgagor's equity of redemption. Such transactions, however, are subject to strict judicial scrutiny so that the mortgagor is protected from the ordinarily superior bargaining power of the mortgagee. If the acquisition is made in bad faith or for inadequate consideration, courts will not recognize it, and the mortgagor will continue to hold an equity of redemption.

1. Deed in Lieu of Foreclosure

Mortgagees often acquire mortgaged property by deed in lieu of foreclosure. Upon default, the mortgagee typically is willing to cancel the mortgage debt and accept a deed to the mortgaged property in lieu of foreclosing the mortgagor's equity of redemption. Such transactions generally are advantageous to both parties. The mortgagee bypasses the frequently complex, expensive, and protracted foreclosure process. The mortgagor sidesteps a potential deficiency judgment. Moreover, each avoids the public attention engendered by foreclosure.

2. Merger

The doctrine of merger provides that when successive real property interests come into the same hands, the lesser interest ends by merging into the greater interest. Thus, when the mortgagee acquires the mortgaged real estate, the mortgage normally merges into the fee. However, because merger is predicated on the actual or presumed intention of the owner of both interests, the mortgage generally is preserved if merger would be detrimental to the mortgagee.

Illustration: A mortgagor owns Blackacre subject to a first mortgage to a first mortgagee and a second mortgage to a second mortgagee. The mortgagor conveys Blackacre to the first mortgagee. Merger does not occur unless the first mortgagee, with knowledge of the mortgage held by the second mortgagee, expresses the intent for it to do so. It is presumed that the first mortgagee does not intend to gratuitously benefit the second mortgagee by giving the second mortgagee's mortgage first lien priority.

III. DUE-ON-SALE CLAUSE

A. GENERAL

Although the mortgagee cannot prohibit the mortgagor from transferring the mortgaged property, the mortgagee may include a provision in the mortgage giving it the right to accelerate the debt if the mortgaged property is conveyed without its consent. A mortgage provision of this type is known as a due-on-sale clause. Such clauses are often broadly worded to cover the transfer of any interest in the property. Transfer by land contract, lease, or junior encumbrance, as well as by outright conveyance, are therefore acts that may trigger acceleration of the debt.

Mortgagees today may freely enforce due-on-sale clauses upon most transfers of mortgaged real estate. A federal statute, discussed later in this section, so mandates. The current situation, however, is a product of years of litigation, regulation, and legislation on the subject. This historical background is traced below.

B. STATE LAW BACKGROUND

At one time, considerable controversy existed regarding the enforceability of due-on-sale clauses. At the beginning of the 1980s, the states were divided into two camps: those following the "automatic enforcement" approach and those subscribing to the "impairment of security" view. This split of authority was primarily the result of differing judicial attitudes as to whether the enforcement of a due-on-sale clause constituted an unreasonable restraint on alienation.

1. Automatic Enforcement Approach

Courts adopting the automatic enforcement approach generally reasoned as follows: To the extent enforcement of a due-on-sale clause directly or indirectly limits the mortgagor's ability to convey the mortgaged realty, such restraint on alienation is reasonable. Mortgagees are justified in using a contractual provision to get rid of low-interest-rate loans in order to maintain their lending portfolios at or near the current market interest rate. Moreover, mortgagors in general benefit from a rule permitting mortgagees to enforce due-on-sale clauses at their discretion. The acceleration of low-interest-rate loans creates additional funds for new borrowers. It also tends to reduce the overall mortgage interest rate by alleviating the mortgagees' need to charge exceptionally high rates on new mortgage loans in order to compensate for low returns on outstanding loans.

Some state courts that adopted the automatic enforcement approach used markedly different analysis in doing so. They determined that due-on-sale clauses are not restraints on alienation in any sense and therefore, are enforceable contract provisions. *See, e.g.*, Occidental Savings and Loan Association v. Venco Partnership, 293 N.W.2d 843 (Neb.1980).

2. Impairment of Security View

Courts in a number of states found due-on-sale clauses enforceable only if the mortgagee established that the conveyance in question would impair the security or enhance the likelihood of default. These courts concluded that it is unreasonable for a mortgagee to exercise a due-on-sale clause merely to improve its financial condition. Additional justification is necessary to tip the balance to the reasonable side of the scale. The grantee's present financial situation, credit history, and background respecting property use and maintenance are factors relevant to this determination.

Some courts espousing the impairment of security point of view concluded that automatic enforcement of a due-on-sale clause constitutes an unreasonable restraint on alienation. *See, e.g.,* Wellenkamp v. Bank of America, 148 Cal.Rptr. 379 (Cal.1978). Other courts adopted the impairment of security view on another theory. They reasoned that it is inequitable for a mortgagee to accelerate the debt under a due-on-sale clause solely for economic reasons. The results of this approach were essentially the same as produced by the restraint on alienation analysis. In addition, some state legislatures enacted statutes incorporating the impairment of security approach.

3. Resolution

As state law became increasingly fractured along the lines discussed above, pressure mounted for a resolution for the due-on-sale clause conflict. The federal government became involved, and in the end, Congress settled the matter by statute. Following is an overview of significant federal activity in the due-on-sale clause area.

C. FEDERAL HOME LOAN BANK BOARD REGULATIONS

The Federal Home Loan Bank Board in 1976 authorized federal savings and loan associations to freely enforce due-on-sale clauses upon most transfers of mortgaged real estate. 12 C.F.R. § 545.8–3(f) & (g) (1982). There was some question, however, as to whether this regulation preempted restrictive state laws on the subject. The Supreme Court answered the preemption question in the affirmative in Fidelity Federal Savings and Loan Association v. de la Cuesta, 458 U.S. 141 (1982), thereby eliminating any doubt about the authority of federal savings and loan associations in this area.

D. GARN-ST. GERMAIN DEPOSITORY INSTITUTIONS ACT OF 1982

1. General

Because of the fragmented law on the enforceability of due-on-sale clauses and the adverse economic impact of due-on-sale restrictions on lending institutions, Congress included provisions in the Garn-St. Germain Depository Institutions Act of 1982 preempting state due-on-sale law and establishing a national standard for the enforcement of due-on-sale clauses. 12 U.S.C.A. § 1701j–3. As a general proposition, the Act permits mortgagees to freely enforce due-on-sale clauses. There are, however, exceptions to this basic rule—one for "window period" loans that is largely only of historical interest and another for certain transfers of residential mortgaged property that retains its vitality.

2. Window Period Loan Exception

A window period loan is one made or assumed before the effective date of the Act (October 15, 1982) in a jurisdiction that had a statewide restriction on the enforcement of due-on-sale clauses in place at the time the loan was executed or assumed. Window period loans remained subject to the restrictive state law for three years (until October 15, 1985) unless the appropriate regulatory body for the originating lender provided otherwise. 12 U.S.C.A. § 1701j–3(c). Under this scheme, state legislatures were given the power to "otherwise regulate" window period loans made by lenders that are not federally chartered. Lawmakers in a few window period jurisdictions extended state law restrictions on such window period loans for various periods beyond October 15, 1985.

Mortgage loans made by federal savings and loan associations were specifically excluded from the window period exception. This is, of course, consistent with the *de la Cuesta* decision discussed above.

3. Exempt Transfers

The Act permanently exempts certain transfers of residential mortgaged property "containing less than five dwelling units." Mortgagees are prohibited from enforcing a due-on-sale clause in the following residential transfer situations: "(1) the creation of a lien or other encumbrance subordinate to the lender's security instrument which does not relate to a transfer of rights of occupancy in the property; (2) the creation of a purchase money security interest for household appliances; (3) a transfer by devise, descent, or operation of law on the death of a joint tenant or tenant by the entirety; (4) the granting of a leasehold interest of three years or less not containing an option to purchase; (5) a transfer to a relative resulting from the death of a borrower; (6) a transfer where the spouse or children of the borrower become an owner of the property; (7) a transfer resulting from a decree of a dissolution of marriage, legal separation agreement, or from an incidental property settlement agreement, by which the spouse of the borrower becomes an owner of the property; (8) a transfer into an inter vivos trust in which the borrower is and remains a beneficiary and which does not relate to a transfer of rights of occupancy in the property; or (9) any other transfer or disposition described in regulations prescribed by the Federal Home Loan Bank Board." 12 U.S.C.A. § 1701j–3(d).

E. PRACTICAL CONSIDERATIONS

When the mortgage contains an enforceable due-on-sale clause and the mortgagor desires to transfer the mortgaged property, the mortgagee has several alternatives, which include the following:

(1) The mortgagee may withhold consent to the transfer, accelerate the debt upon transfer, and then reinvest the funds at the current market interest rate. Some lenders also have sought a prepayment penalty under these circumstances, but such attempts generally have been rejected by the courts on the ground that once the lender accelerates the debt there can no longer be any *pre*payment. Moreover, regulations issued under the Garn-St. Germain Depository Institutions Act of 1982 prohibit mortgagees from charging a prepayment penalty in connection with the enforcement of a due-on-sale clause in a mortgage on a borrower-occupied residence. 12 C.F.R. § 591.5(b)(2) (2017).

(2) The mortgagee may consent to the transfer conditioned upon the grantee's assumption of the mortgage and the payment of a transfer fee or an increased interest rate. The Garn-St. Germain Depository Institutions Act of 1982 contains an

unusual provision that "encourage[s]" the lender to consent to transfer upon the grantee's assumption of the mortgage at a blended interest rate not more than the average of the original rate and the current market rate. 12 U.S.C.A. § 1701j–3(b)(3) (2017). If the lender consents to an assumption of a loan on a borrower-occupied residence, it apparently must by regulation release the mortgagor from personal liability. 12 C.F.R. § 591.5(b)(4) (2008). This regulation, however, has been interpreted in various ways. *See* Nelson, Whitman, Burkhart & Freyermuth, Real Estate Finance Law 352–353 (6th ed. 2015)

(3) The mortgagee may promote customer relations by consenting to the transfer without imposing any conditions.

IV. FURTHER ENCUMBRANCE OF MORTGAGED PROPERTY

A mortgagor may place a junior mortgage on the mortgaged property. Such further encumbrance, however, may permit the mortgagee to accelerate the debt under a due-on-sale clause, at least when the mortgaged property is commercial or multi-unit residential in excess of four units.

V. TRANSFER AT MORTGAGOR'S DEATH

On the mortgagor's death, the mortgaged property passes to the mortgagor's heirs or devisees. Because the mortgage debt is a personal obligation, the heir or devisee generally may compel the decedent's personal representative to pay the debt. In some states, however, statutes relieve the personal estate of this burden. In addition, specific testamentary directions regarding the payment of mortgage debts may render the general rule inapplicable in individual cases.

CHAPTER 8

TRANSFER OF MORTGAGEE'S INTEREST

I. MORTGAGEE'S INTEREST

Legal problems that arise from the transfer of the mortgagee's interest are some of the most complicated in real estate finance. This is primarily because the mortgagee's interest in the mortgage loan consists of two types of property—the obligation which is personalty and the mortgage which is realty. The material in this chapter is more easily understood if the reader remains constantly aware of this duality.

II. ASSIGNMENT OF MORTGAGE LOAN

A. BASIC CONCEPT

Like other interests in property, a mortgage is freely alienable or assignable. However, a mortgage cannot be transferred except in connection with the transfer of the obligation it secures. The mortgage or security interest secures an underlying obligation. The underlying obligation can exist without the security interest, but the security interest cannot exist without an underlying obligation. This principle has two facets. First, when the mortgagee assigns only the underlying debt, the mortgage is automatically carried to the assignee as an inseparable incident of the debt. The assignee then may require the mortgagee to execute a formal mortgage assignment. Second, when the mortgagee assigns only the mortgage, the transaction generally is invalid, and the assignee acquires no interest in either the mortgage or the debt. *See, e.g., In re* Affordable Home Corp., Bankr. 2013 WL 6048836, at *153 (Bankr. N.J. 2013) (stating "[t]he assignment of a mortgage, without assignment of a promissory note secured thereunder, confers no rights upon the assignee). If, however, the mortgagee intends the separate mortgage assignment to operate also as an assignment of the secured indebtedness, the transaction usually is valid, and the assignee receives an equitable right to the debt.

> *Illustration*: A mortgagor executes a promissory note and a mortgage to a mortgagee. The mortgagee assigns the note to an assignee who purchases it without knowledge that it is secured by the mortgage. Nonetheless, the assignee has an equitable right to the mortgage. The mortgagee holds the mortgage in trust for the assignee and must transfer it to the assignee upon request.

> *Illustration*: A mortgagor executes a promissory note and a mortgage to a mortgagee. The mortgagee assigns the mortgage to an assignee, but keeps the note under the mistaken belief that both parties (the mortgagee and assignee) have rights against the mortgagor. The attempted transfer is ineffective. The assignee acquires no interest in the mortgage loan.

Illustration: A mortgagor executes a promissory note and a mortgage to a mortgagee. The mortgagee gives the note to the mortgagee's attorney for safekeeping. Later the mortgagee requests the attorney to return the note so that the mortgagee can transfer it to an assignee. The attorney refuses on the ground that the mortgagee has failed to pay for legal services rendered. Undeterred, the mortgagee assigns the mortgage to the assignee with the express intention that the assignment also operate as an assignment of the note. The assignment is effective. The assignee may enforce both the note and mortgage subject to the attorney's lien rights, if any. *See* Beaty v. Inlet Beach, Inc., 9 So.2d 735 (Fla.1942).

As a general rule, an assignee must gain possession of a negotiable note in order to enforce it. Under the Uniform Commercial Code, a note or obligation is transferred when a person other than its issuer delivers it to an assignee to give the assignee the right to enforce the note or obligation. *See* U.C.C. § 3–203(a).

The usual transfer of a mortgage loan involves separate assignments of the obligation and the mortgage. The validity of the assignment of the underlying obligation is determined by reference to contract and commercial paper law. The formal assignment of the mortgage must comply with the legal requirements for the conveyance of an interest in land.

B. ORDINARY ASSIGNMENT/ASSIGNMENT AS SECURITY DISTINCTION

An ordinary assignment of a note and mortgage must be distinguished from an assignment of a note and mortgage as security (collateral assignment). An ordinary assignment involves the sale of a note and mortgage to an assignee (purchaser). A collateral assignment involves the pledge of a note and mortgage to secure a loan from a collateral assignee (lender). The bulk of this chapter focuses on the ordinary sale assignment and the legal status of the assignee. One section deals exclusively with collateral assignments.

C. ASSIGNEE'S RIGHTS

The assignee of a properly transferred note and mortgage is entitled to collect payment of the debt from the mortgagor and in the event of default, is empowered to foreclose the mortgage. The assignee's rights, however, are subject to the limitations discussed in the following sections on defenses that may be available against the assignee and on payment problems that may arise after the assignment.

D. APPLICABILITY OF UCC ARTICLE 9

Article 9 of the Uniform Commercial Code (UCC) covers ordinary assignments (sales) of mortgage loans in addition to assignments of mortgage loans as security. *See* U.C.C. § 9–109(a) & (b). Under Article 9, an assignee (purchaser) of a promissory note and mortgage is shielded from claims of the mortgagee-assignor's future lien creditors and bankruptcy trustee without recording in the real estate records, filing under the UCC, possessing the note, or doing anything else. In other words, the assignment (sale) is "perfected" automatically. *See* U.C.C. § 9–309(4).

E. RECORDING MORTGAGE ASSIGNMENT

A mortgage assignment is valid even if an assignee fails to record it. *See, e.g.*, Kan. Stat. Ann. § 382.360(1) (2017) (failure to record doesn't affect the validity or perfection of a mortgage under state law); Mass. Gen. Laws Ann. ch. 183, § 6C (2017) (failure to record assignment of a mortgage doesn't affect its validity); S.C. Code Ann. § 30–7–100 (B) & (C) (2017) (providing that it is not necessary to record the assignment but this rule must be reflected in the mortgage in bold print). However, the statutes in several jurisdictions provide that the recording of an assignment by itself is not notice to the mortgagor which invalidates any payments made by the mortgagor to the mortgagee. *See, e.g.*, Alaska Stat. 34.20.010 (2016); N.D. Cont. Code § 35–03–05.1 (2017); N.Y. Real Prop. § 324 (Consol. 2017); Utah Code Ann. § 57–1–15 (2017); Wyom. Stat. Ann. 34–1–128 (2017).

Even if an assignment is valid without recordation, there are several reasons why the assignee should record the assignment. For example, in Michigan, if a party is foreclosing a mortgage by advertisement and is not the original mortgagee, a record chain of title is required before the foreclosure sale. Mich. Comp. Laws § 600.3204(3) (2017). In Minnesota, a mortgagee is entitled to foreclosure only if the assignment has been recorded. *See* Minn. Stats. § 580.02 (3) (2017). In Ruiz v. 1st Fid. Loan Servicing, LLC, 829 N.W.2d 53 (2013), the Supreme Court of Minnesota determined that the mortgagee must strictly comply with section 580.02. Id. at 54. In *1st Fidelity*, there were multiple assignments but the third assignment was recorded after the assignee began foreclosure by advertisement. Id. at 55. The court held that the foreclosure was void because the assignee did not strictly comply with the statute as all of the assignments needed to be recorded before the foreclosure. Id. at 59.

In addition, the assignee must record the mortgage assignment to preserve its interest against subsequent purchasers or encumbrancers of the mortgaged property in the event the mortgagee-assignor improperly releases the mortgage.

> *Illustration*: A mortgagor owns land worth \$20,000. The mortgagor executes a \$10,000 promissory note and a mortgage on the property to a mortgagee. The mortgagee assigns and delivers the documents to an assignee, but the assignee does not record it. The mortgagee and mortgagor enter into a scheme to defraud the assignee. The mortgagee executes a release of the mortgage to the mortgagor who records it. The mortgagor then conveys the land to an innocent purchaser for \$20,000, an amount that is twice as much as the mortgagor normally could have obtained. The purchaser owns the land free from the mortgage because the land

records did not reflect the assignee's current lien on the property. The assignee's only recourse is against the mortgagor and mortgagee.

Recording also may protect the assignee if the mortgagee-assignor should assign the same note and mortgage to another party, at least under the traditional approach. Moreover, in some circumstances recording imparts notice that mortgage loan payments should be directed to the assignee.

In response to problems associated with recording numerous and frequent mortgage assignments, entities connected with the secondary mortgage market devised the Mortgage Electronic Registration System (MERS). Under this privately organized, funded, and managed scheme, MERS becomes the nominal record holder of entered mortgages and then maintains current information on-line about assignments and other aspects of these mortgage loans.

F. SECONDARY MORTGAGE MARKET

The assignment process occurs innumerable times each business day. Many mortgagees originate mortgage loans and then sell and assign them to permanent investors. The aggregate of these assignment transactions constitutes the secondary mortgage market.

III. DEFENSES AVAILABLE AGAINST ASSIGNEE

As a general rule, the right of a mortgage loan assignee to foreclosure the mortgage upon default depends on its ability to enforce the underlying obligation. This doctrine rests on the basic concept that the obligation is the essential aspect of the transaction, while the mortgage is just an appendage. The form of the underlying obligation (negotiable/nonnegotiable), therefore, is of primary importance in determining what defenses the mortgagor may assert against an assignee of the mortgage loan.

A. NONNEGOTIABLE OBLIGATION

If the underlying obligation is nonnegotiable, the assignee takes the note and the mortgage subject to all defenses the mortgagor had against the mortgagee. *See* Hammelburger v. Foursome Inn Corp., 54 N.Y. 2d 580, 586 (1981).

> *Illustration*: A mortgagee agrees to loan \$3,000 to a mortgagor. The mortgagor executes a \$3,000 nonnegotiable note and a mortgage to the mortgagee. The mortgagee however, does not actually advance any money to the mortgagor. The mortgagee immediately assigns the documents to an assignee, who is a bona fide purchaser for value without notice of the mortgagee's failure to advance funds. The mortgagor refuses to pay the assignee. The assignee cannot recover on the note nor can the assignee foreclose the mortgage. The assignee

took the documents subject to the mortgagor's defense of failure of consideration.

B. NEGOTIABLE OBLIGATION

It is more difficult to determine what defenses the mortgagor may assert against an assignee when the underlying obligation is negotiable. The answer primarily depends upon whether the assignee qualifies as a holder in due course. An assignee may become a holder in due course only if certain requirements are met. First, the obligation, of course, must be negotiable. *See* U.C.C. § 3–104(a). Second, it must have been transferred to the assignee by negotiation. *See* U.C.C. § 3–201. Third, the assignee must have obtained the obligation for value, in good faith, and without notice of any defect, such as an alteration, claim, or defense. *See* U.C.C. § 3–302(a).

If the underlying obligation is negotiable and the assignee is a holder in due course, the assignee normally takes the note *and* the mortgage free from "personal" defenses the mortgagor had against the mortgagee. Personal defenses include mistake, failure of consideration, and fraud in the inducement. *See* U.C.C. § 3–305.

The negotiable mortgage concept rests on the theory that negotiable notes should be freely transferable and that the mortgage, as mere security, should travel with the note. A handful of jurisdictions, however, apparently reject this principle on the ground that a mortgage is a property interest for all purposes and thus, cannot assume the characteristics of commercial paper. Under this minority approach, even a holder in due course takes the mortgage subject to personal defenses the mortgagor had against the mortgagee.

> *Illustration*: A mortgagee agrees to loan \$3,000 to a mortgagor. The mortgagor executes a \$3,000 negotiable note and a mortgage to the mortgagee. However, the mortgagee does not actually advance any money to the mortgagor. The mortgagee immediately negotiates the note and assigns the mortgage to an assignee, a holder in due course. As a holder in due course, the assignee takes the note free from any personal defenses the mortgagor had against the mortgagee. The defense of failure of consideration is a personal defense. The assignee, therefore, may recover \$3,000 on the note from the mortgagor. In the vast majority of states, the assignee also may foreclose. This result is based on the theory that the mortgage is clothed with the negotiable characteristics of the note and thus, the assignee also takes the mortgage free from personal defenses. In a handful of jurisdictions, however, the assignee apparently cannot foreclose. This view is predicated on the notion that a mortgage can never become negotiable and therefore, the mortgagor can assert the mortgagor's personal defense in a foreclosure suit.

Even if the assignee qualifies as a holder in due course, it still takes subject to "real" defenses the mortgagor has on the negotiable obligation. Real defenses include incapacity, duress, infancy, and fraud in the fact. *See* U.C.C. § 3–305(a)(1) & (b).

> *Illustration*: Assume the same fact situation as in the immediately preceding illustration except that the mortgagor was mentally incompetent at the time the mortgagor executed the note and mortgage. Even though the note is negotiable and the assignee is a holder in due course, the assignee takes the note subject to the real defense of incapacity. Because the mortgagor has a valid defense against enforcement of the negotiable note, the mortgagor also has a defense against enforcement of the mortgage. Thus, the assignee can neither recover on the note nor foreclose.

Of course, if the assignee does not qualify as a holder in due course, it takes the note and the mortgage subject to both real and personal defenses the mortgagor had against the mortgagee. *See* U.C.C. § 3–305(a).

C. ESTOPPEL CERTIFICATE

A prospective assignee may be unwilling to accept an assignment of a mortgage loan unless it receives an estoppel certificate from the mortgagor specifying the unpaid balance of the obligation. An estoppel certificate also benefits an assignee by including a statement that the mortgagor claims no defenses against its enforcement. The assignee may thereby protect itself from all defenses, whether real or personal. In Hammelburger v. Foursome Inn Corp., 54 N.Y. 2d 580 (1981), the mortgagor executed an estoppel certificate stating that there were no defenses or offsets to the mortgage 10 days before the mortgagee assigned it to an assignee. Id. at 585. After the mortgagor defaulted on the mortgage, the assignee initiated foreclosure proceedings. Id. The mortgagor moved for summary judgment asserting an affirmative defense of usury. Id. The assignee also moved for summary judgment based on the estoppel certificate. Id. The court explained that the assignee's rights are based on the mortgagor's representation in the estoppel certificate and that enforcement of a defense would allow the mortgagor to obtain an unfair advantage at the assignee's expense. Id. at 587. The estoppel certificate doesn't validate the mortgage but prevents the mortgagor from asserting it to be void after representing its validity to the assignee's detriment. Id. However, the estoppel certificate must have influenced the assignee; hence, if the assignee takes the mortgage with knowledge that it is unenforceable, it will defeat an estoppel claim. Id. at 588. The court of appeals in *Hammelburger* addressed the impact of a usurious interest rate on the estoppel certificate. The court remanded the case because it was unclear whether the assignee had knowledge of the usury, which would have invalidated the estoppel certificate. Id. at 588. If the assignee relied on the estoppel certificate in good faith, the mortgagor would not have been able to successfully assert a defense of criminal or civil usury. Id. at 592.

Similarly, in Resolution Trust Corp. v. Hidden Ponds Phase IV Dev. Assocs., 873 F. Supp. 799 (1995), the mortgagor acknowledged in an estoppel certificate "that the mortgage assignment was to be made and that there were no defenses or offsets to the note or the mortgage." Id. at 803. The mortgagor eventually defaulted on the mortgage loan, and the mortgagee's receiver initiated foreclosure proceedings. Id. The mortgagor unsuccessfully raised several defenses, including asserting that the mortgage was void and unenforceable because it lacked consideration. Id.

Estoppel certificates are not limited to assignments. For example, in Shelton v. Kennedy Funding, Inc., 622 F.3d 943 (2010), in applying for a bridge loan, the lender requested the mortgagee/seller to execute an estoppel certificate because the lender could not determine the outstanding balance of the seller's mortgage loan. Id. at 947. After negotiations, the seller reduced the mortgage loan to a sum certain of $675,000, and issued the estoppel certificate to the lender that included a promise from the lender to place $675,000 of its loan in an escrow account. Id. The seller signed the certificate. Id. at 948. The lender did not sign the estoppel certificate but a "sticky note" was attached to settlement documents stating that the lender would remit the $675,000 to the seller if the mortgagor defaulted on the loan. Id. at 948–949. Subsequently, the mortgagor defaulted on the bridge loan, and the lender initiated foreclosure proceedings. Id. at 949. The court determined that the lender's promise to remit the $675,000 to the seller was enforceable under the statute of frauds even though the lender did not sign the certificate. Id. at 954.

IV. PAYMENT PROBLEMS AFTER ASSIGNMENT

The assignee of a mortgage loan is entitled to receive all payments made after the assignment. Nonetheless, the mortgagor or a grantee may continue to pay the original mortgagee through inadvertence or ignorance. In most instances, the original mortgagee merely forwards the payment to the assignee, and the parties eventually work out the administrative details. Problems arise, however, when the original mortgagee absconds with the funds or becomes insolvent. Who bears the loss, the payor or the assignee? In order to answer this question, one must ascertain who made the payment (the mortgagor or a grantee), the form of obligation involved (negotiable or nonnegotiable), and the type of payment made (part or final). Because the mortgage is a mere incident of the obligation, contract and commercial paper law generally dictates the outcome. The result is not always consistent with the policy underlying the recording statutes.

A. PAYMENT BY MORTGAGOR

1. Negotiable Obligation

a. Established Principles

If the underlying obligation is negotiable, the commonly accepted view is that the mortgagor pays the original mortgagee at the mortgagor's peril. Proper payment, whether part or full, ordinarily can be made only to the holder of a negotiable instrument. *See* U.C.C. § 3–602(a). The mortgagor is protected by the right to demand production of the instrument and its surrender if the payment is final, or an endorsement thereon of part payment if that is the case. If, however, the holder is not a holder in due course and the mortgagor paid the original mortgagee without notice of the prior assignment, the mortgagor may be able to assert successfully the contract defense of payment against the holder. *See* U.C.C. § 3–305(a)(2).

In a handful of states, statutes authorize the mortgagor to pay the mortgagee until an assignment of the mortgage is recorded. Such statutes, of course, run contrary to basic commercial paper policy stated above.

b. Amended UCC Position

UCC § 3–602 was amended to significantly modify the basic pay-the-holder requirement in 2002. The UCC now permits the mortgagor to pay a negotiable obligation to the mortgagee until the mortgagor receives "adequate" notice of a mortgage loan assignment and of the duty to pay the assignee. Such notice must identify the instrument, include a payment address, and bear the signature of the mortgagee or the assignee. *See* U.C.C. § 3–602(b). The pace at which states will enact this amendment is unpredictable.

2. Nonnegotiable Obligation: Notice Problem

If the underlying obligation is nonnegotiable, the mortgagor may safely pay the mortgagee until receiving notice of an assignment. However, the mortgagor may obtain notice in various ways and frequently is on notice of an assignment.

a. Actual Notice

The mortgagor may receive actual notice of the assignment from the assignor, the assignee, or otherwise.

b. Record Notice

The recordation of a mortgage assignment generally is not considered constructive notice to the mortgagor because recording imparts notice only to subsequent purchasers, not to prior interest holders. There is, however, some authority that recording the assignment puts the mortgagor on notice.

c. Inquiry Notice

By weight of authority, the mortgagor receives inquiry notice of an assignment if upon final payment the mortgagee does not produce and surrender the note or give a reasonable excuse for its inability to do so. This view is based on the belief that it is prudent business practice for the mortgagor to demand production of a nonnegotiable note when paying it off. In some jurisdictions, however, the mortgagor is not on inquiry notice of an assignment when the mortgagee fails to produce the note upon final payment. This stance is supported by the fact that the assignee could have easily protected itself by notifying the mortgagor of the assignment.

The mortgagor's part payment of a nonnegotiable obligation is viewed in a different light. It is not common business practice to require production of a nonnegotiable note upon part payment. The mortgagor, therefore, is typically not on inquiry notice of an assignment just because the mortgagee fails to produce the note each time an installment payment is made.

B. PAYMENT BY GRANTEE

When the mortgagor transfers the mortgaged property to another party, additional payment problems arise.

1. Negotiable Obligation

a. Established Principles

If the underlying obligation is negotiable, the grantee ordinarily must pay the holder of the note. *See* U.C.C. § 3–602(a). The grantee cannot safely pay the mortgage owner of record because commercial paper law makes a negotiable instrument freely transferable. The grantee, therefore, must demand production of the note before making either part or full payment. However, the defenses discussed above in connection with payment of a negotiable obligation by the mortgagor also may be available to a grantee.

b. Amended UCC Position

The notice provisions of amended UCC § 3–602, as analyzed in the immediately preceding section on payment by the mortgagee, apply to payment by a grantee as well. *See* U.C.C. § 3–602(b).

2. Nonnegotiable Obligation: Notice Problem

If the underlying obligation is nonnegotiable, the grantee may pay the mortgagee until the grantee receives notice of an assignment. Again, notice may come from several sources.

a. Actual Notice

The grantee may receive actual notice of the assignment from the mortgagor, the assignor, the assignee, or otherwise.

b. Record Notice

The grantee also may receive notice from the public records. A properly recorded mortgage assignment is constructive notice to a subsequent grantee.

> *Illustration*: A mortgagor executes a nonnegotiable note and a mortgage to a mortgagee. The mortgagee assigns the documents to an assignee who records the mortgage assignment. The mortgagor then sells and conveys the mortgaged property to a purchaser subject to the mortgage. The purchaser has no actual knowledge of the assignment, so the purchaser makes part payment to the mortgagee. The payment is not good against the assignee. The purchaser was on constructive notice of the assignee's interest because the records reflected the assignment at the time the purchaser purchased the mortgaged property.

c. *Inquiry Notice*

The grantee generally may receive inquiry notice of an assignment in the same fashion as the mortgagor. Thus, the discussion of inquiry notice found in the above section on payment by the mortgagor is applicable here.

C. SERVICING ARRANGEMENTS

The severity of the established general rule that the mortgagor or a grantee ordinarily must pay the holder of a negotiable instrument is softened by the realities of mortgage financing. Often the assignee of the negotiable note and mortgage will authorize the mortgagee to "service" the loan. The mortgagee thereby continues to collect payments, but now as agent for the assignee. Naturally, such payments are good against the servicing agent's principal—the holder of the negotiable note.

Servicing arrangements also may affect the application of legal principles governing the payment of nonnegotiable obligations. Even if the mortgagor or a grantee has notice of an assignment, payment of a nonnegotiable obligation to the mortgagee will be effective if the mortgagee is servicing the mortgage loan for the assignee. This analysis applies as well to the payment of assigned negotiable instruments in states that have enacted amended UCC § 3–602 with its notice provision.

V. CONFLICTING ASSIGNMENTS

An unscrupulous or careless mortgagee may sell and assign the mortgage loan to two or more parties. The conflict among these assignees is not easily resolved. The traditional approach to this issue has two branches—one for nonnegotiable obligations and another for negotiable obligations. Article 9 of the UCC now also addresses the conflicting assignments question, but in a somewhat different manner. Since the traditional approach provides relevant background for the Article 9 approach and to a certain extent coexists with Article 9, both approaches are analyzed in this section.

A. TRADITIONAL APPROACH

1. Nonnegotiable Obligation

Under the traditional approach, if the underlying obligation is nonnegotiable, priority among assignees is generally governed by applicable real estate recording statutes. This means that the first assignee prevails unless a subsequent assignee fits within the protection afforded by the local recording statute.

> *Illustration*: A mortgagor executes a nonnegotiable note and a mortgage to a mortgagee. The mortgagee sells, assigns, and delivers the documents to a first assignee who records the mortgage assignment. The mortgagee then sells and assigns to a second assignee, but, of course, cannot deliver the documents. The first assignee and the second assignee each claim ownership of the mortgage

documents. The first assignee prevails over the second assignee, because the first assignee recorded first and the second assignee received constructive notice of the first mortgagee's prior assignment from the real estate records. The second mortgagee also received inquiry notice from the mortgagee's failure to deliver the documents.

2. Negotiable Obligation

Under the traditional approach, if the underlying obligation is negotiable, commercial paper law, not a recording statute, usually determines the rights of competing assignees. Hence, the assignee who takes possession of the note and the mortgage normally prevails.

Illustration: A mortgagor executes a negotiable note and a mortgage in favor of a mortgagee who records. The mortgagee sells and assigns the loan to a first assignee, but retains possession of the documents. The first assignee records the mortgage assignment. The mortgagee then sells the loan to a second assignee. The mortgagee negotiates the note, assigns the mortgage, and delivers the documents to the second assignee who takes in good faith without actual notice of the prior assignment. The first assignee and second assignee each claim ownership of the note and the mortgage. Under the commonly accepted view, the second assignee prevails over the first assignee because constructive notice from the land records does not prevent the second assignee from becoming a holder in due course. *See* U.C.C. § 3–302(b). However, authority to the contrary exists.

Illustration: A mortgagor executes a negotiable note and a mortgage to a mortgagee. The mortgagee sells the loan to a first assignee. The mortgagee negotiates the note and assigns the mortgage to the first assignee who takes possession of the documents, but does not record the mortgage assignment. The mortgagee then sells and assigns the documents to a second assignee who relies on the land records, but, of course, does not receive the documents. The first assignee and second assignee each claim ownership of the note and the mortgage. Under the generally held view, the first assignee prevails because the second assignee is not a holder in due course and therefore, takes subject to the first assignee's claim of legal title.

B. UCC ARTICLE 9 APPROACH

Article 9 of the UCC resolves the conflict among assignees by providing that typically whoever takes possession of the mortgage note prevails. Specifically, UCC § 9–330(d) states that the "purchaser of an instrument has priority over a security interest in the instrument perfected by a method other than possession if the purchaser gives value and takes possession of the instrument in good faith and without knowledge that the purchase violates the rights of the secured party." *But see* U.C.C. § 9–

331(a) (noting exceptions). The purchaser is considered to have knowledge of the violation if the note bears notice of the prior assignment. *See* U.C.C. § 9–330(f).

VI. FRACTIONAL ASSIGNMENTS (LOAN PARTICIPATION)

A. FORMS OF LOAN PARTICIPATION

Mortgagees commonly assign fractional interests in large mortgage loans to other investors. This technique is referred to as loan participation. This technique may allow a mortgagee to give a loan to a mortgagee that exceeds its lending ability. A loan participation is normally structured in either of two ways. (1) The mortgagee takes a single mortgage note from the mortgagor, holds it, and issues participation certificates to the investors; or (2) the mortgagee takes a series of notes from the mortgagor, each note for a fraction of the mortgage debt. The mortgagee then assigns some of the notes to the investors.

Although the series-of-notes method of participation was formerly quite common, today the certificate approach is employed extensively. In either case, priority problems arise when the foreclosure sale proceeds are insufficient to pay all the investors.

B. AGREEMENT ESTABLISHING PRIORITY

Most modern participations are governed by a separate participation agreement that establishes priority among the parties. (An agreement regarding priority, of course, could be included in the mortgage.) The agreement ordinarily provides that all investors, including the mortgagee, have equal priority and share ratably in the foreclosure sale proceeds.

C. PRIORITY ABSENT AGREEMENT—PARTICIPATION CERTIFICATES

Each loan participant's interest is usually represented by a participation certificate. The participant does not have a legal relationship with the mortgagor. First Bank of WaKeeney v. Peoples State Bank, 12 Kan. App. 2d 788, 790 (1988). The participant's rights are derived from the terms of the participation agreement. Id. As previously indicated, priority among the investors is almost invariably covered by a participation agreement. In the rare instances where no agreement exists, the pro rata rule applies because the certificates do not purport to assign any specific part of the mortgage loan. Thus, absent an agreement to the contrary, all investors, including the mortgagee, hold undivided interests having equal priority.

An exception to this rule exists. If the mortgagor guarantees payment of a certificate, the certificate holder is given priority over the mortgagee on the ground the guaranty indicates the intent to grant the certificate holder a superior claim.

D. PRIORITY ABSENT AGREEMENT—SERIES OF NOTES

Participations originally involved the assignment of a series of notes. The parties to these participations often failed to make provision in the mortgage for priority among the holders of the notes. Absent such an agreement, the courts were forced to develop principles governing the allocation of foreclosure sale proceeds. A tangle of conflicting rules and exceptions resulted.

1. Pro Rata Rule

The general rule is that, absent agreement fixing priority, the mortgage is enforced on a pro rata basis in favor of the mortgagee and all assignees. This rule is predicated on the theory that equality is equity.

> *Illustration*: A mortgagor executes five $1,000 promissory notes and a mortgage to a mortgagee. The mortgagee sells and assigns one note to each A, B, C, and D. The mortgagee retains one note. The parties make no agreement regarding the priority of their interests. The mortgagor defaults, and a foreclosure sale produces $2,000. Under the pro rata rule the mortgagee, A, B, C, and D are each entitled to 1/5 of the $2,000 proceeds ($400).

a. Guaranty Exception

Courts in most pro rata states make an exception to the general rule when the mortgagee assigns a note with a guaranty of payment. In such case, the assignee is normally awarded priority over the mortgagee on the theory that the assignee has the greater equity.

b. Priority-for-Assignees Exception

In a few pro rata jurisdictions, the general rule is not available to the mortgagee. The note or notes that the mortgagee retains are postponed in priority to those held by the assignees.

> *Illustration*: Assume the same fact situation as in the immediately preceding illustration. In a state that applies the pro rata rule only to assignees, A, B, C, and D have a $4,000 first lien as a group, and the mortgagee has a $1,000 second lien. Each assignee receives 1/4 of the $2,000 proceeds obtained at foreclosure ($500). The mortgagee recovers nothing because the proceeds are not sufficient to pay off the assignees' $4,000 first lien.

Priority for assignees is justified on a variety of equitable grounds that have a common source—the theory that assignment of part of the debt operates also as a pro tanto assignment of the mortgage lien. Thus, the priority-for-assignees exception to the pro rata rule is sometimes inaccurately referred to as the pro tanto rule. The label is misleading because the pro tanto assignment concept is applied only between the mortgagee and the assignees. The assignees themselves share pro rata. The priority-for-assignees exception is, therefore, at most a severely limited pro tanto approach. As discussed below, the true pro tanto rule establishes priority among assignees in the order they acquire their notes.

c. *Order-of-Maturity Exception*

Some pro rata states do not apply the general rule if the mortgage debt is represented by a series of notes having different dates of maturity. In these states, priority is awarded the parties in the order of maturity of their notes.

> *Illustration*: A mortgagor executes to the mortgagee a series of three $1,000 promissory notes: #1 matures in one year, #2 matures in two years, and #3 matures in three years. The notes are all secured by a single mortgage. The mortgagee sells and assigns note #1 to A and note #2 to B. The parties make no agreement regarding the priority of their interests. The mortgagor defaults, and a foreclosure sale produces $1,500. Under the order-of-maturity exception, A receives $1,000, B receives $500, and the mortgagee receives nothing.

2. Priority of Assignment Rule (Pro Tanto Rule)

A few jurisdictions reject the pro rata rule with its various exceptions in favor of the principle that, absent agreement to the contrary, assignees have priority in the order the assignments were made. This approach, known as the priority of assignment rule or the pro tanto rule, is based on the theory that each assignee receives that portion of the mortgage necessary to secure the interest assigned. Under this approach, subsequent participants take subject to the rights of prior assignees, and the mortgagee takes subject to all.

> *Illustration*: A mortgagor executes to the mortgagee a series of three $1,000 promissory notes maturing in three successive years. The notes are secured by a single mortgage. The mortgagee assigns one of the notes to A and then assigns another note to B. The mortgagee retains one note. The parties make no agreement regarding the priority of their notes. The mortgagor defaults, and the foreclosure sale produces $1,500. Under the pro tanto rule, A receives $1,000, B gets $500, and the mortgagee receives nothing. The maturity dates of the notes are irrelevant.

VII. ASSIGNMENT BY OPERATION OF LAW (SUBROGATION)

Courts may imply an assignment of the mortgage by operation of law under the equitable doctrine of subrogation. In real estate finance law, subrogation is the substitution of one who pays the mortgage debt to the position of the mortgagee.

The Restatement does a good job in explaining the purpose of subrogation. It states that subrogation prevents unjust enrichment. Restatement (Third) of Property, Mortgages § 7.6(a) (1997). Further, the Restatement notes that it is designed to prevent a mortgagee with a junior interest from receiving an unearned windfall. Restatement (Third) of Property, Mortgages § 7.6 cmt. a (1997). It also states that the subrogation concept should be construed broadly and that the situations where a junior mortgagee will be unjustly enriched noted in subsection (b) of the Restatement, such as misrepresentation, duress or undue influence, are illustrations. Id.

In addition, the Restatement only permits subrogation when a person fully discharges a mortgage loan. *Accord* U.S. Bank, N.A. v. JPMortgage Chase Bank, N.A., 768 Ariz. Adv. Rep. 6 (Ct. App. 2017). According to the Restatement:

> Where subrogation to a mortgage is sought, the entire obligation secured by the mortgage must be discharged. Partial subrogation to a mortgage is not permitted. The reason is that partial subrogation would have the effect of dividing the security between the original oblige and the subrogee, imposing unexpected burdens and potential complexities of division of the security. . . However, if the payor can negotiate a full settlement of the obligation for less than its face value, subrogation will be recognized.

Restatement (Third) of Property, Mortgages § 7.6 cmt. a (1997).

A. PARTIES FOR WHOM SUBROGATION IS AVAILABLE

A payor who is neither the primary obligor nor a mere volunteer may be subrogated to the rights of the mortgagee. However, the primary obligor and the volunteer are not eligible for subrogation because they have no compelling equities in their favor.

Following are situations in which the payor commonly qualifies for this form of equitable relief.

1. Mortgagor as Surety After Conveyance

Upon conveying away the mortgaged real estate subject to the mortgage, the mortgagor becomes a surety. If the grantee fails to pay the obligation and the mortgagor is forced to do so, justice demands that the mortgagor be subrogated to the rights of the mortgagee.

Illustration: A mortgagor executes a promissory note and a mortgage to a mortgagee. The mortgagor sells and conveys the mortgaged property to a purchaser subject to the mortgage. The purchaser fails to pay the obligation, so the mortgagor as surety pays the mortgagee. The mortgagor is thereby subrogated to the mortgagee's right to foreclose. If the purchaser assumed the obligation, the mortgagor also receives the mortgagee's right to recover a deficiency judgment against the purchaser.

2. Junior Mortgagee

When a junior mortgagee pays off a prior lien for the protection of its own security interest, it is subrogated to the rights of the mortgagee receiving payment.

Illustration: A mortgagor executes a $10,000 promissory note and a mortgage on the mortgagor's land to a first mortgagee. The mortgagor then executes a $5,000 note and a second mortgage on the same land to a second mortgagee. The mortgagor becomes insolvent and defaults on both obligations. Property values have recently declined, and it is projected that a foreclosure sale will produce only $10,000. Because the second mortgagee will receive nothing in that case, the second mortgagee desires to postpone foreclosure. Therefore, the second mortgagee pays the first mortgagee and is subrogated to that mortgagee's rights. The land remains subject to two liens, both in favor of the second mortgagee who can wait until property values rise to foreclose.

3. Lender of Pay-Off Funds

One who loans funds to pay off an existing mortgage may be subrogated to the rights of the mortgagee receiving payment. For example, assume that a first mortgagee holds a first mortgage on a mortgagor's land, and a second mortgagee holds a second mortgage. The mortgagor borrows money from a lender to pay off the first mortgage. The lender is ignorant of the second mortgagee's mortgage even though it is recorded. The mortgagor executes a promissory note and a mortgage to the lender. The mortgagor uses the loan proceeds to pay the first mortgage loan. The lender then discovers the second mortgagee's mortgage. Courts following the generally accepted view subrogate the lender to the first mortgagee's priority position on the theory that equity demands it and the second mortgagee is not prejudiced. Indeed, a growing number of decisions reach the same result when the lender actually knows of the second mortgagee's mortgage, notwithstanding the traditional rule to the contrary.

In Bank of Am., N.A. v. Prestance Corp., 160 P.3d 17 (Wash. 2007), the court considered the meaning of equitable subrogation in the context of a refinancing mortgagee. Id. at 18. In the case, a lender foreclosed on its deed of trust that secured a loan granted after a senior deed of trust loan but before that senior lien was refinanced. Id. at 19. The court considered whether it should adopt the Restatement approach that a refinancing mortgagee's actual or constructive notice of an intervening lien would not prevent it from being entitled to subrogation. Id. The court explained that one of the purposes of equitable subrogation is to "maintain the proper order of priorities." Id. at 20 (citations omitted). Further, the court noted that a new lien is not created; rather, the refinancing mortgagee takes over the position of the refinanced mortgage loan. Id.

The court adopted the Restatement's approach that subrogation is allowed even if the refinancing mortgagee has actual or constructive notice because notice is irrelevant where the refinancing mortgagee "reasonably expected to get security with a priority equal to the mortgage being paid." Id. at 28. *See* Restatement (Third) of Property, Mortgages § 7.6 cmt. e (1997).

The dissenting judge rejected the Restatement's approach and adopted the traditional approach that permits subrogation where the refinancing mortgagee has constructive notice but not if the mortgagee has actual notice. Prestance Corp., 160

P.3d at 29 (Owens, J., dissenting). The dissenting judge's approach may represent the majority approach, but the Restatement approach is the modern trend and is followed in many jurisdictions. Nelson, Whitman, Burkhart & Freyermuth, Real Estate Finance Law 942–943 (West 2015). *See, e.g.*, Investors Sav. Bank v. Keybank Nat'l Ass'n, 424 N.J. Super. 439, 444 (2012) (stating that in New Jersey a mortgagee is not entitled to subrogation if the mortgagee has actual notice).

A minority of jurisdictions refuse to apply the doctrine of subrogation because the lender's loss was the result of the lender's own negligence in failing to check the records. Sometimes a line is drawn between ordinary negligence and unjustifiable negligence. Prestance Corp., 160 P.3d at 21.

4. Purchaser of Mortgaged Property

When a purchaser of the mortgaged property assumes and pays the mortgage debt under the mistaken belief that no junior encumbrances exist, the purchaser may be subrogated to the rights of the mortgagee. There is, however, a division of opinion on the question.

> *Illustration*: A mortgagor owns land subject to a first mortgage in favor of a first mortgagee and a second mortgage in favor of a second mortgagee. The mortgagor sells the land to a purchaser who assumes the obligation to the first mortgagee. The purchaser is ignorant of the second mortgagee's mortgage even though it is recorded. If the purchaser pays the first

mortgage loan, many courts will subrogate the purchaser to the first mortgagee's priority position to prevent the gratuitous advancement of the second mortgagee's lien priority. Other courts, however, deny subrogation for various reasons, including the notion that the purchaser is now the primary obligor, a party for whom subrogation is unavailable.

B. CONVENTIONAL SUBROGATION

The mortgagor and the payor sometimes enter an agreement that subrogation should occur in the payor's favor. Although subrogation consistent with this agreement is called conventional subrogation, the actual legal effect of the agreement is subject to dispute. Some courts treat conventional subrogation as solely contractual in nature and, therefore, separate from equitable subrogation. (Equitable subrogation is sometimes referred to as legal subrogation.) Many courts, however, view the agreement calling for subrogation as merely an important factor that often influences equity to act to prevent injustice in individual cases.

> *Illustration*: A mortgagor obtains a construction loan from a mortgagee and executes a promissory note and a mortgage to the mortgagee. During the course of construction, a contractor performs work on the project, but is not paid. Under local law, the contractor may file a mechanic's lien on the property within ninety days after completion of the project. The lien will relate back to when

construction began. The mortgagee's construction loan mortgage was recorded prior to commencement of construction and thus, under local law has priority over all mechanics' liens. Sixty days after completion of construction, a bank makes a permanent mortgage loan to the mortgagor to "take-out" the mortgagee's construction mortgage loan. The mortgagor executes a new promissory note and mortgage to the bank that is justifiably ignorant of the contractor's claim. The mortgage contains a provision that the bank is subrogated to any lien discharged by proceeds of the bank's loan. Eighty days after completion of construction, the contractor records a mechanic's lien that relates back to the beginning of construction and therefore, is prior to the lien of the bank's mortgage. The bank, however, is subrogated to the mortgagee's priority position. This conclusion may be reached on various grounds. One approach is that subrogation is enforced as a contractual right. Another view is that subrogation occurs by operation of law and that the existence of the agreement merely indicates the bank is entitled to equitable relief.

C. RIGHT TO FORMAL ASSIGNMENT

A subrogee usually may compel the mortgagee to formally assign the obligation and the mortgage.

VIII. ASSIGNMENT AS SECURITY

The mortgagee may assign the note and mortgage as security for a loan received by the mortgagee. Such collateral assignments are common practice, notably among mortgage bankers who frequently employ this technique to obtain financing.

A lender that takes a collateral assignment of a note and mortgage may perfect its security interest against the mortgagee's future lien creditors and bankruptcy trustee by filing pursuant to the requirements of UCC Article 9. *See* U.C.C. §§ 9–312(a), 9–317(a). A collateral assignee, however, must obtain possession of the note, or place notice of the assignment on the note, to be shielded from claims of subsequent ordinary or collateral assignees of the mortgage loan. *See* U.C.C. § 9–330(d) & (f). Under the theory that the mortgage travels with the note, recording in the land records is not required, indeed is insufficient, to protect the collateral assignee's security rights in the mortgage vis-à-vis the potential claimants noted above. *See* U.C.C. §§ 9–109(b); 9–308(e). Nonetheless, the prudent collateral assignee will record the assignment for other purposes, such as to prevent improper release of the mortgage.

IX. TRANSFER AT MORTGAGEE'S DEATH

The mortgagee's interest in the mortgage loan passes as personal property at the mortgagee's death on the theory that the mortgage, the realty aspect of the mortgage loan, is merely an incident of the obligation, the personalty aspect. This rule is, however, of waning significance. Two reasons exist for its decline in importance. First, most mortgagees are institutions that may last in perpetuity. Second, even when the mortgagee is an individual, modern intestacy statutes generally provide that personalty and realty descend in the same way.

CHAPTER 9

AFTER DEFAULT AND BEFORE FORECLOSURE

I. DEFAULT

A. DEFINITION AND SIGNIFICANCE OF DEFAULT

Default occurs when the mortgagor fails to pay the underlying debt or to perform some other obligation secured by the mortgage. PNC Bank, Nat'l Ass'n v. Zubel, 24 N.E.3d 869, 874 (2014). What constitutes default in each case, therefore, can be determined only by examining the mortgage loan documents in question.

Default activates a set of mortgage law principles that determine the rights and obligations of the mortgagor and the mortgagee until foreclosure occurs. This chapter is devoted to an analysis of these principles.

B. COMMON TYPES OF DEFAULT

1. Failure to Pay Principal and Interest

One of the most common types of defaults is where the mortgagor fails to pay the required installments of principal and interest. Ordinarily, the loan documents will allow a mortgagor a grace period (e.g., 10 days) before the loan is in default. After the grace period, the mortgagee needs to decide whether to accelerate the balance of the payments and initiate foreclosure proceedings.

2. Failure to Pay Taxes or Insurance

A mortgagee will frequently include as a default in the loan documents the mortgagor's failure to pay property taxes and hazard insurance to protect the mortgagee's security interest. If the mortgagor lacks hazard insurance and a fire destroys the mortgaged property, the mortgagee loses its security interest and can only sue the mortgagor for a deficiency upon default. In addition, if the mortgagor fails to pay state and local real estate taxes, the local and state governments can foreclose on the tax liens which may result in the mortgagee's loss of its security interest.

The mortgagor's failure to pay real estate taxes or insurance premiums was once a common type of default. However, many mortgagors use escrow accounts for these expenses which has reduced the frequency of default in these areas. When the property taxes are due, the escrow agent or a servicing mortgagee will likely send a check to the mortgagor when the taxes are payable. The check is usually made payable to the mortgagor and the government. This is to ensure that the mortgagor uses the escrow funds to pay the taxes. If the escrow amount is insufficient to cover the entire balance due, the mortgagor must pay the balance. If the amount escrowed exceeds the amount due, the government will reimburse the mortgagor for the excess. For hazard insurance, it is common for the escrow agent or servicing mortgagee to submit payment to the insurance company directly from the escrow account.

3. Waste

Mortgages commonly provide that the commission of waste on the mortgaged property constitutes default. The mortgagor's commission of waste jeopardizes the mortgagee's security interest. The mortgagee agrees to make a mortgage loan based on a requisite loan-to-value ratio. If the mortgagor commits waste, it may increase the intended loan-to-value ratio and make the loan riskier. More importantly, the waste may ultimately impair the security to such a degree to essentially transform the loan from secured to unsecured.

For example, assume that the mortgagor purchases a house for $200,000 and takes out a $160,000 mortgage loan from a mortgagee. Several years later, the mortgagor's roof begins to leak during rainstorms. The mortgagor does not repair it, and it continues to leak when it rains. Eventually, the water damage causes toxic mold. The local housing authority condemns the house. The house becomes worthless. However, if the loan documents considered the mortgagor's commission of waste to be a default, the mortgagee could have accelerated the loan upon the default if it had notice of it and taken possession after the waste to prevent additional damage and protect the mortgagee's security interest.

4. Construction Difficulties

Construction loan mortgages present additional possibilities for breach. These loans provide interim financing during the construction of a project. They are usually interest-only during the construction of the improvements with a balloon payment due at the end of the loan term. Construction lenders have special risks because the improvements have not been completed. Hence, the security is less secure.

One of the most common types of defaults is where the mortgagor fails to make the interest payments. In addition, default often occurs when the mortgagor is unable to complete the contemplated improvements in accordance with the terms of the construction loan agreement. The loan documents can include other types of defaults. For example, in Nat'l Bank of Arizona v. Thruston, 218 Ariz. 112 (2008), the loan documents stated that the construction lender could consider the loan in default if the mortgagor did not complete construction before the stated deadline. Id. at 113. The loan documents also stated that a default occurred if the mortgagor neglected to pay real estate taxes and homeowner's association assessments. Id.

C. WAIVER OF DEFAULT

The mortgagee may waive default by accepting late payment or other tardy performance. Lenders usually are willing to make some allowance for the borrower's financial difficulties because a modicum of tolerance often reaps greater monetary return than hasty invocation of expensive and protracted foreclosure procedures.

Waiver of one late performance traditionally has not been viewed as constituting waiver of subsequent late performances. Some courts, however, may require a mortgagee who has regularly accepted late performance to give the mortgagor notice of its intention to require timely performance in the future. Many mortgages address this issue by providing that forbearance does not constitute waiver. For example, in First Nat'l Bank of Omaha v. Centennial Park, LLC, 48 Kan. App. 2d 714 (2013), the court noted that a mortgagee waives the right to accelerate if the mortgagee has accepted a late or partial payment. Id. at 715. However, according to the court, if the mortgage unambiguously includes an anti-waiver provision, the mortgagee is entitled to accelerate the loan after accepting an earlier late payment. Id. *See also* Duena-Redon v. Wells Fargo Bank, N.A., 354 P.3d 1037, 1041–1042 (Alaska 2015) (concluding that acceleration and foreclosure were proper even though the mortgagee had previously accepted late payments because the agreement expressly stated that the mortgagee did not waive its right to accelerate the loan for a later default); McCool v. Katz, 480 N.E. 2d 596, 598 (Ind. App. 1985) (concluding that because of a contractual non-waiver clause, the mortgagee had not waived its right to declare the loan in default even though the mortgagee had previously accepted late payments).

Clauses permitting the mortgagee to assess a charge for late payment also are common.

II. ACCELERATION

A. ACCELERATION CLAUSE

One of the most significant provisions in the modern amortized mortgage is the clause that authorizes the mortgagee to accelerate the entire debt when the mortgagor defaults in the payment of a single monthly installment or in the performance of any other obligation secured by the mortgage. These clauses are very common and are generally enforceable pursuant to their terms unless they are fraudulent or unconscionable. Key Intern. Mfg. Inc. v. Stillman, 103 A.D.2d 475, 477 (N.Y. Sup. Ct. App. Div. 2d Dep't 1984). Without an acceleration clause, the mortgagee can initiate foreclosure proceedings to recover only the amount in default. If foreclosure proceedings are withdrawn after acceleration, that debt is then reinstated on the pre-acceleration terms. PNC Bank, N.A. v. Tidwell, 762 S.E.2d 119 (2014) (citing statute). Further, if the mortgagee does foreclose in such a situation, authorities are in conflict as to whether the lien for the amount not in default survives foreclosure.

Illustration: A mortgagor executes a $40,000 promissory note and a mortgage to a mortgagee. The documents provide for equal monthly payments of $300 over a thirty-year term, but do not include an acceleration clause. The mortgagor misses two payments. The mortgagee may institute foreclosure proceedings, but the mortgagee is only entitled to that part of the proceeds sufficient to satisfy the partial default

($600). In some states, the mortgage lien continues on the property to secure the unpaid balance of the debt. Any surplus goes to the mortgagor. In other jurisdictions, however, the property is sold free from the mortgage lien. In such case, the surplus is usually either applied immediately to the unpaid balance of the loan or placed in trust to cover the debt as it matures.

An acceleration clause should be included in both the note and the mortgage. These clauses should coincide in all respects. In this regard, the note may refer to the mortgage for acceleration rights. The note's negotiability is not affected by such reference. *See* U.C.C. § 3–106(b).

If an acceleration clause is included only in the mortgage, the mortgagee may have trouble in accelerating the loan. Authorities are divided concerning the significance of its omission from the note. One view is that the mortgagee can accelerate under both documents on the theory that the note and mortgage are integral components of a single contract. The other view is that the mortgagee can only accelerate under the mortgage.

Illustration: A mortgagor executes a promissory note and a mortgage to a mortgagee. An acceleration clause is included in the mortgage, but it is omitted from the note. The mortgagor defaults by failing to make two monthly payments. The mortgagee can accelerate under the mortgage, foreclose, and apply the foreclosure sale proceeds to the entire debt. In some states, the mortgagee also can obtain a deficiency judgment against the mortgagor on the note. In others, the mortgagee cannot.

B. CURING DEFAULT BEFORE ACCELERATION

The mortgagor may reinstate the mortgage loan by curing default before the mortgagee accelerates. For example, assume that a mortgagor executes a promissory note and a mortgage in favor of a mortgagee. The documents contain identical acceleration clauses. The mortgagor defaults by missing one monthly payment. If the mortgagor makes a late payment to the mortgagee before the mortgagee accelerates, the loan is reinstated. The mortgagee may not use the cured default as a basis for acceleration. The mortgagee, of course, may accelerate after a later default.

Today, residential mortgages often provide that, with certain exceptions, the mortgagee must give the mortgagor notice of impending acceleration and the opportunity to avoid it by curing default. *See, e.g.*, Iowa Code Ann. § 654.2D(3) (West 2016) (giving mortgagors thirty days from the time the notice is given to cure the default before a mortgagee can accelerate); 41 Pa. Cons. Stat. Ann. § 403(a) and (c)(4) (West 2016) (requiring a residential mortgagor be given at least thirty days' notice prior to accelerating the maturity of any residential mortgage obligations by a lender); Tenn. Code Ann. § 45–20–104(b) and (d) (West 2017) (stating that the mortgagee must provide notice not less than thirty days prior to publishing notice of the foreclosure, but the right to cure cannot be invoked more than once during a 12-month period).

C. TRIGGERING ACCELERATION

Acceleration clauses are either self-operating or optional. If the clause is automatic or self-operating, a mortgagee is not required to provide notice to the mortgagor before accelerating the debt. Snow v. Wells Fargo Bank, N.A., 156 So. 3d 538, 541 (Fla. Dist. Ct. App. 2015). Acceleration clauses are usually activated at the mortgagee's option. A self-operating clause can result in acceleration contrary to the mortgagee's best interest. Optional acceleration is triggered by the mortgagee's performance of an act that clearly evidences the intent to treat the entire debt as due. In most states, formal notice of acceleration is unnecessary. But, some states require notice where the acceleration clause is optional. Montenegro v. Ocwen Loan Servicing, LLC, 419 S.W.3d 561 (Tex. App. 2013). In *Montenegro*, the court noted that equity demanded that the mortgagee provide notice of intent to the mortgagor before accelerating the loan. Id. at 569. The filing of a foreclosure complaint is generally sufficient to indicate an election to accelerate. The mortgage may also require the mortgagee to provide notice before acceleration. *See, e.g.*, Jackson v. Wells Fargo Home Mortgage, N.A., 159 So. 3d 58 (Ala. Civ. App. 2014) (both notice of intent to accelerate and notice of acceleration required under the mortgage).

D. CURING DEFAULT AFTER ACCELERATION

1. General Rule

The general rule is that after the mortgagee accelerates, the mortgagor cannot reinstate the loan by curing the original default. The mortgagor must pay the entire debt or face foreclosure. Courts will enforce a mortgagee's right to accelerate the mortgage indebtedness and foreclose thereafter regardless of a mortgagor's sudden financial hardship. *See* New England Mutual Life Ins. Co. v. Luxury Home Builders, Inc., 311 So.2d 160, 163 (Fla. Ct. App. 3d Dist. 1975). In *Luxury Homes*, the mortgagor argued that its inability to maintain mortgage payments resulted from its lessee's default and should bar the mortgagee from accelerating the mortgage debt. Id. at 162. Although the court held it could estop a party's exercise of an acceleration clause when acceleration would be unconscionable, there was no evidence of unconscionability in this case. Id. at 163. In particular, the mortgagee had not "lulled or misled" the mortgagor into believing it would not accelerate the mortgage debt upon the mortgagor's default. Id. Likewise, the court noted that once a mortgagee elects to accelerate the debt, a mortgagor's payment of all amounts due will not stop the foreclosure. Id. To be effective, such a tender must be made before the mortgagee accelerates the mortgage indebtedness. Id.

Similarly, in Graf v. Hope Building Corp., 254 N.Y. 1, 3 (N.Y. Ct. App. 1930), the mortgage permitted the mortgagee to accelerate the debt if the mortgagor had been in default of any payment for 20 days or longer. The case involved a set of unfortunate circumstances: the president and treasurer of the mortgagor's corporation was the only officer authorized to sign checks on the corporation's behalf; he left for Europe after signing a check that was erroneously $400 short of the proper mortgage interest payment; and though the president returned during the 20-day period, his office staff did not inform him of the error until the 20 days expired. Id. at 3–4. As permitted under the mortgage, the mortgagee did not permit the mortgagor to cure its default by tendering the deficiency. Id. at 4. The court upheld the mortgagee's right to do this although it noted the mortgagee "may be ungenerous." Id. Nonetheless, the court held that the mortgagor's default did not require judicial relief because the contract was fair on its face, consented-to by both parties, and free of coercion, oppression, and unconscionability. Id.

Likewise, a Florida court upheld a mortgagee's right to accelerate even though the mortgagors offered to pay all the interest it owed after the mortgagee elected to accelerate. Harris v. Siegel, 438 F. Supp. 510, 511 (S.D. Fla. 1977). In *Harris*, the parties executed a promissory note for over $730,000 that provided the mortgagee with the right to accelerate the debt after the mortgagors' failure to pay any interest installment for 15 days after it was due. Id. When the mortgagors missed an interest payment, the mortgagee issued written notice of its intent to exercise its power under the acceleration clause. Id. Thereafter, the mortgagors offered to pay the mortgagee all interest they owed. Id. The mortgagors argued that paying the interest they owed ought to prevent acceleration of the mortgage debt. Id. at 513. Because the mortgagors' offer to pay what they owed did not come until after the mortgagee elected to accelerate the mortgage indebtedness, the court held that the mortgagors could not cure the default by paying the payments in default and that acceleration was proper. Id. at 513–14.

However, several state legislatures have enacted statutes that permit mortgagors to nullify acceleration by paying just the amount originally in default. For example, in Pennsylvania, a mortgagor can cure a default of a residential mortgage by paying the missed payments, reasonable costs and late penalties and performing any required obligation up to one hour before bidding begins at the foreclosure sale. Pa. Stat. Ann. tit. 41, § 404(a) & (b) (West 2017). The mortgage is restored after the residential mortgagor cures the default as if the default had not occurred. Pa. Stat. Ann. tit. 41, § 404(c) (West 2017). Similarly, in New Jersey, a mortgagor of a residential mortgage can cure a default up to the entry of final judgment and de-accelerate and reinstate the residential mortgage. N.J. Stat. Ann. § 2A:50–57(a) (West 2017). Generally, the mortgagor can exercise this right only once every 18 months. Id. To cure the default, the mortgagor must pay the missed payments and late charges, perform a required obligation, pay court costs and any attorneys' fees. N.J. Stat. Ann. § 2A:50–57(b) (West 2017). However, the mortgagee cannot require the mortgagor to pay any penalties attributable to curing the default. N.J. Stat. Ann. § 2A:50–57(c) (West 2017).

Moreover, some commonly used mortgage forms give the mortgagor a similar contract right.

2. Equitable Relief

Mortgagors occasionally seek to set aside an acceleration because the default which triggered it resulted from misunderstanding or excusable neglect. Equitable relief is commonly unavailable in such cases. Many courts view an acceleration clause as an agreement regarding the time for payment whose enforcement does not exact a penalty or involve a forfeiture. Thus, the mortgagee may enforce the clause as written unless it has acted fraudulently, unconscionably, or in bad faith. In many jurisdictions, courts refuse to recognize an acceleration that would produce inequity or injustice. Assume, for example, that a mortgagor executes a promissory note and grants a mortgage in favor of a mortgagee. The documents contain identical optional acceleration clauses. The mortgagor goes to Europe on business but advises an assistant to make the next required payment to the mortgagee. The mortgagor's assistant uses the wrong mathematical formula to compute the interest and pays a little less than is due. The mortgagee elects to accelerate and foreclose because of this minor default. The mortgagor returns from Europe, makes late tender of the unpaid interest, and requests the court to set aside the acceleration. In many states, courts will not grant relief for breach of contract resulting from the mortgagor's negligence. *See* Graf v. Hope Building Corp., 171 N.E. 884 (N.Y.1930). The general approach is to grant the mortgagor relief when acceleration is inequitable or unjust under the circumstances. Although the mortgagor's willingness to cure the default is not sufficient reason to grant equitable relief under this emerging view, other factors, such as mortgagor's good faith and the unusual situation, indicate that the acceleration should be set aside. *See* Fed. Home Loan Mortgage Corp. v. Taylor, 318 So.2d 203 (Fla.App.1975). *See also* First Nat'l Bank of Omaha v. Centennial Park, LLC, 303 P.3d 705, 712 (Kan. App. 2013) (citing equitable principles that disallow acceleration when a default is the result of a mortgagee's fraud or other inequitable conduct); Althouse v. Kenney, 182 So. 2d 270, 272 (Fla. Dist. Ct. App. 1966) (stating that courts of equity could refuse to foreclose on a mortgage if the acceleration due date of debt would be an "inequitable or unjust result and circumstances would render acceleration unconscionable").

E. DUE-ON-SALE CLAUSE

Mortgages often provide for acceleration if the mortgagor transfers any interest in the mortgaged property without the mortgagee's consent. These due-on-sale clauses present special legal problems that are discussed in Chapter 7.

III. RIGHT TO POSSESSION AND RENTS

A. SIGNIFICANCE OF MORTGAGE THEORIES

Title, intermediate, and lien mortgage theories are significant today primarily as they relate to possession of the mortgaged real estate. Possession is important because with it comes the right to rents and profits produced by the property.

A basic tenet of common law is that possession is an attribute of legal title. Thus, in title theory states, the mortgagee receives the right to possession when the mortgage is executed. However, the mortgagee usually allows the mortgagor to possess the mortgaged property. It is much easier for the mortgagee to take possession after a default in a title theory jurisdiction because the mortgage conveyed title to the mortgagee. The mortgagee doesn't need to establish a basis for possession, such as waste or abandonment, to take possession. While a mortgagee in a title theory jurisdiction has title to the property, the mortgagee is not the owner of it. Once a mortgagor defaults on a mortgage, the mortgagee may take possession of the mortgaged property, but the mortgagee takes the property subject to the mortgagor's equity of redemption. Bevilacqua v. Rodriguez, 955 N.E. 2d 884, 895 (Mass. 2011). A mortgagee does not incur the responsibility of a mortgagee in possession unless the mortgagee has officially become a mortgagee in possession. Case v. St. Mary's Bank, 63 A.3d 1209, 1213–1214 (N.H. 2013).

In intermediate theory jurisdictions, the mortgagee ostensibly receives legal "title," but is allowed by law to take possession only upon default. In these jurisdictions, the mortgagee can immediately take possession upon default.

In lien theory states, a mortgage does not convey equitable or legal title to the mortgagee. Mere default by a mortgagor generally does not give the mortgagee the right of possession until the mortgaged property is foreclosed. However, a mortgagee may be able to take possession if the mortgagor voluntarily relinquishes possession. Kerr v. Miller, 159 Or. App. 613, 621, 977 P. 2d 438, 444 (Or. Ct. App. 1999). The mortgagee may also request the court to grant possession to the mortgagee if the mortgagor has committed waste or has abandoned the property.

The confusion created by these conflicting theories has been somewhat alleviated by the common practice of dealing with the issue of possession in the mortgage contract itself. The modern mortgage often provides that the mortgagor has the right to possession until default and the mortgagee has the right thereafter. Courts in some lien theory states, however, refuse to enforce mortgage agreements of this type for public policy reasons. But even in those jurisdictions, the mortgagor may give possession to the mortgagee after default.

Hence, as a practical matter, default frequently gives the mortgagee the right to possession either by operation of law or by mortgage provision. The consequences of this right are explored in the next section.

B. MORTGAGEE IN POSSESSION

1. Definition

A mortgagee may lawfully gain possession of the mortgaged property prior to the foreclosure sale. When the mortgagee lawfully exercises dominion and control over the mortgaged property pursuant to the mortgage, it is known as a mortgagee in possession. A mortgagee may take possession without physically entering or occupying the property, so long as it exercises substantially the same control as the mortgagor normally would exert. For example, assume that a mortgagor grants a mortgage on a vacant farm in favor of a mortgagee, and the mortgage authorizes the mortgagee to take possession upon default. If the mortgagor defaults, the mortgagee need not actually occupy the farm to become a mortgagee in possession if the mortgagee is maintaining the farm and seeking tenants to rent it.

2. Rights

A mortgagee in possession may control the property until either redemption or foreclosure occurs and collect all rents and profits arising from the mortgaged property during that time, but the mortgagee must apply them on the mortgage debt and account to the mortgagor for any surplus. Prince v. Brown, 856 P.2d 589, 590 (Okla. App. 1993). The mortgagee, of course, does not acquire title to the mortgaged property merely by taking possession of it under the mortgage.

One issue is whether a mortgagee in possession is entitled to reimbursement for repairs and improvements made after the mortgagor retakes possession of the mortgaged property by curing the default. The general approach is that a mortgagee in possession is entitled to reimbursement for reasonable and necessary repairs. Herman v. Herman, 707 P.2d 1374, 1378 (Wash. App. 1985). Under common law, a mortgagee in possession was entitled only to reimbursement for necessary expenses but not improvements. Kerr v. Miller, 159 Or. App. 613, 622, 977 P. 2d 438, 444 (Or. Ct. App. 1999). That approach has been replaced by a more flexible approach based on principles of equity. Id. at 445.

3. Obligations

All states impose trustee-like obligations on a mortgagee in possession. The mortgagee's duty is to act as a provident or prudent owner.

a. Management

A mortgagee in possession must manage and maintain the property, apply receipts that exceed expenses to the mortgage debt, and account to the mortgagor for any surplus. Brooks v. Adams, 115 So. 2d 578, 582 (Fla. Dist. Ct. App. 1959); Prince v. Brown, 856 P.2d 589, 590–591 (Okla. App. 1993). A mortgagee in possession is also responsible for maintaining and repairing the property. Case v. St. Mary's Bank, 63 A.3d 1209, 1214 (N.H. 2013). The obligation of prudent management requires that a mortgagee in possession use reasonable efforts to make the property productive. The mortgagee is, therefore, chargeable for rent it could have secured but for lack of reasonable diligence. A mortgagee in possession is liable to the mortgagor for grossly mismanaging the property and for wrongful acts that damage the property. Prince v. Brown, 856 P.2d 589, 590 (Okla. App. 1993). Further, if the mortgagee occupies the property for its own use, it is generally accountable for the fair rental value of its occupancy without regard to whether the property produces more or less than that amount.

b. Accounting

A mortgagee in possession does not act free from judicial scrutiny. A mortgagee in possession must account to the mortgagor for rents received during the mortgagee's possession. Kerr v. Miller, 977 P.2d 438, 450 (1999). The mortgagor can require the mortgagee to make a detailed accounting of receipts and expenses but only in a foreclosure action or upon redemption.

c. Liability to Third Parties

A mortgagee in possession may incur liability to third parties. For example, the mortgagee is responsible in tort for its negligence in managing the mortgaged real estate. Hence, a mortgagee in possession may be liable in tort to injured plaintiffs. In Klatt v. Hoboken Bank for Savings, 18 A.2d 602, 602–03 (N.J. 1941), the mortgagee in possession contracted an awning mechanic to remove awnings from a commercial building. Id. 602–03. After already removing 120 awnings during the day, a falling piece of stone struck the awning mechanic as he removed the building's final awning. Id. at 603. The court applied the doctrine of *res ipsa loquitur* because the falling stone, which was the instrument that caused injury, was under the mortgagee in possession's sole management and control. Id. Accordingly, the court affirmed the jury verdict in the amount of $1,000 in the plaintiff's favor. Id. *See also* Scott v. Hoboken Bank for Savings, 126 N.J. 294, 298–299 (1941) (finding mortgagee in possession liable to a third party for personal injuries suffered after a fall caused by its negligent maintenance of a common stairway); Mortimer v. East Side Savings Bank, 251 A.D. 97, 100 (N.Y. Sup. Ct. App. Div. 4th Dep't 1937) (holding a mortgagee in possession was responsible for maintaining a restaurant's elevator shaft into which the plaintiff fell).

In addition, the mortgagee in possession is responsible for the cost of goods and services properly supplied to the property during the mortgagee's possession based on an implied or express contract. Essex Cleaning Contractors, Inc. v. Amato, 317 A.2d 411, 412 (N.J. Super. Ct. App. Div. 1974) (considering whether the mortgagee in possession was liable based on implied or express contract for the cost of janitorial services rendered during the possessory period); Woodview Condo. Ass'n, Inc. v. Shanahan, 917 A.2d 790, 794 (App. Div. 2007) (citations omitted) (determining that the mortgagee in possession of two condominium units was liable for common monthly condominium fees to the condominium association related to utilities, administration, and maintenance supplied to him as the mortgagee in possession).

The mortgagee in possession may also be liable for the payment of taxes. In United Nat'l Bank v. Parish, 750 A.2d 238 (N.J. Super. Ct. App. Div. 1999), the court determined that payment of taxes is a specific obligation that is mandated by the mortgagee in possession's general responsibility for a property's management and preservation. Id. at 241. Because a mortgagee in possession receives the benefit of rents collected on the property, it must apply those rents to any taxes due and payable on the property during the possessory period. Id. at 242. However, the court in *Parish* limited the extent of a mortgagee in possession's obligation to pay taxes, requiring payment only "to the extent the rents collected are sufficient to bear that expense." Id.

However, if a mortgagee has not become a mortgagee in possession, the mortgagee will not be liable to third parties even in a title theory jurisdiction because the mortgagee is not the owner of the property even though the mortgagee has legal title. Case v. St. Mary's Bank, 63 A.3d 1209, 1213 (N.H. 2013) (holding that the mortgagee was not liable to a tenant for alleged trespass or violation of a state quiet enjoyment statute).

4. Problem of Leases Existing at Default

When mortgaged property is subject to a lease at the time of default, a mortgagee who has the right to take possession either by law or by agreement can ascertain its rights and duties vis-à-vis the lessee only by determining whether the lease was made before or after the execution of the mortgage. It is assumed in the following discussion that all instruments were promptly recorded, so that the order of their execution is also the order of their priority under applicable recording statutes.

a. Prior Leases

If the lease was executed before the mortgage, the mortgagee in possession is bound by the lease because the mortgagee's security extends only to the interest the mortgagor owned at the time the mortgage was created. The lessee under a prior lease is also bound because the mortgagee in possession succeeds to the mortgagor's reversion and thereby establishes privity of estate. Hence, the lessee may remain on the property but must pay rent to the mortgagee in possession.

b. Junior Leases

If the lease was executed after the mortgage, the mortgagee may take possession and thereby terminate the lease on the theory that the lessee can have no greater right to possession than the lessor. Although the mortgagee appears to be in a generally favorable position in this situation, it is really at an advantage only if it desires to terminate the junior lease. If the mortgagee wants to continue the junior lease and collect rent from the junior lessee, difficulty arises because the lessee is liable only to one with whom the lessee is in either privity of contract or privity of estate. The junior lessee clearly has no contractual obligation to the mortgagee. In addition, no privity of estate exists between the junior lessee and the mortgagee because the mortgage could not transfer the mortgagor's reversion against a lessee not then in existence. The mortgagee, therefore, faces "Catch 22" of real estate finance law. Because the mortgagee cannot force the junior lessee to enter a contract, the mortgagee is entitled to receive rent only if it can establish privity of estate with the lessee. If, however, the mortgagee attempts to do so by taking possession, the junior lease and the lessee's obligations thereunder are destroyed because the mortgagee's possession relates back to when the mortgage was executed.

The mortgagee in possession may avoid this dilemma by persuading the junior lessee to enter an attornment agreement recognizing the mortgagee as lessor. This arrangement establishes the privity of contract necessary for the mortgagee to enforce the lease. The attornment agreement is in reality a new lease. Hence, the lessee and the mortgagee in possession may choose to set entirely new terms.

Although some junior lessees attorn to a mortgagee in possession, others take advantage of the situation to rid themselves of what they consider to be an undesirable lease. This may be disastrous to the mortgagee who was depending upon their rents to pay the mortgage debt.

The mortgagee, therefore, should take steps to ensure that it can preserve and enforce junior leases after default. Several options are available. First, the mortgagee could subordinate the mortgage to junior leases so that they would be treated as prior leases and therefore, survive the mortgagee's possession as well as foreclosure. Second, the mortgagee could require the mortgagor to negotiate an attornment provision in each valuable junior lease whereby the junior lessee agrees to recognize the mortgagee as landlord if the lessor-mortgagor defaults on the mortgage. The lessee, of course, may seek to have the mortgagee execute a non-disturbance agreement in return. Indeed, such a combination of attornment and non-disturbance agreements may be employed to maintain a junior lease beyond foreclosure. Third, the mortgagee could require that the mortgagor assign rents generated by the mortgaged property, an alternative explored in the following section. Fourth, after default, the mortgagee could seek the appointment of a receiver of rents, a course of action that is discussed later in this chapter.

C. ASSIGNMENT OF RENTS

The mortgagee may require the mortgagor to execute an assignment of rents giving the mortgagee an interest in all present and future leases and in all rents arising from the mortgaged real estate independent of any right the mortgagee may have to take possession of the property. The practical effect of an assignment of rents is that upon default the mortgagee, as assignee of the mortgagor's rights, may collect rents without taking possession under the mortgage. Thus, the mortgagee can preserve and enforce junior leases until foreclosure. Moreover, in most jurisdictions the mortgagee may establish the priority of its interest in rents over subsequent claimants by recording the assignment, without taking any step to activate it. In certain states, however, priority dates from activation because the assignment is "inchoate" before then.

A division of opinion exists as to how an assignment of rents may be activated so that the mortgagee can begin collecting rents. The precise language of the assignment may be determinative. There is authority that an assignment of rents is an "absolute" assignment triggered automatically upon default. However, the generally accepted view is that an assignment of rents constitutes a security interest that the mortgagee must trigger by taking some affirmative step after default. The type of action required varies among the states. Depending upon the jurisdiction, the mortgagee may activate the assignment of rents by making formal demand of the mortgagor, by giving notice to the lessees, by filing a foreclosure suit seeking the appointment of a receiver, by taking possession of the property, or by obtaining the appointment of a receiver.

An assignment of rents also protects the mortgagee from being bound by agreements for advance rental payment, rent reduction, or lease cancellation commonly used by mortgagors in distress to milk the mortgaged property of all potential revenue. If the mortgagee obtains an assignment of rents, records it, and gives notice to existing lessees, all lessees enter advance payment, rent reduction, and cancellation agreements with the mortgagor at their peril.

In 2005, the National Conference of Commissioners on Uniform State Laws sought to reconstruct the fragmented assignment-of-rents legal framework by crafting the Uniform Assignment of Rents Act (UARA). UARA sets forth many rules, such as clarifying the timing of the perfection of a security interest, abolishing absolute assignment of rents, and expanding the definition of rents. This measure has been enacted in only a few states, including Nevada, New Mexico, Texas and Utah.

The majority of states have not enacted UARA, and their approach to assignment of rents depends in part on whether the jurisdiction follows the title, lien or intermediate theory of mortgages.

D. RECEIVER

1. Background

The mortgagee may seek to have a receiver for rents and profits appointed in an action for foreclosure. This is a particularly valuable option in lien theory states where the mortgagee cannot obtain possession and reach rents and profits absent the mortgagor's agreement that the mortgagee may do so.

Even when the mortgagee has the right to possession of the mortgaged real estate upon default, it may want to have a receiver appointed rather than take possession itself. Several reasons support such an approach. First, the stringent accounting duties imposed on a mortgagee in possession are avoided. Second, the potential tort and contract liabilities of a mortgagee in possession are eliminated. Third, junior leases are preserved and rents may be collected under those leases even when there is no assignment of rents.

2. Grounds for Appointment

A receivership is an equitable remedy designed to preserve the mortgaged property pending foreclosure. The appointment of a receiver is generally within the court's sound discretion bounded only by the traditional requirement that due consideration be given to the security's adequacy, the existence or likelihood of waste, and the mortgagor's financial position. For example, in Florida Reinvestment Corp. v. Cypress Sav. Ass'n., 509 So. 2d 1352 (Fla. Dist. Ct. App. 1987), the mortgagee filed a motion for the appointment of a receiver for Florida Reinvestment's mortgaged property, townhouse units. Id. at 1353. The mortgagee believed that Florida Reinvestment's rental practices were detrimental to its security interest and that Florida Reinvestment was not using the rental income to maintain the townhouses. Id. The court stated that when a mortgagor was receiving rents but not applying them to the mortgage debt, the court could appoint a receiver unless the mortgagor showed that the value of the mortgaged property and additional security covered the entire debt. Id. 1353–1354. Because Florida Reinvestment did not meet its burden, the court upheld the appointment of a receiver. Id. at 1354.

Judicial authority in this area has been further broadened by the common use of a mortgage clause authorizing the mortgagee to obtain the appointment of a receiver.

Courts have exercised their largely unbridled discretion in markedly different ways. In a number of states, the appointment of a receiver is virtually automatic upon request. Indeed, such a result is dictated by statute in certain jurisdictions when the mortgage contains a receivership clause. Residing at the opposite end of the spectrum are states in which a receiver is appointed only in the most compelling circumstances. The bulk of jurisdictions take various positions somewhere between these polar approaches.

3. Receiver's Powers

Once appointed, the receiver generally is empowered to preserve the mortgagee's security by taking possession of the mortgaged real estate and collecting rents and profits. A receiver takes rents out of the mortgagor's control, but the mortgagee has no control and therefore does not have not have a claim to rents and profits in the receiver's hands. Sargent v. Smith, 865 A.2d 1129, 1133 (Conn. 2005). Rather, the court has legal possession of the rents and profits, and they are to be distributed as ordered by the court. Id. The appointment of a receiver may appear to benefit one party and oftentimes arises from the request of one party, but a receiver's responsibility is to the court alone. Hart v. Ed-Ley Corp., 482 P.2d 421, 425 (Colo. App. Div. 1 1971). As an officer of the court, a receiver is responsible for protecting and maintaining property while also collecting any rent or income from the property. Id.

This section will analyze a receiver's authority related to collecting rent from junior lessees and mortgagors who are in possession of the mortgaged property as a residence and operating the mortgagor's business.

a. Collecting Rent from Junior Lessees

A mortgagee may utilize a receiver to reach rent payable under a lease entered after the execution of the mortgage even when there is no assignment of rents. Where a mortgage agreement does not address assignment of rents or profits, the mortgagee's right to those rents or profits arises by taking possession of the property or having a receiver appointed to collect the property's rents or profits under foreclosure law. *In re* Somero, 122 B.R. 634, 638 (Bankr. D. Maine 1991). In *Somero*, the parties had executed an assignment of rents agreement, but the issue in the case was whether the assignment of rents agreement was valid if a mortgagee hadn't taken possession of the mortgaged property or a receiver hadn't been appointed to collect rental income. Id. at 638. Under the agreement, the mortgagors were entitled to the rents unless they were in default under the mortgage. Id. at 637. While the court held parties to a mortgage may modify entitlements to rents or profits under an assignment of rents agreement without the mortgagee's possession or appointment of a receiver, it acknowledged the appointment of a receiver was one such way to reach rents payable under a lease even without an assignment of rents clause. Id. at 637.

The receiver's action is that of the court, not the mortgagee, so it does not automatically destroy junior leases.

b. Collecting Rent from Mortgagor in Residence

A vexing rent collection problem arises when the mortgagor occupies the mortgaged property as a residence. Although some authority exists that a receiver may collect rent from the mortgagor in such cases, courts may be hesitant to permit a receiver to do so. *See* Holmes v. Gravenhorst, 188 N.E. 285 (N.Y.1933). A court may authorize a receiver to collect rent from mortgagors who live in the mortgaged property. Carlin Trading Corp. v. Bennett, 24 A.D.2d 91, 91 (N.Y. App. Div. 1st Dep't 1965) (per curiam). However, unless the mortgage contains specific language allowing otherwise, a receiver may not interfere with a mortgagor's possession of the property during the pendency of the foreclosure action even if the mortgagor fails to pay the rent to the receiver. Id. The court in *Bennett* reversed a lower court's order directing the sheriff to evict a mortgagor who lived in the mortgaged property but refused to pay rent to the receiver and noted that there was "a marked distinction between the right to collect rent and the right to obtain possession." Id. at 91–92. Two judges dissented in the *Bennett* decision, noting the decision frustrated the mortgagee's ability to enforce the court's order that the mortgagor pay rent to a receiver. Id. at 93 (Valente, dissenting).

c. *Operating Mortgagor's Business*

Mortgagees may request the appointment of a receiver to operate the mortgagor's business pending foreclosure. A court generally will grant the request only if the business is either specifically covered by the mortgage or based primarily on the rental value of the mortgaged real estate, as in the case of an apartment building. For a greater discussion of whether a receiver can exercise control of the mortgagor's business see Nelson, Whitman, Burkhart & Freyermuth, Real Estate Finance Law § 4.41, at 240–242 (West 2015).

In *In re* 29 Brooklyn Avenue, LLC, 535 B.R. 36, 39 (Bankr. E.D. N.Y. 2015), a receiver was appointed when a bank brought foreclosure proceedings regarding the LLC's single asset, its property at 29 Brooklyn Avenue. Id. at 40. The mortgagor-LLC sued objecting to the receiver's request to be paid nearly $80,000 to cover expenses it incurred in operating the property. Id. These expenses required to operate the business included tens of thousands of dollars for heating oil, roughly $1,500 for extermination services and thousands of dollars for ordinary maintenance and janitorial services. Id. at 53–54. The court ordered the mortgagor to reimburse the receiver for these aforementioned fees, which comprised the vast bulk of the receiver's claim. Id. at 59–60. However, the court did not order the receiver's reimbursement for landlord-tenant counsel expenses totaling approximately $3,300 because the receiver failed to properly account for those expenses. Id. at 56, 59.

Cases have considered whether receivers are liable for damages while operating a mortgagor's business. In *In re* Sundance Corp., Inc., 149 B.R. 641 (Bankr. E.D. Wash. 1993), Scott Property Management, Inc. (SPM) was appointed as receiver during the foreclosure of a mortgage on a 2,000-acre fruit orchard. Id. at 646. The court order authorized SPM to incur costs required for the orchard's operation and preservation. Id. In particular, SPM reviewed an inspection report that called for the orchard's trees to be "staked" to correct the trees' improper growth that was caused by wind. Id. at fn. 1. Before SPM began this operation, it treated the 300,000 stakes it planned to use with a combination of pentachlorophenol and diesel fuel to prevent their deterioration. Id. at 647. After serving as receiver for over four years, SPM filed a motion to discharge its custodianship. Id. at 647–48. The mortgagee's successor in interest, Pacific and Holeman, objected, however, claiming SPM was liable for the costs to clean up chemicals used in the orchard. Id. at 648. In particular, Pacific and Holeman argued SPM's use of chemicals was "abnormally dangerous," giving rise to strict liability under the common law, the Comprehensive Environmental Response Compensation and Liability Act (CERCLA), Washington's Model Toxics Control Act (MTCA), and Washington's Hazardous Waste Management Act (HWMA). *Id.* In a lengthy opinion, the court addressed the claims in turn. The court held summary judgment could not be granted on the common law claim. Id. at 655. When a receiver's court-approved course of action is within the spectrum of reasonable business judgment, the receiver is immune from liability. Id. Only inconclusive evidence regarding SPM's business judgment was presented, however, so the court could not decide the issue at hand. Id.

Likewise, the court held that receivers, acting as court officers, were not liable under CERCLA, MTCA, or HWMA for actions within the scope of their court-ordered authority. Id. at 664. The court held SPM was not liable under CERCLA because the statute limited liability to a "person." Id. at 658. Though acknowledging the term's ambiguity, the court held that judicial immunity and derivative judicial immunity existed under CERCLA so long as a judge or officer of the court was carrying out judicial functions as SPM was here. Id. at 661. The court likewise disposed of the two claims brought pursuant to Washington state's statutes. Id. at 661–63.

Likewise, other courts follow the court's rationale in *Sundance* in holding that receivers were not liable for damages arising under CERCLA violations when receivers acted within the scope of their court-appointed duties. *See., e.g.,* Hervey v. Dyer, 972 P.2d 42, 43 (Okla. Civ. App. 1st Div. 1998) (refusing to join as party defendant a court-appointed receiver because that receiver acted within his authority to operate a party's businesses, including its landfill).

IV. EQUITY OF REDEMPTION

A. AVAILABILITY

Certain qualified individuals may prevent foreclosure by paying off the mortgage debt before the foreclosure sale. This right of late payment is known as the equity of redemption. The equity of redemption doctrine was established to provide mortgagors with relief against forfeiture by allowing them to cure default within a reasonable time. Scott v. Dorothy B. Schneider Estate Trust, 783 S.W.2d 26, 28 (Tex. App. 1990). The equitable right to redeem is included in every mortgage, and it is commonly stated that there cannot be a clog on equity of redemption. The *Scott* court states that there are three requirements for equitable redemption. First, the person seeking to exercise equitable redemption must establish that the person has a legal or equitable interest in the mortgaged property. Id. at 28. *Id.* Any person who has an interest in the property and who would suffer a loss because of a foreclosure would meet this requirement. Second, the person must establish that the person is "ready, able or willing" to exercise the redemption rights. Id. Finally, the person's attempt to equitably redeem the property must be timely. Id.

B. PARTIES WHO MAY REDEEM

The mortgagor, of course, may redeem. In addition, any party acquiring an interest in, or a lien on, the mortgaged property after the attachment of the mortgage may redeem because its interest will be cut off by foreclosure. Other eligible individuals able to exercise redemption rights include grantees, heirs, devisees, junior lessees, and junior encumbrancers. When several parties have equitable redemption rights, they may redeem in the order of the priority of their interests, subject to the mortgagor's ultimate right to redeem.

C. AMOUNT REQUIRED FOR REDEMPTION

Equitable redemption generally can be accomplished only by paying the entire mortgage debt, late fees and any additional lawful charges and fees. However, if the entire debt is not in default, as in the case of an unaccelerated amortized loan, the mortgagor may reinstate the loan and avoid foreclosure by making late payment of the overdue amount. In the following discussion, it is assumed that the entire mortgage debt is in default.

D. RESULT OF REDEMPTION

1. By Mortgagor or Mortgagor's Successor

Redemption by the mortgagor or the mortgagor's successor discharges the mortgage in default. Junior interests survive the mortgagor's redemption unless also paid off. The mortgagor is entitled to ownership in the property unencumbered by the redeemed mortgage. However, all other encumbrances are revived because the mortgagor's ownership is restored to reflect the mortgagor's interest before the foreclosure action. Coursey v. Fairchild, 436 P.2d 35, 38 (Okla. 1967).

2. By Junior Interest Holder

Redemption by a junior interest holder does not terminate the mortgage from which the property is redeemed. On the contrary, the mortgage survives, and the one who redeems is subrogated to the rights of the mortgagee. Portland Mortgage Co. v. Creditors Protective Ass'n, 262 P.2d 918, 924 (Or. 1953) (stating "[w]hen a junior lienholder has redeemed the senior incumbrance and steps into the shoes of the prior mortgagee, he must foreclose his lien and have the property sold, in order to realize on his security, unless the purchaser at the prior foreclosure, who has acquired the mortgagor's equity of redemption, chooses to redeem from him"). As a result, the redeeming junior mortgagee can initiate foreclosure proceedings.

Illustration: A mortgagor executes a $10,000 first mortgage to a first mortgagee on land, then a $5,000 second mortgage to a second mortgagee, and finally a $2,000 third mortgage to a third mortgagee. The mortgagor defaults on all loans, and each mortgagee accelerates. The mortgagor may pay the first mortgagee $10,000 and free the land from the first mortgage. In that case, the second and third mortgages will continue to encumber the land. The second mortgagee also may pay the first mortgagee $10,000 before the mortgagor does so. This will not terminate the first mortgage. All three mortgages will remain, but now the second mortgagee will hold both the first and second mortgages. The third mortgagee can then redeem from the second mortgagee by paying the second mortgagee the total amount of the first and second liens ($15,000). This will not terminate either the first or second mortgages. All three mortgages remain, but they now are held by the third mortgagee. However, the mortgagor has the ultimate right to redeem. Based on these facts, the mortgagor must pay the third mortgagee the total of all mortgage liens ($17,000) to redeem the land free from the encumbrances.

E. ENFORCEMENT OF RIGHT TO REDEEM

If the parties cannot agree on the question of redemption, the one asserting a right to redeem may file a bill in equity to enforce this right.

F. WAIVER/CLOGGING

The equitable redemption right is a "substantive property right," and any attempt to destroy that right is against public policy and void. Coursey v. Fairchild, 436 P.2d 35, 38 (Okla. 1967). Therefore, courts will not recognize mortgage clauses that waive or otherwise clog the mortgagor's equity of redemption. *See, e.g.,* C. Phillip Johnson Full Gospel Ministries, Inc. v. Investors Financial Services, LLC, 12 A.3d 1207, 1215 (Md. 2011) (stating that the mortgagor's equity of redemption is "inseparately connected with a mortgage" and cannot be waived at the time the mortgage is granted); Humble Oil & Refining Co. v. Doerr, 123 N.J. Super. 530, 303 A.2d 898, 905 (N.J. Super. Ct. App. Div. 1973) (stating that any agreement that clogs the equity of redemption is against public policy and therefore void and unenforceable). The court in *Humble Oil* stated that "[t]he very purpose of the anti-clogging rules, based upon strong public policy, is to prevent mortgagors from being 'outbargained' in mortgage transactions and to protect them from the consequences of their acts done through infirmity of will because of their inferior bargaining positions." Id. at 915. The waiver of equitable redemption will allow the mortgagee to thwart the fundamental principles underlying equity of redemption by allowing title to vest in the mortgagee immediately upon the mortgagor's default. *See* Swift v. Kirby, 737 S.W.2d 271, 276 (Tenn. 1987).

Some courts allow waiver in other limited circumstances. For example, in Oakland Hills Development Corp. v. Lueders Drainage Dist., 212 Mich. App 284, 537 N.W.2d 258 (Mich. Ct. App. 1995), the court noted that courts must "carefully scrutinize" situations where a mortgagor waives redemption rights. Id. at 263. Further, the court stated that a mortgagor is entitled to release or sell the equitable right of redemption for bona fide consideration where there is no fraud or undue influence and it is not done by a contemporaneous or subsequent executory contract where the equity of redemption will be forfeited if the debt is not paid on a day set forth in the contract. Id. at 264.

G. WHEN RIGHT OF REDEMPTION ENDS

1. Foreclosure

The completion of foreclosure terminates the equity of redemption of all party defendants. If foreclosure is by judicial sale, the right to redeem generally ends when the court confirms the sale. If foreclosure is by power of sale, the right to redeem ends when the sale is final under local law.

A junior interest holder omitted from the foreclosure proceedings retains both the junior interest and an equity of redemption. The omitted junior interest holder, therefore, may seek to assert the right to redeem even after foreclosure.

2. Termination by Other Means

A mortgagor's equitable right to redeem may be barred by estoppel, laches, or a statute of limitations. Generally, none of these possibilities will arise if the mortgagor remains on the mortgaged property. *See* Nelson, Whitman, Burkhart & Freyermuth, Real Estate Finance Law § 575 (6th ed. West 2015). It is when the mortgagee takes possession that circumstances are ripe for the development of these bars to redemption.

V. ALTERNATIVES TO FORECLOSURE

Although a mortgagee is entitled to commence foreclosure proceedings after default, it may decide to pursue another course of action initially.

A. LOAN MODIFICATION AND WORKOUT ARRANGEMENT

1. Workout Arrangement

Institutional mortgage lenders desire to avoid foreclosure and may enter into a workout agreement with a mortgagor. Their business is to obtain a reasonable return on their investments, not to engage in litigation or manage real estate. Consequently, they often lower monthly payments, extend the time for payment, waive late charges, or make any other reasonable arrangement that allows the mortgagor to work out of temporary financial difficulty.

Care should be taken in writing these agreements to avoid ambiguous terms. In Multifamily Mortgage Trust 1996–2 v. ARA Associates-Shangri-La, Ltd., 530 S.E.2d 217 (Ga. App. 2000), the mortgagor and the U.S. Department of Housing and Urban Development, the assignee of the mortgagor's note, entered into a provisional workout agreement to prevent foreclosure. Id. at 219. Under the agreement after the mortgagor was required to pay for "operating expenses," any funds remaining in the operating account would be used to pay down the note. Id. at 219. The mortgagee initiated foreclosure proceedings after the mortgagor paid for extensive repairs from operating expenses rather than paying down the note from the operating account, and the mortgagor moved to enjoin the foreclosure action. Id. at 218. The term "operating expenses" was not defined under the workout agreement, and the court determined that the term was ambiguous. Id. at 219. The court looked at context of the term and precedent establishing that the repairs must benefit the project rather than the owner and concluded that the repairs benefited the project in this case. Id. at 219–220. Therefore, the court determined that the mortgagor was not in default under the agreement and enjoined the foreclosure action.

2. Government Loan Modification Programs

After the subprime loan crisis, the federal government established several programs that permitted eligible homeowners who were underwater or upside down in their home mortgage loans to modify their loans. One of these programs was the Home Affordable Modification Program (HAMP). HAMP allowed for the reduction of principal loan payments. The Department of Treasury and the Federal Housing Finance Agency established HAMP to incentivize mortgagees to modify loans for homeowners who were in danger of losing their homes through foreclosure. Edwards v. Aurora Loan Services, LLC, 791 F. Supp. 2d 144, 147 (D.D.C. 2011) (providing a good discussion of the program and the reasons for its creation).

3. Tax Consequences of Loan Modification

Mortgagors must be aware of the tax consequences of the discharge or reduction of mortgage debts. Under the Internal Revenue Code, gross income includes income from the discharge of indebtedness. IRC § 61(a)(12) (2017). When a debt is discharged, the mortgagor usually receives Form 1099-C, Cancellation of Debt. However, it is possible that the mortgagor will qualify for an exclusion under IRC § 108(a). If the mortgagor's debt is discharged in bankruptcy, the entire amount of the discharged debt is excluded from gross income. If the debt is discharged outside of bankruptcy but the mortgagor is insolvent, the discharge is excluded as well but only up to the amount of the insolvency. *See* IRC § 108(a)(3) (2017). If the mortgagor is insolvent and in bankruptcy, the bankruptcy exclusion takes precedence. IRC § 108(a)(2)(A) (2017).

There are exclusions for "qualified farm indebtedness" and "qualified real property business indebtedness." IRC § 108(a)(1)(C) & (D) (2017). Finally, homeowners were entitled to an exclusion up to $2 million for qualified principal residence indebtedness for discharges occurring before January 1, 2017. IRC §§ 108(a)(1)(E) & 108(h)(2) (2016). The qualified principal residence indebtedness exclusion was created by the Mortgage Forgiveness Debt Relief Act of 2007, Pub. L. No. 110–142, which inserted the new subparagraph (E) for principal residence indebtedness. This change was effective for debt discharges after December 31, 2006. This exclusion was enacted because of the collapse of the real estate market during the Great Recession. In a press release upon signing the Mortgage Forgiveness Debt Relief Act of 2007, Former President George W. Bush noted the uncertainty and strains on the housing market and stated that the exclusion would be an incentive for homeowners and lenders to have loans reduced without the fear of incurring a tax liability.

Statement by George W. Bush Signing HR 3648 2007 U.S.C.C.A.N. S31–S32.

The qualified principal residence exclusion's deadline was continuously extended. First, the Emergency Economic Stabilization Act of 2008, Pub. L. No. 110–343, extended the deadline from January 1, 2010, to January 1, 2013. Thereafter, the American Taxpayer Relief Act of 2012, Pub. L. No. 112–240, extended the deadline to January 1, 2014. The Tax Increase Prevention Act of 2014, Pub. L. No. 113–295, again pushed the deadline until January 1, 2015. Finally, the Protecting Americans from Tax Hikes Act of 2015, Pub. L. No. 114–113, extended the deadline for the exclusion to discharges occurring before January 1, 2017. No extension has since been made.

Generally, the exclusions under section 108 result in a deferral of income rather than a complete forgiveness because the mortgagor is required to reduce certain tax attributes, including net operating losses, capital loss carryovers, adjusted basis and passive loss carryovers. IRC § 108(b) (2017). For example, assume that a mortgagor's principal loan balance is reduced by $20,000, the mortgagor is insolvent to that extent and has a capital loss carryover of $25,000. The entire $20,000 is excluded from the mortgagor's gross income under IRC § 108, but the mortgagor must reduce the capital loss carryover to $5,000. If the mortgagor realizes $25,000 in capital gains in the future, the mortgagor will be taxed on the vast majority of the capital gains because the capital loss carryover is only $5,000. If the mortgagor is not required to reduce the capital loss carryover by $20,000, the capital loss will fully offset the $25,000 capital gains in its entirety. With respect to the principal residence indebtedness exclusion, the mortgagor's adjusted basis in the residence had to be reduced but not below zero. *See* IRC § 108(h)(1) (2017). The principal residence exception took precedence over the insolvency exclusion unless the mortgagor elected otherwise. IRC § 108(a)(2)(C) (2017). While the principal residence exception only applied to discharges occurring before January 1, 2017, it remains relevant as the Internal Revenue Service can assess deficiencies related to that tax year for three years after the tax return is filed.

B. DEED IN LIEU OF FORECLOSURE

1. Meaning of a Deed in Lieu of Foreclosure and General Rules

If the mortgagor cannot possibly pay the mortgage obligation, the mortgagee may be willing to accept a deed to the mortgaged real estate in lieu of foreclosure. There are numerous advantages for both the mortgagor and the mortgagee. The mortgagor and mortgagee can avoid the delays and costs associated with foreclosure actions, and the mortgagor avoids having a foreclosure on the mortgagor's credit report. Decon Group, Inc. v. Prudential Mortgage Capital Co., LLC, 227 Cal. App. 4th 665, 670 (2014). It is a convenient and efficient way to transfer title to the mortgagee when the mortgagor defaults on the mortgage. Morrison v.

Christie, 266 S.W.3d 89, 92–93 (Tex. Ct. App. 2008). The mortgagee avoids statutory redemption in the states that permit it, and the mortgagor avoids a potential deficiency judgment. Restatement (Third) of Property, Mortgages § 8.5 cmt. b (1997).

The parties can agree that the deed in lieu of foreclosure partially satisfies a debt. For example, in *Morrison*, the parties agreed that the mortgagee would sell the property conveyed in the deed in lieu of foreclosure, the sales proceeds from the sale would be used to pay off the unpaid balance on the debt, and the mortgagee could collect a deficiency to cover the remaining balance due on the debt. Morrison, 266 S.W.3d at 91.

The mortgagee must accept the deed in lieu of foreclosure. If so, junior encumbrances are not extinguished as they are when there is an actual foreclosure provided they are named as party defendants to the foreclosure action.

2. Tax Consequences of a Deed in Lieu of Foreclosure

When a mortgagor conveys real property to a mortgagee in a deed in lieu of foreclosure, the mortgagor must include the mortgage relief in the amount realized for purposes of determining the mortgagor's gain or loss. Treas. Reg. § 1.1001–2(a) (2017). The mortgage relief is included irrespective of whether the discharged loan is recourse or nonrecourse. Crane v. Comm'r, 331 U.S. 1 (1947). However, to the extent that the mortgage secures a recourse loan and the mortgagor has discharge of indebtedness income under IRC § 61(a)(12), the amount realized on the deed in lieu of foreclosure will not include the amount that is discharge of indebtedness income. Treas. Reg. § 1.1001–2(a)(2) (2017). If, for example, a mortgagor owned real property that had a fair market value of $200,000 that was subject to a mortgage debt of $250,000. As a result, the mortgagor was underwater. Although the mortgagor was personally liable on the debt, the mortgagee agreed to a deed in lieu of foreclosure and discharged $50,000 on the deed in lieu of foreclosure. The mortgagor has $50,000 in discharge of indebtedness income per IRC § 61(a)(12). In addition, the mortgagor must recognize gain on the conveyance of the property to the mortgagee in the deed in lieu of foreclosure. The mortgagor's gain will be determined under Treas. Reg. § 1.1001–2(a)(2). Assume that the mortgagor's adjusted basis in the property is $100,000 at the time of the conveyance to the mortgagee. The mortgagor's amount realized includes the mortgage relief of $250,000 less the $50,000 discharge of indebtedness income, and the mortgagor's gain equals $100,000 ($200,000 amount realized less $100,000 adjusted basis). The purpose of this rule is to prevent double taxation. Without this rule, the income will be taxed as discharged of indebtedness income under section 61(a)(12) and taxable gain under section 61(a)(3) as gains derived from the dealings in property.

Conversely, if the debt was nonrecourse, the mortgagor's amount realized would equal $250,000, the entire mortgage relief, and the mortgagor would be required to recognize gain of $150,000 ($250,000 amount realized less $100,000 adjusted basis) on the conveyance of the property to the mortgagee.

The net gain is the same whether the loan is recourse or nonrecourse, $150,000. However, the character of the gain is not the same. In the case of the deed in lieu of foreclosure involving a nonrecourse debt, the entire $150,000 is capital gain presuming that the property is a capital asset. In the recourse loan scenario, $100,000 of the gain is taxed as capital gain, but the $50,000 discharge of indebtedness income is taxed at the ordinary income rates under IRC § 1.

C. SHORT SALES

A mortgagor in default may decide to sell the mortgaged real estate and satisfy the mortgage loan with the proceeds of the sale. If, however, the balance of the mortgage loan exceeds the market value of the realty, this route to discharging the loan is seemingly unavailable. Nonetheless, a mortgagee may agree to a "short sale" in such a situation. Short sales were relatively uncommon prior to 2008 but became more prevalent during the subprime loan crisis. For example, in California, short sales grew from almost none in 2007 and a few thousand in 2008 to 110,000 in 2010. Coker v. JPMorgan Chase Bank, N.A., 364 P.3d 176, 179 (Cal. 2016).

One of key differences between a short sale and a foreclosure sale is that the former is a voluntary sale by the mortgagor with the consent of the mortgagee, and the latter is a sale by the mortgagee involuntarily entered into by the mortgagor. Rex v.

Chase Home Finance LLC, 905 F.Supp.2d 1111, 1138 (C.D. Cal. 2012). In addition, it is advantageous to the mortgagor because it prevents a negative entry on the mortgagor's credit report, and it is advantageous to the mortgagee because it saves money and time. Id. at 1139. Even though there is not a foreclosure sale with a short sale, the court in *Rex* determined that the anti-deficiency statute applied which precluded a deficiency after the short sale. Id. at 1144–1145.

As a general matter, a "short sale" arrangement involves selling the property at a price lower than the outstanding mortgage debt, applying the sale proceeds to reduce the debt, cancelling the obligation that remains or establishing terms for its full or partial repayment, and releasing the mortgage. *See* Coker, 364 P.3d, at 178. *See also* Rex v. Chase Home Finance LLC, 905 F.Supp.2d at 1138 (stating that in a short sale the mortgagor "secures the agreement of the [mortgagee] to release the mortgage upon a bona fide sale to a third party for an agreed upon price below the mortgage loan balance").

Courts recognize that a short-sale agreement is a form of contract and will enforce them so long as the agreements adhere to ordinary contract principles. Jones v. SunTrust Mortgage, Inc., 274 P.3d 762, 764 (Nev. 2012). The mortgagors in *Jones* purchased a home in 2006 using a loan provided by Home Mortgage Direct Lenders, which apparently assigned the loan to the mortgagee. Id. at 763. The mortgagors subsequently defaulted, voluntarily entered Nevada's Foreclosure Mediation Program, and signed an agreement to resolve the pending foreclosure through a short sale of the property during a specified two-month time period. Id. The mortgagors first argued they did not receive the necessary short-sale documents, but the district court quickly disposed of this argument based on evidence that the mortgagee twice mailed such documents. Id. at 764. The court determined that the parties entered an enforceable short-sale agreement. Id. Although the mortgagors argued their agreement lacked consideration, this court held the agreement was supported by consideration. Id. Namely, in exchange for the mortgagors agreeing to a short sale, the mortgagee suspended foreclosure proceedings during the agreed-upon two-month period. Id. The court held the mortgagee properly could foreclose on the property because a short sale was not accomplished during the two-month period specified in the enforceable agreement. Id. at 764–65.

Courts will not enforce a short-sale agreement if the mortgagor violates the terms of the agreement. In Gould v. Bank of New York Mellon, 123 F.Supp.3d 197 (D. Mass. 2015), the mortgagor (Gould) failed to make her mortgage payments for several years, and the property's value had dropped below the outstanding mortgage amount. Id. at 200. Gould faced the prospect of foreclosure in 2012 and agreed to execute a short sale of the property instead. Id. If Gould found a buyer who would pay a price approved by the mortgagee, her mortgage would be discharged. Id. Bank of America was the servicing agent at that time and required that a short sale be an arm's length transaction, meaning the buyer and seller be "unrelated." Id. Gould's husband formed SPI, Inc., to act as purchaser of the property to "skirt" Bank of America's requirement. Id. After negotiations between SPI and Bank of America, the two parties settled on a selling price of $422,500 in August of 2012. Id. at 201. Then, in October of 2012, Bank of America stated it would not approve the short sale after uncovering the relationship between the prospective buyer and Gould. Id. After finding an enforceable contract was never even formed, the court went on to hold that the lender would be excused from performance if an enforceable contract had been formed because of the buyer and seller's relationship. Id. at 204. The court held it was a material requirement that the buyer and seller of Gould's property be unrelated. Id. In holding the lender would have been excused if an enforceable contract had been formed, the court articulated the basic contract principle that one party's material breach excuses the other party's performance. Id.

While the remaining outstanding balance of the loan is usually discharged where there is a short sale, the agreement may require the mortgagor to pay a deficiency. In Bank of Am., N.A. v. Roberts, 217 Cal. App. 4th 1386 (2013), the mortgagor defaulted on her home equity loan, the home was sold in a short sale and in the agreement with the bank she acknowledged that she would be responsible for repaying the unpaid balance that wasn't covered by the short sale. Id. at 1390. She later argued that the bank was barred from the remaining deficiency because they had accepted the lesser amount in the short sale. Id. at 1391. The trial court determined that there was no evidence to show that the bank waived its right to recover the deficiency and so the mortgagor still owed that amount since she acknowledged that she would still be responsible for it. Id. at 1391–1392. The mortgagor argued that an amendment to the statute that prohibited the collection of a deficiency in the case of a short sale should be applied retroactively. Based on the legislative history, jurisprudence of the court and language of the statute itself, the court determined that the statute should not be applied retroactively in this case. Therefore, the mortgagee could seek the deficiency judgment even though there was a short sale. Id. at 1398.

D. RECOVERY ON THE NOTE ALONE/ONE ACTION RULE

Even if litigation is necessary, the mortgagee generally may sue on the note without foreclosing the mortgage. This principle is predicated on the notion that because the underlying obligation is the essential element of the transaction, the mortgagee may treat the note as unsecured if it so wishes. In California and a few other states, however, the mortgagee's only remedy on default is to foreclose and obtain a deficiency judgment if appropriate. Cal. Civ. Pro. Code § 526(a) (2016). Other states following the one action rule include Idaho, Montana, Nevada and Utah. *See* Idaho Code Ann. § 6–101(1) (2016); Mont. Code Ann. § 71–1–222(1) (2015); Nev. Rev. Stat. § 40.430(1) (2016); Utah Code Ann. § 78B–6–901(1) (2016). Even in jurisdictions that follow the one action rule, there are several acts that may not be an "action." For example, in Idaho, these acts include the ability to appoint a receiver, enforce an assignment of rents, and enforce a mortgage on property located outside of the state that is security for the same debt secured by the real property that is being foreclosed. *See* Idaho Code Ann. § 6–101(3)(a)–(c) (2016). *Accord* Mont. Code Ann. § 71–1–222(4)(a)–(c) (2015); Nev. Rev. Stat. § 40.430(6)(a)–(c) (2016).

The "one action" rule is based on several factors. First, it is based on the theory that because the mortgaged property is the primary fund for repayment of the debt, the mortgagee must exhaust it before seeking satisfaction from the mortgagor's other assets. *See* Bank of Am., N.A. v. Roberts, 217 Cal. App. 4th 1386, 1397 (2013). The rule also is designed to protect the mortgagor from multiple actions arising from the same loan transaction. Moreover, the rule is designed to prevent creditors from receiving a windfall by obtaining the foreclosed property for much lower than its fair market value while pursuing the mortgagor for the full outstanding balance on the underlying note. Machock v. Fink, 137 P.3d 779, 782 (Utah 2006). Further, the one action rule is intended to "eliminate harassment of debtors and multiple litigation" that is possible under the common law rule. Id. at 784.

Where suit on the note alone is permitted, the mortgage is not affected by the resulting personal judgment against the mortgagor. The debt merges into the judgment, and the judgment becomes the underlying obligation. Whatever the mortgagee then collects from the mortgagor's other assets is credited against this obligation. The only significant change in the legal relationship of the parties is that enforcement of the underlying obligation is now governed by the statute of limitations on judgments rather than by the statute of limitations on promissory notes.

CHAPTER 10
PRIORITIES

I. GENERAL PRINCIPLES

When foreclosure is imminent, the mortgagee and other parties holding interests in the mortgaged property become particularly concerned about the priority of their respective interests. Their concern is well founded. First, interests acquired before the mortgage survive foreclosure. Those acquired after the mortgage are extinguished provided that the holders of these interests are named as parties to the foreclosure action. Second, the mortgagee and subsequent interest holders are paid from the proceeds of the foreclosure sale in the order of their priority, but the proceeds may be insufficient to pay everyone. As a result, a senior mortgagee is more likely to recoup its investment after a foreclosure sale than a junior mortgagee. Mortgagees usually record their mortgages to ensure that subsequent mortgagees have notice of their mortgages.

Mortgagees commonly turn to title insurance for assurance of lien priority. Mortgage loan arrangements frequently call for the acquisition of a lender's title insurance policy at the mortgagor's expense.

II. RECORDING STATUTES

The principle "first in time, first in right" determines the order of priority among interest holders in the mortgaged property unless a subsequent purchaser or mortgagee fits within the protection afforded by the local recording statute. There are three types of recording statutes: notice, race-notice, or race. In all jurisdictions, the prior interest holder may preserve the holder's original priority position by recording the interest immediately following its acquisition. Assume that a mortgagor grants a first mortgage in favor of a mortgagee who promptly records it. If the mortgagor then executes a mortgage in favor of a second mortgagee, the first mortgage has priority over the second mortgage under any type of recording statute because the second mortgagee is on constructive notice of the first mortgage and the first mortgagee is the first to record.

In jurisdictions with notice recording statutes, a subsequent mortgagee who has no notice of a prior mortgage at the time the mortgagor grants a mortgage to the mortgagee will prevail against a prior mortgagee. Argent Mortgage Co., LLC v. Wachovia Bank N.A., 52 So.3d 796, 799 (Fla. Dist. Ct. App. 2010). In *Argent*, the mortgagors borrowed $90,000 on August 31, 2004 and recorded that mortgage on January 5, 2005. Id. at 798. The mortgagors borrowed $65,000 on December 10, 2004, securing the loan with a mortgage on the same property. Id. The subsequent mortgage was recorded on January 31, 2005. Id. The trial court made undisputed findings of fact, including the execution and recording dates and—most notably—that the subsequent mortgagee lacked actual or constructive notice of the first mortgage when it was granted the second mortgage. Id. The primary disagreement in this case was the type of recording statute under Florida law. Id. The trial court mistakenly determined that an amendment to a state statute had changed the state's recording statute to a race-notice statute, but the court of appeals determined that the amendment did not impact Florida's notice statute. As a result, the subsequent mortgagee prevailed because it did not have notice at the time the mortgagor granted the mortgage to the subsequent mortgagee. Id. at 800–801.

In jurisdictions with race-notice recording statutes, subsequent mortgagees receive priority when they record before a prior mortgagee records and the subsequent mortgagees do not have notice of the prior mortgage at the time the mortgage is granted to the subsequent mortgagees. *See* Spickler v. Ginn, 40 A.3d 999, 1002 (Me. 2012). For example, in January a mortgagor grants a mortgage in favor of her brother. The brother fails to immediately record the mortgage. In February, the mortgagor grants a mortgage to a bank. The bank does not have actual knowledge of the brother's mortgage at the time it is granted its mortgage. The bank also lacks constructive notice because the brother recorded its mortgage too late. The bank has priority because it is a subsequent mortgagee without notice of the brother's mortgage and it recorded first.

In jurisdictions with pure race recording statutes, the first party to record a mortgage has priority regardless of whether that mortgagee knows of a prior unrecorded mortgage. Eastern Savings Bank, FSB v. Cach, LLC, 124 A.3d 585, 589 (Del. 2015) (concluding that a judgment lien had priority over a mortgage because it was recorded eight days before the mortgage was recorded). Only a few jurisdictions have pure race statutes. There are equity concerns with race statutes because a mortgagee who records first is given priority even if that mortgagee was aware of a prior encumbrance when its mortgage was granted.

III. SELECTED ISSUES

Priority issues are inextricably entwined with the development of certain fundamental mortgage concepts. This chapter discusses several important priority concepts.

A. PURCHASE MONEY MORTGAGE

1. Distinguishing Features

A purchase money mortgage is a mortgage taken by the seller of real estate as security for part of the purchase price or by a third-party lender as security for purchase funds advanced. In either situation, purchase money mortgage status is available only when the deed and the mortgage are components of a single transaction. However, if the mortgage is an inseparable aspect of the acquisition of the mortgaged property, it need not be executed at the same time as the deed. *See* Stewart v. Smith, 30 N.W. 430 (Minn.1886). *See also* Nelson v. Stoker, 669 P.2d 390, 395 (Utah 1983) (stating that the test is whether the deed and mortgage were intended as parts of a single continuous transaction and concurrent dates of execution or recording is a strong presumption of such intent) (citations omitted).

Where there is little or no evidence of a single continuous transaction, a court is unlikely to hold a mortgage is a purchase money mortgage. In Gores v. Schultz, 777 N.W.2d 522, 529 (Minn. Ct. App. 2009), the purchasers agreed to purchase real property for $100,000, and the mortgagee (their realtor) offered to loan the same amount if secured by a residential mortgage. Id. at 523. The wife did not sign the mortgage, and it would have been void under the state statutory law unless one of the allowable exceptions applied, including an exception for purchase money mortgages. Id. at 527. The purchasers purchased the property after borrowing $135,000 from the mortgagee, but they did not provide her a mortgage securing the loan at that time. Id. at 524. Instead, nine days after closing the purchase, the purchasers provided the mortgagee with a note and mortgage covering two business properties. Id. However, the mortgagee did not accept the note and mortgage because she was unfamiliar with the business partner. Id. Finally, three months after the closing, the purchasers executed a $150,000 mortgage to the mortgagee. Id. The court in *Gores* held the mortgage was not a purchase money mortgage because the deed and mortgage were not part of a continuous transaction. Id. at 528. While the lack of concurrent execution or recording of the deed and mortgage, alone, was not dispositive of the issue, the parties lacked agreement at closing that a mortgage would even result—and this showed the mortgage and deed were not part of a single continuous transaction. Id. Therefore, the court concluded that the mortgage was void because it did not meet an allowable exception.

2. Preferred Priority Position

Purchase money mortgages take precedence over any prior liens arising through the mortgagor. BancFlorida v. Hayward, 689 So.2d 1052, 1054 (Fla. 1997). Additionally, purchase money mortgages' "superpriority" takes precedence over prior recorded liens even though the purchase money mortgagee had constructive notice of these interests under the recording statutes. Id. Underlying this principle is the equitable theory that when the mortgagor receives the property, it is already encumbered with a lien in favor of the purchase money mortgagee whose willingness to extend credit or advance funds made the acquisition possible. Id. Accordingly, a purchase money mortgage takes precedence over judgment liens against the mortgagor, liens arising from after-acquired property clauses in other mortgages executed by the mortgagor, and claims against the mortgagor for dower or homestead. For example, assume that a creditor obtains a judgment against a mortgagor and receives a judgment lien on all real estate owned by a mortgagor. Later, the mortgagor borrows money from a mortgagee to purchase a parcel of land. The mortgagor executes a mortgage on the land to the mortgagee to secure repayment of the loan. Under the purchase money mortgage rule, the mortgagee's mortgage has priority over the creditor's judgment lien.

The superpriority extends beyond the traditional claims and liens. The court in Commerce Savings Lincoln, Inc. v. Robinson, 213 Neb. 596, 597 (1983), determined that purchase money mortgages even take precedence over child support judgment liens. Id. In *Robinson*, a father's divorce decree ordered him to pay child support and alimony. Id. The father failed to make several payments, however, and a court attached a judgment lien to any property he owned or might acquire. Id. The father purchased real property after executing a purchase money mortgage to a mortgagee. Id. The issue here arose when purchasers acquired the real property subject to the purchase money mortgage and executed a new mortgage consolidating the loans in favor of the same bank. Id. at 598. When the new mortgage was granted, the lender released the father's original purchase money mortgage. Applying the general rule that a release and new mortgage continues the original mortgage, the court held the second mortgage likewise had purchase money mortgage status and had priority over the child support judgment lien. Id. at 600. *See also* American General Financial Services, Inc. v. Carter, 39 Kan.App.2d 683 (2008) (finding that a later purchase money mortgage has priority over sales tax liens); Westinghouse Elec. Co. v. Vann Realty Co., 568 S.W.2d 777 (Mo. 1978) (en banc) (stating that mechanic's liens are not exempt from the general rule that purchase money mortgages take priority over all liens).

The priority of a lien or other interest existing on the property at the time of its acquisition by the mortgagor is not affected by the purchase money mortgage rule. Hence, when a mortgagor acquires property with a purchase money mortgage and there is a preexisting lien on the land, the purchase money mortgage does not take priority over the lien. Bednarowski & Michaels Development, LLC v. Wallace, 293 F.Supp.2d 728, 734 (D. Mich. 2003). In *Wallace*, the mortgagor purchased a piece of property from a seller encumbered by a tax lien. Id. at 729. Though the mortgagor used a purchase money mortgage to obtain the property, the court held the mortgagor inherited the seller's preexisting tax lien. Id. at 734. Accordingly, unlike the general rule where purchase money mortgages have superpriority, the preexisting tax lien took priority over the purchase money mortgage in this case. Id.

> *Illustration*: An owner owns land. A creditor obtains a judgment against the owner and receives a judgment lien on all real estate owned by the owner, including the land in question. The owner then conveys the land to a mortgagor. The judgment lien is not discharged. The mortgagor pays the owner with funds borrowed from a mortgagee and executes a mortgage on the land to the mortgagee to secure repayment of the loan. Although the mortgagee's mortgage qualifies as a purchase money mortgage, it does not take precedence over the creditor's prior judgment lien on the land.

B. SUBORDINATION AGREEMENTS

Established priorities may be altered by agreement. Such an agreement is called a subordination because it involves a senior interest holder voluntarily subordinating its rights to those of a junior interest holder. Three common subordination situations are treated here.

1. Subordination of Purchase Money Mortgage to Construction Loan Mortgage

a. Background

Subordination agreements are frequently employed as part of the real estate development process. Developers, of course, need raw land upon which to construct shopping centers, apartment houses, office buildings, subdivisions, and other projects. Because developers may be unable to purchase land outright and because construction lenders commonly may be unwilling to make land acquisition loans, sellers often finance the sale themselves. This form of financing is not difficult to implement. The seller agrees to convey the land to the developer in exchange for a small down payment and a note for the balance of the purchase price secured by a purchase money mortgage on the land. The developer then obtains financing for the actual development. Construction lenders, however, normally demand a first lien on the property as security. Without the subordination agreement, the construction lender's mortgage can be extinguished if the purchase money mortgagee forecloses its mortgage. For the planned development to occur, the seller, therefore, must subordinate the purchase money mortgage to the construction loan mortgage. The seller is usually willing to take this risk on the expectation that the development will enhance the property's value to the extent that the seller will be in a better security position as a second mortgagee of improved land than as a first mortgagee of unimproved land. Moreover, the seller ordinarily can demand a higher than normal purchase price for the property as compensation for agreeing to the subordination.

A purchase money mortgage may be subordinated by the parties' agreement, the express terms of which will be strictly construed because such an agreement eliminates the superpriority usually attributed to purchase money mortgages. Citizens & Southern Nat'l Bank of South Carolina v. Smith, 277 S.C. 162, 164 (S.C. 1981). Additionally, superpriority of the subordinated purchase money mortgage will be reinstated if the debt terms are materially changed without first obtaining the subordinated mortgagee's consent. Id. at 165. However, courts will not nullify a subordination agreement and restore a subordinated purchase money mortgage's priority merely because a construction loan fails to achieve its intended purpose and the infusion of capital is unsuccessful in saving the project. Conshohocken Federal Sav. & Loan Ass'n v. Period & Country Homes, Inc., 287 Pa. Super. 520, 533 (Pa. Super. Ct. 1981).

b. Subordination Agreement in General

The subordination is normally part of the original agreement between the seller and the developer and is covered in either the real estate contract, the purchase money mortgage, or a separate document.

An advance subordination agreement may take either of two forms: (1) an agreement that subordination occurs automatically when the construction loan mortgage is executed or (2) an agreement to execute a formal subordination upon request once the construction loan is obtained.

c. *Describing Construction Loan*

The subordination agreement must contain an adequate description of the construction loan. If the subordination agreement does not, courts refuse to enforce the agreement on the ground it is impossible to tell what has been promised.

The question of whether the description of the construction loan is so indefinite as to render the subordination contract unenforceable is frequently difficult to resolve. Although courts generally agree that the maximum amount of the construction loan must be stated and often also require that an interest rate cap be specified, they disagree as to whether the maturity, use of proceeds, or other loan details must be spelled out. Furthermore, some courts may enforce a less detailed subordination agreement when the missing terms are left for determination to an institutional construction lender. This approach is based on the rationale that institutional lenders are bound by regulation, custom, and usage to impose reasonable loan terms.

In California, the indefinite description issue is further complicated by a court decision requiring all subordination agreements to be just and reasonable with respect to the seller-purchase money mortgagee.

Handy v. Gordon, 55 Cal.Rptr. 769 (Cal.1967). What this "fairness" doctrine demands regarding precision in describing the construction loan remains an open question. The Court of Appeal of California in Roskamp Manley Assocs., Inc. v. Davin Dev. & Inv. Corp., 184 Cal. App. 3d 513 (1986), addressed this issue and reinforced the *Handy* precedent. The court in *Roskamp* stated that an agreement's terms must be specific enough for a court to determine the agreement's fairness and reasonableness to the seller. Id. According to the court, fairness is important, but it needs to be defined to be meaningful. Id. at 520.

In *Roskamp*, the mortgagor agreed to purchase the seller's property for $525,000 financed with a $275,000 cash down payment and a $250,000 purchase money mortgage. Id. at 516. Initially, the parties agreed that the seller would subordinate his purchase money mortgage to a subsequent construction loan. Id. The issue in this case arose when the mortgagor deleted the seller's right to approve the construction loan's principal amount from the subordination agreement and, instead, substituted a term that did not limit the loan's principal but provided that the loan could not exceed 80% of the completed project's value as appraised by the construction lender. Id. The parties disagreed as to how a subordination agreement's validity was determined—whether specific terms needed to be included or whether overall fairness and reasonableness was the standard. Id. at 517.

In analyzing the issue, the court noted that other courts have oftentimes required subordination agreements to include, at a minimum, terms related to the maximum principal, interest rate, and term and the mode of the new loan's repayment. Id. at 518. However, specificity in terms is not enough—a principle first articulated by the state's supreme court in *Handy*. Id. at 520. According to the court, subordination agreements must additionally be just and reasonable to the seller. Id. This means that an agreement must have terms specific enough for a court to determine the agreement's fairness to a seller while other terms may be left unspecified or to be determined by usage and custom. Id. at 521. Although the subordination agreement in this case included the specific term limiting a loan to 80% of the completed project's value, this court held that the seller's control over the principal was "illusory," thus neither fair nor reasonable. Id. at 522.

d. Obtaining Construction Loan Described

If the developer obtains a construction loan that varies materially from the loan described in the subordination agreement, subordination does not occur.

e. Diversion of Construction Loan Funds

Priority problems may arise even after the specified construction loan is obtained. Occasionally, a mortgagor-developer diverts loan proceeds from the project with the result that the property is not sufficiently enhanced in value to adequately secure the subordinated purchase money mortgage loan. In such case, the seller-purchase money mortgagee is likely to claim that the subordination agreement has been breached and that the original lien priority has been restored. When this issue first arose, the courts typically held that, absent an agreement to the contrary, a construction loan mortgagee acting in good faith had no duty to monitor the application of construction funds. *See, e.g.,* Parker v. Columbia Bank, 604 A.2d 521, 531 (Md. Ct. Spec. App. 1992) (stating that a mortgagee's duty to act in good faith only requires it to perform its contractual obligations while exercising good faith, but does not require a mortgagee to undertake affirmative actions beyond those required by the parties' agreement); Pimental v. Wachovia Mortgage Corp., 411 F.Supp.2d 32, 37–39 (D. Mass. 2006) (finding that the contract included only permissive language related to monitoring loan funds, and the mortgagee's failure to act in good faith could present a claim if the mortgagee knowingly disbursed funds to a party whose work was "substandard and incomplete"). The construction lender, therefore, retains the lien priority granted to it in the subordination agreement unless it advances money to the developer in bad faith. *See* Cambridge Acceptance Corp. v. Hockstein, 102 N.J. Super. 435, 438 (Ct. App. Div. 1968) (reciting the general view that unless there was collusion or an express stipulation, a mortgagor's diversion of construction loan funds will not affect the agreed upon priority).

Absent an express assumption of a fiduciary relationship, a construction lender ordinarily owes no fiduciary duty to a mortgagee who subordinated its purchase money mortgage to the construction mortgage. Inversiones Inmobiliarias Internacionales de Orlando Sociedad Anomina v. Barnett Bank of Cent. Florida, N.A., 584 So.2d 110, 111 (D. Fla. 1991). Because no fiduciary relationship will be construed, a landowner who subordinates its purchase money mortgage to a construction mortgage bears the risk of a mortgagor-developer diverting funds from the project. Id. A landowner may recover, however, if he shows fraud or collusion between the mortgagor-developer and mortgagee. Id.

In addition, some courts have recognized other situations that impose conditions on subordination. First, sellers-purchase money mortgagees commonly condition subordination upon actual use of the construction loan funds for construction purposes. Second, a similar condition may be implied in certain limited situations. *See* Middlebrook-Anderson Co. v. Southwest Savings & Loan Ass'n, 96 Cal.Rptr. 338 (Cal.App.1971). *But see* Swiss Property Management Co., Inc. v. Southern California IBEW-NECA Pension Plan, 60 Cal. App. 4th 839, 846 (1997) (holding that the implied condition rule established by *Middlebrook-Anderson* does not survive when parties explicitly contract to eliminate any such implied agreements). Third, some courts have concluded that construction lenders owe subordinated lienors a duty to exercise reasonable care in disbursing construction loan funds.

When subordination is expressly or impliedly conditioned upon the proper application of loan proceeds and funds are diverted, the seller-purchase money mortgagee is entitled to relief. *See* Cambridge Acceptance Corp. v. Hockstein, 102 N.J. Super. 435, 439 (N.J. App. 1968) (stating "[w]here, however, the construction mortgagee expressly agrees with the subordinator to see to it that the proceeds of his loan will be applied to construction of the improvement he will be held to his agreement and will lose his priority as to any advance not going into the construction").

The purchase money mortgage ordinarily should be restored to priority over the construction loan mortgage to the extent of the diverted funds. For example, in Miller v. Citizens Sav. & Loan Ass'n, 248 Cal.App.2d 655 (1967), the sellers sold several lots to Westglen Corp., and Westglen granted them a purchase money mortgage that included a subordination agreement. Id. at 657. The subordination agreement contained a "purpose" clause that set forth the reason for the subordination and the use of the disbursed funds secured by a subsequent deed of trust, including improving the land and paying hazard insurance. Id. at 657–58. Westglen thereafter borrowed a total of $349,500 from Citizens Savings & Loan Association, granted it a deed of trust and constructed houses on the property. Id. at 658–659. Most of the funds that Citizens paid out satisfied the purpose clause, but about $26,341 was used for other purposes. Id. at 659. When the houses failed to sell, Westglen defaulted and gave the property back to the sellers. Id. The court considered whether the sellers' purchase money mortgage was subordinate to the $26,341. The court determined that the subordination agreement should to be construed as only subordinating the purchase money mortgage to loan funds that were used for a purpose outlined in the subordination agreement. *See id.* at 664. Accordingly, the court held the $26,341 payment by Citizens to Westglen did not have priority over the purchase money mortgage because its use was not within the purpose of the subordination agreement. Id. at 665.

Thus, lien priority generally should be established as follows: (1) construction lender for funds properly applied to the project, (2) seller-purchase money mortgagee for the full amount of the purchase money mortgage, and (3) construction lender for diverted funds. There is, however, authority that the seller-purchase money mortgagee should be reinstated to first lien priority when the construction lender breaches an express condition to subordination.

2. Subordination of Lease to Mortgage and Vice Versa

A mortgagee may desire to enhance its security position by switching priorities with a lessee of the mortgaged property. Reversal of priorities may occur in either direction. If a lease is unattractive to the mortgagee and has original priority, the mortgagee may demand subordination of the lease to the mortgage as a condition of making the mortgage loan. The subordination enables the mortgagee to terminate the lease if the mortgagee takes possession after default or foreclosure. If an attractive lease is originally junior to the mortgage, the mortgagee may grant the lessee a nondisturbance agreement because the rental stream of income is the primary security for income-producing property. If the mortgagee forecloses, the mortgagee or other purchaser at the foreclosure sale takes the property subject to the lease. Therefore, the mortgagee can collect rents from the lessee upon default and preserve the lease beyond foreclosure.

3. Subordination of a Mortgage on the Fee to Leasehold Mortgage

A leasehold mortgage is a mortgage on the improvements (e.g., an apartment building). If there is a senior mortgage on the fee/land and the fee mortgagee forecloses, the leasehold mortgage is extinguished if the leasehold mortgagee is named as a party to the foreclosure action. As a result, the leasehold mortgagee frequently requires the fee mortgagee to subordinate its mortgage to the leasehold mortgage. In such a case, if the fee mortgagee forecloses, the purchaser at the foreclosure sale must take the property subject to the leasehold mortgage.

C. FIXTURES

A mortgage is a lien on all fixtures on the mortgaged property. These fixtures also may be subject to the lien of a security interest that attached to them before they became fixtures. In that event, a contest results between the mortgagee and the holder of the security interest regarding the priority of their respective liens. Section 9–334 of the Uniform Commercial Code (UCC) is designed to resolve this priority issue. Following is a summary of its most significant provisions.

Generally, under UCC § 9–334 priority between the holder of a security interest in fixtures and the mortgagee goes to the first one to properly file in the public records. A purchase money security interest filed before or within twenty days after items of personal property become fixtures. U.C.C. § 9–334(d). However, a security interest in property takes priority over existing nonconstruction loan mortgages on the theory that the party who supplies the money used to acquire the fixtures should be favored. But, because a construction lender provides funds for the entire improvement and expects all parts thereof to serve as collateral for its loan, existing construction loan mortgages take priority over purchase money security interests in items of personal property that become fixtures during construction. U.C.C. § 9–334(h). Finally, regarding the recordation process, the UCC requires that fixture financing statements be filed and indexed in local real estate records so a person conducting a title search can discover them. *See* U.C.C. §§ 9–501(a), 9–519(d).

D. OBLIGATORY/OPTIONAL ADVANCES

A mortgagee who holds a properly recorded mortgage for future advances may receive priority over parties who subsequently acquire an interest in the mortgaged property. Courts, however, sometimes limit the priority of a mortgage for future advances to preserve the marketability of the mortgaged property for subsequent encumbrance or sale. The necessity for limitation depends in large part upon whether the future advance is obligatory or optional. Whether future mortgage advances are "optional" or "obligatory" is not determined by the surrounding circumstances but, instead, by the controlling documents' terms alone. Home Lumber Co. v. Kopfmann Homes, Inc., 535 N.W.2d 302, 304 (Minn. 1995). Accordingly, a court must consider the relevant contractually created legal relationships in each case. Id. at 305.

1. Obligatory Future Advances

If a mortgagee is contractually obligated to make future advances, the lien for each advance has priority over any encumbrance that attaches to the property subsequent to the execution of the mortgage. This rule applies even when the mortgagee makes an advance with knowledge of an encumbrance that arose in the interim between the execution of the mortgage and the advance. No policy reason exists to change the principle that priority for future advances dates from the day the mortgage was executed. Because the mortgagor has the right to additional future advances, the mortgagor is not prejudiced by the fact that secondary financing on the property is probably unavailable from another lender.

Illustration: A mortgagor and construction lender enter a construction loan agreement that the lender is required to advance funds up to a total of $1,000,000 as construction on the

> mortgaged property progresses. The mortgagor executes a $1,000,000 promissory note and a mortgage to the construction lender who records the mortgage. The construction lender advances $500,000 as construction progresses in accordance with the agreement. At that point, the mortgagor borrows $200,000 from a second mortgagee and gives the second mortgagee a $200,000 promissory note secured by a mortgage on the same property. The second mortgagee records its mortgage. The construction lender knows of this lien, but because mortgagor fully complies with the construction loan agreement, the construction lender advances the remaining $500,000. The construction lender has a first lien for $1,000,000 because it was obligated to advance the entire loan amount. The second mortgagee has a second lien for $200,000.

In Home Lumber Co. v. Kopfmann Homes, Inc., 535 N.W.2d 302 (Minn. 1995), Kopfmann Homes obtained a $450,000 construction loan mortgage from MidAmerica Bank Maplewood (the Bank) to build a spec home, but the Bank quit making disbursements after paying out approximately $271,000 in five separate disbursements. Id. at 303. Home Lumber, along with other businesses that provided materials or labor for the project, filed mechanic's liens, which attached no later than May 16, 1990. Id. Notably, the Bank made three disbursements before May 16, 1990, and two after that date. Id. While the trial court held the disbursements made after May 16, 1990, were optional—and thus junior to the mechanic's lien, the Supreme Court of Minnesota held that the Bank's disbursement after May 16, 1990, were obligatory—thus retaining priority over mechanic's liens that arose on the same date—because the Bank was required to advance the mortgage's full value for the property's completion and improvement. Id. at 305–06. Additionally, the court held the construction loan agreement clearly stated the conditions under which the Bank was to make additional disbursements regardless of the Bank's decision to waive certain conditions of the agreement. Id. at 306. The Bank's decision to waive certain conditions of the loan agreement, namely its right to first receive lien waivers, was immaterial here because a party is free to waive a condition when the condition was imposed for its own benefit. Id. at 305. Accordingly, the advances here were obligatory and retained their priority over the mechanic's liens. Id.

In another case, a couple obtained a $2.4 million construction loan from Bank One to construct ten six-unit apartment buildings, and the couple hired Schalmo Builders as the general contractor to construct the building. Schalmo Builders, Inc. v. Malz, 629 N.E.2d 52, 52 (Ohio Ct. App. 1993). The couple defaulted on their loan payments, and Bank One brought a foreclosure action. Id. There was an issue of the priority between Schalmo and Bank One. In making its decision, the court of appeals addressed Schalmo Builders' argument that Bank One was not obligated to make future advances under the construction loan. Id. at 54. According to the court, a mortgagee is obligated to make future advances when it contractually committed to make such advances regardless of whether the making of such advances is conditioned upon the occurrence or non-occurrence of some event. Id. at 55. Here, the court held Bank One's advances were obligatory and entitled to priority because the loan agreement required Bank One to disburse $2.4 million for the buildings' construction—regardless of the fact that the advances were conditioned on the couple's compliance with certain procedures. Id.

2. Optional Future Advances

Many mortgages for future advances provide that future advances are optional with the mortgagee. Mortgages for optional future advances are sometimes referred to as open-end mortgages. An advance will be considered optional if the mortgagee has discretion to make the advances. *See, e.g.*, Kraus-Anderson Constr. Co. v. Superior Vista LLC, 2010 WL 2650481 *12 (Minn. Ct. App. 2010) (concluding that advances were optional even though the construction lender was obligated to make advances pursuant to the plans because the obligation was conditioned on the lender's ability to obtain the necessary funds to make the advances); Rosenthal & Rosenthal, Inc. v. Benun, 441 N.J. Super. 184, 187 (2015) (concluding that advances were optional because the agreement stated that the mortgagee could make them in its "sole discretion").

A construction lender is in a quandary. There are valid reasons why it should maintain some control over the advances, but too much control may result in a loss in priority. A construction lender should monitor the construction to ensure that it is consistent with the plans and specifications. If the developer/mortgagor strays from these plans, the permanent lender may refuse to take out the construction loan causing the construction lender to either foreclose its mortgage or become the permanent lender.

a. Priority Problems

Controversy often arises regarding the priority of optional advances over encumbrances that attach to the mortgaged property following the execution of the mortgage. The outcome depends upon which of three possible fact patterns is presented: (1) The lien for optional future advances made *before* the attachment of a subsequent encumbrance clearly has priority under the fundamental principle of "first in time, first in right." (2) The lien for optional future advances made *after* the attachment of a subsequent encumbrance and *without notice* of that encumbrance also has priority on the theory that it arose at the date that the mortgage for future advances was executed. (3) The lien for optional future advances made *with notice* of the attachment of a subsequent encumbrance is generally postponed to the lien of the intervening encumbrance because the marketability of the mortgagor's land for subsequent encumbrance or sale would otherwise be virtually destroyed. If other lenders were unable to ensure the priority of their encumbrances over the lien of later optional future advances, they certainly would not make mortgage loans on the property. The mortgagor then would be left to the whim of the original mortgagee for additional financing. Likewise, it is improbable that potential purchasers would be willing to acquire the property subject to a mortgage arrangement that put the original mortgagee in such a dominant position.

b. Notice Issue

The "notice" limitation on the priority of optional future advances is clouded by disagreement over the type of notice required. There are two views on the subject. The generally accepted view is that the lien of an optional future advance loses priority to the lien of an intervening encumbrance only if the mortgagee has actual notice of the encumbrance when it makes the advance. Tenn. Code Ann. § 47–28–103(c) (2017) (providing that optional advances have priority unless mortgagee has actual notice of an intervening lien); Rosenthal & Rosenthal, Inc. v. Benun, 441 N.J. Super. 184, 191 (2015) (stating the rule is clear that actual notice of an intervening lien is required for subordination of optional advances); Daniels v. Elks Club of Hartford, 192 Vt. 114, 135 (2012) (stating that Vermont aligns itself with most states that require actual notice).

Some states, however, postpone the lien of an optional future advance to the lien of an intervening encumbrance when the mortgagee has either actual or constructive notice of the encumbrance. In these jurisdictions, recording the encumbrance imparts constructive notice of its existence to the mortgagee. This approach, however, is inconsistent with established legal principles. Recording systems are designed to work prospectively only; subsequent purchasers, not prior interest holders, receive constructive notice of a recorded document. A mortgagee who makes optional future advances after an intervening encumbrance is recorded can be considered a subsequent purchaser only if the future advance is viewed as a separate loan. This is, of course, contrary to the fundamental notion that the lien for future advances arises at the date of the execution of the mortgage, not when the advance is made.

Illustration: A mortgagor borrows $20,000 from a construction lender and gives the construction lender a $20,000 promissory note and a mortgage. The mortgage contains an optional future advances clause and provides for a maximum total indebtedness of $30,000. The construction lender records the mortgage. The mortgagor then borrows $5,000 from a bank and gives the bank a $5,000 promissory note secured by a mortgage on the same property. The bank records its mortgage. The construction lender next advances an additional $10,000 to the mortgagor under the optional future advances clause in the original mortgage. The generally accepted view is that the construction lender has a first lien for $30,000 unless it had actual notice of the bank's lien at the time it made the future advance. In some jurisdictions, however, the construction lender's lien for the future advance is postponed in priority to the bank's lien because the construction lender was on constructive notice of the bank's encumbrance.

In these states, the construction lender has a first lien for $20,000, the bank has a second lien for $5,000, and the construction lender has a third lien for $10,000.

3. Obligatory/Optional Distinction Rejected by Statute

Certain state legislatures have enacted statutes eliminating the distinction between obligatory and optional future advances with respect to various mortgage loan transactions. In these jurisdictions, the lien of all future advances dates from the execution of a mortgage covered by the statute even if the mortgagee makes the advance with notice of an intervening encumbrance. In other words, obligatory and optional advances are treated the same; each takes priority over intervening encumbrances. Almost all statutes that produce this result, however, require that the mortgage specify the total amount to be secured. *See, e.g.*, Haw. Rev. Stat. § 506–1 (2017) (providing that a mortgage securing future advances up to a maximum stated amount has priority over a subsequently recorded mortgage even for advances made subsequent to that recorded mortgage); Kan. Stat. Ann. § 58–2336 (2017) (stating that priority of advances up to the maximum stated amount is determined by the date that the mortgage is recorded until the mortgage is released); Md. Code Ann., Real Property § 7–102 (2017) (stating that whether an advance is obligatory or optional, it's priority up to the aggregate amount provided in the mortgage is based on the date that the mortgage is recorded). Accord N.M. Stat. Ann. § 48–7–9 (2017); Wash. Rev.

Code § 60.04.226 (2017). Moreover, some of these legislative measures allow the mortgagor to restrict the operation of a future advances clause to funds already disbursed by filing a prescribed notice.

4. Construction Lender's Dilemma

The distinction between obligatory and optional future advances for priority purposes has been severely criticized by construction lenders because its application to advances made under a construction loan mortgage often produces inequitable results. Because the construction lender is obligated to make advances as construction progresses, it receives first lien priority for all advances when the project is completed according to the plans. Problems arise, however, when construction does not progress smoothly and the borrower-developer defaults. Construction loan documents typically give the lender the right to stop advancing funds upon the mortgagor's default. Hence, any advances made thereafter are optional and may lose priority to intervening liens. If, however, the construction lender does not make additional advances, the incomplete project probably will not be of sufficient value even to cover the amount of the lien for obligatory advances made before the default.

Courts may struggle with the optional/obligatory future advance rule in this situation because completion of the project enhances the value of the security for both the construction lender and any intervening lienor. Although the hazy line dividing optional and obligatory advances gives the judiciary ample opportunity to exercise discretion, generally judges mechanistically apply the optional/obligatory rule and conclude that advances made after default are optional. A few courts, however, apparently will award the construction lender complete lien priority if the lender makes post default advances in good faith and under economic compulsion. This result, long favored by commentators, is reached by statute in those states in which the legislature has eliminated the distinction between obligatory and optional future advances.

E. MECHANICS' LIEN STATUTES

1. In General

Mechanics' lien statutes protect parties supplying services, labor, or materials to a construction project by affording them a lien on the realty for payment due. These statutes are designed to incentivize the construction or improvement of property by affording laborers and materialmen the right to a mechanic's lien on the property if the owner fails to pay for the services or materials pursuant to the terms of the contract. They also reduce the likelihood of unjust enrichment. However, these universally enacted measures vary greatly among the states regarding parties protected, lien amount, lien priority, and other matters. This section addresses amount, priority, and constitutional issues. It also discusses other protection for mechanics and materialmen.

2. Amount

Mechanics' lien statutes generally take one of two markedly different approaches regarding the amount that a lien claimant may recover. Some states, following the New York system, view the rights of mechanics' lienors as derived from the general construction contract and thus limit recovery to the balance due on the contract at the date the lien is filed. *See, e.g.*, Seaman v. Climate Control Corp., 436 A.2d 271, 274 (Conn. 1980) (stating that a mechanic's lien cannot exceed the amount the owner agreed to pay); Kirkland v. Oberquell, 405 N.W.2d 21, 23 (N.D. 1987) (voiding the subcontractor's mechanic's liens because the owner of the property had already paid the contractor the full value of the subcontractors' total contributions); Stolz v. Honeycutt, 42 S.W.3d 305, 310 (Tex. App. 2001) (stating a subcontractor doesn't have a direct lien against property owner; rather, the subcontractor has derivative rights to recover money that is due from the owner to the primary contractor). Other jurisdictions, adopting the Pennsylvania system, give mechanics' lien claimants direct rights and therefore permit recovery for the full value of their labor, goods, or services. *See, e.g.*, H&M Heating Co. v. Andrae, 35 Wis. 2d 1, 5 (1967) (stating that under Wis. Stat. § 779.01 a subcontractor has a direct lien on property of the owner and this lien is not dependent on the rights of the general contractor).

3. Priority

Priority problems frequently arise between mechanics' lienors and mortgagees, particularly construction mortgage lenders. To resolve these issues, it is necessary to ascertain the priority accorded mechanics' liens under local statutes. The statutes are far from uniform on this subject.

a. Relation Back to Commencement of Construction

In numerous states, a mechanics' lienor's priority relates back to when construction begins. For example, Wisconsin follows the relation back rule. Under Wisconsin law, for new construction, commencement of construction occurs when there is substantial excavation for the foundations, footings or base of the new construction. Wis. Stat. § 779.01(4) (2017). For additions or renovations, the commencement takes place the earlier of the beginning of substantial excavation or when there is substantial preparation of the existing structure to receive the new construction. Id. *See also* Minn. Stat. 514.05 (2017) (lien attaches when the first item of material or labor is furnished but "[v]isible staking, engineering, land surveying, and soil testing services do not constitute the actual and visible beginning of the improvement"); Tex. Prop. Code Ann. § 53.124(a) & (b) (2015) (mechanic's liens relate back to visible commencement of construction or visible delivery of materials at the construction site). Under this approach, the construction lender can protect its mortgage lien against all mechanics' lienors by recording the construction loan mortgage before construction commences. But, if the lender fails to do so, it loses priority to all mechanics' lienors, not just those who did work before the mortgage was recorded.

> *Illustration*: A mortgagor decides to construct a building on the mortgagor's property. The mortgagor hires a contractor to clear the land and do the necessary excavation work. The contractor completes the job and the mortgagor pays the contractor for the excavation work. Six weeks later, the mortgagor obtains a construction mortgage loan from a construction lender who promptly records the mortgage. After the mortgage is recorded, a second contractor does work on the building. The second contractor is not paid. Therefore, the second contractor files a mechanics' lien. The second contractor's lien relates back to when the contractor performed the initial construction work on the project (the excavation work) and thereby takes priority over the construction lender's mortgage.

Even if the construction loan mortgage is recorded before work begins, controversy may develop as to the priority of future advances made by a construction lender over an intervening mechanic's lien. This issue usually arises when a mechanic's lienor contends that all construction advances made after the attachment of its mechanic's lien are optional, not obligatory, and thereby lose priority to its encumbrance.

b. Other Approaches

The remaining states take a wide variety of approaches to the mechanic's lien priority issue. Certain jurisdictions grant lien priority from the date the mechanic's lienor began work or supplied materials. *See, e.g.,* Ind. Code Ann. § 32–28–3–5(b) (Michie 2017); N.C. Gen. Stat. § 44A–10 (2016). In some states, the lien receives priority as of the day the lien claimant files. *See, e.g.*, Miss. Code Ann. § 85–7–405(2)(b) (2017) (providing priority based on date of filing except mechanics' liens don't have priority over tax liens). Other jurisdictions base lien priority on additional considerations, such as the time the general construction contract was entered. *See, e.g.*, 770 Ill. Comp. Stat. 60/16 (2016).

4. Constitutionality of Mechanics' Lien Statutes

Mechanics' lien statutes generally authorize mechanics and materialmen to perfect their liens without judicial involvement and sometimes without prior notice to the property owner. This procedure has been attacked in several jurisdictions as a denial of the owner's Fourteenth Amendment due process rights.

Most courts faced with this issue have upheld the mechanics' lien statutes in question on the theory that a mechanics' lien does not constitute a taking of property within the meaning of the Fourteenth Amendment. For example, in Spielman-Ford, Inc. v. Hanson's Inc., 379 F. Supp. 997 (D. Ariz. 1973), aff'd 417 U.S. 901 (1974) (per curiam), the plaintiffs argued that Arizona's mechanics' and materialmen's lien statutes were unconstitutional because they did not provide for notice and hearing prior to the filing of the lien. Id. at 998. However, the court rejected their argument and concluded that the filing of the lien was not a taking of a property interest; therefore, the filing did not violate due process of law under the Fourteenth Amendment. Id. at 999. *Accord* Tucker Door & Trim Corp. v. Fifteenth St. Co., 235 Ga. 727, 728 (1975) (concluding that there was no deprivation until after the judicial foreclosure proceeding). Courts reason that the attachment of the lien does not deprive the owner of possession, use, or enjoyment of the property and any impairment of the owner's ability to sell or encumber the property is merely a de minimis taking that does not trigger the application of procedural due process safeguards. *See* Cook v. Carlson, 364 F. Supp. 24, 27 (S.D.S.D 1973). A few courts, however, have concluded that a mechanic's lien affects a Fourteenth Amendment property interest by impairing the property owner's ability to alienate the property and by reducing the value of the owner's equity. Some of these courts further held that local statutory procedures for perfecting mechanics' liens were constitutionally defective on due process grounds.

Significantly, in Connecticut v. Doehr, 501 U.S. 1 (1991), a property owner challenged the constitutionality of Connecticut's ex parte prejudgment attachment procedure, successfully arguing in the United States Supreme Court that it violated his right of due process. Id. at 2107. According to the Court, the possibility of "erroneous deprivation" was too great without notice and a hearing. Id. at 2108. The Court determined that the property interests affected by the attachment were significant, including clouding title, impacting the owner's credit history, reducing the opportunity to mortgage the property and impairing the ability to sell the property. Id. at 2113. The *Doehr* case did not involve a mechanic's lien issue. However, the Court distinguished its summary affirmance of *Spielman-Ford*. Id. at 2113 n.4. The Court stated:

> The facts of *Spielman-Fond* presented an alternative basis for affirmance in any event. Unlike the case before us, the mechanic's lien statute in *Spielman-Fond* required the creditor to have a pre-existing interest in the property at issue. As we explain below, a heightened plaintiff interest in certain circumstances can provide a ground for upholding procedures that are otherwise suspect.

Id. (citations omitted). For a greater discussion of the constitutionality of mechanic's liens, see Nelson, Whitman, Burkhart & Freyermuth, Real Estate Finance 1074–1083 (West 6th ed. 2015).

5. Other Protection for Mechanics and Materialmen

It is noted earlier in this section that in most states a prudent construction lender may secure priority over a mechanic's lienor by recording the construction loan mortgage before construction commences. Hence, if the project fails and the mortgagee forecloses, mechanic's lienors usually receive nothing from the foreclosure sale. To correct this inequity, some states have given mechanics and materialmen lien rights in addition to those they receive under the traditional mechanics' lien statutes.

a. Stop Notice Statutes

In some jurisdictions, parties who have supplied services, labor, or materials to a construction project may obtain a statutory lien on construction loan money not yet disbursed by the lender. Legislation of this type is known as a stop notice statute. As a general proposition, a stop notice statute permits an unpaid mechanic or materialman to file a notice of claim with the lender who then must stop advancing funds for construction or, at least, withhold funds to cover the claim. These statutes differ in various respects. For example, in Arizona, a stop notice prevents payment from a construction lender to a borrower or to a person the borrower must make a payment in an amount that is sufficient to cover certain claims. Ariz. Rev. Stat. § 33–1058 (2017). In New Mexico, upon receipt of a stop notice claim from a contractor, the construction lender must withhold the funds set forth in the stop notice claim until it has been fulfilled or settled by a court. N.M. Stat. Ann. § 48–2A–8 (2017). In Washington, unless there is a payment bond of at least 50 percent, lien claimants that have not received payment for labor or materials supplied within five days of the contract payment date can file a stop notice within 35 days of the required payment date. Wash. Rev. Code § 60.04.221

(2017). If the lender does not comply with the stop notice, it can lose its priority. Id.

b. Equitable Liens

Many courts have used the equitable lien concept to fashion a remedy for mechanics and materialmen like that available under stop notice statutes. Under the equitable lien approach, unpaid lien claimants may reach undisbursed funds if they show special equities or verify that the lender has been unjustly enriched in order to reach undisbursed construction loan funds. In Richard F. Kline, Inc. v. Signet Bank/Maryland, 651 A.2d 442 (Md. Ct. Spec. App. 1995), a subcontractor who was unable to get a mechanic's lien sued the construction lender to recover the amounts that the bankrupt general contractor had not paid to the subcontractor. Id. at 443. The construction lender had purchased the property at the foreclosure sale. Id. The subcontractor claimed unjust enrichment because the subcontractor's work on the property increased its value and the construction lender was obligated to notify the subcontractor of the general contractor's default. Id. at 445. In rejecting the subcontractor's unjust enrichment argument, the court reasoned that the subcontractor failed to show that the construction lender had received an unjust benefit or that the construction lender had misled the subcontractor by inducing the subcontractor to continue working on the project. Id. at 446. Hence, the equitable remedy was unavailable.

F. TAX LIENS

1. State and Local Real Estate Tax Liens

Statutes in most states impose a lien on real estate to secure the payment of taxes or assessments levied on the real estate. Usually these real estate tax and assessment liens are allowed to leapfrog existing encumbrances to the first lien priority position. *See, e.g.*, Ariz. Rev. Stat. Ann. § 42–17153(c)(3) (2016) (real estate tax liens are prior to all liens except liens held by the state and for taxes accruing in prior years); Ga. Code Ann. § 48–2–56(b) (2016) (lien for taxes is prior to other liens with a lien for state taxes ranking above county real estate taxes); 35 Ill. Comp. Stat. 200/21–75 (2016) (real estate tax liens are prior and superior to all other liens); N.H. Rev. Stat. Ann. § 80:19 (2017) (real estate taxes and special assessments given priority over other liens). To minimize the risk of losing priority to subsequent tax liens, mortgagees commonly require the mortgagor to escrow funds for the payment of real property taxes.

2. Federal Income Tax Liens

The federal government may obtain a lien against the real property of a delinquent income taxpayer. Under IRC § 6321, the government is entitled to a lien on a taxpayer's real or personal property if the taxpayer defaults on taxes, interest or penalties. The tax lien is valid until the liability is paid or unenforceable because of the statutory period. IRC § 6322 (2017).

The tax lien arises by operation of law, attaches to all real and personal property of the taxpayer and is perfected against the taxpayer even if the government has not filed a Notice of Federal Tax Lien. *In re* Aquatic Pools, Inc., 567 B.R. 376, 381 (Bankr. D. N.M. 2017) (citations omitted). Unlike state and local real estate tax liens, a federal tax lien does not receive priority over existing encumbrances. It also is not valid against subsequent mortgages until the Notice of Federal Tax Lien is filed in the public land records. IRC § 6323(a) (2017). The IRS is required to send written notice to the taxpayer of the filing of a notice of lien and the taxpayer's right to an administrative hearing on this matter. IRC § 6320 (2017). At the hearing, the taxpayer is entitled to raise any relevant issues and can challenge the appropriateness of the collection action. Pitner v. Comm'r, 112 T.C.M. (CCH) 720 (2016). The notice of tax lien does not need to be updated to reflect any increase in the accruing interest and penalties. *Aquatic Pools*, 567 B.R. at 383. Even a properly filed federal tax lien loses priority to certain interests that arise subsequent to its filing, such as real estate tax liens and certain mechanics' liens. Id.

G. LIS PENDENS

Under common law, a lis pendens provides constructive notice of claims asserted against the real estate in the pending litigation. U.S. Bank Nat'l Ass'n v. Bevans, 138 So.3d 1185, 1189 (Fla. Dist. Ct. App. 2014). It alerts lenders, creditors, prospective purchasers and others that title to real estate is subject to litigation. Therefore, one who acquires an interest in real estate involved in litigation is bound by the court's judgment or decree. Id. In *Bevans*, the mortgagor was delinquent in paying condominium fees and mortgage payments. Id. at 1187. The condominium association initiated foreclosure proceedings. Id. Before the foreclosure sale in that action, the senior mortgagee initiated foreclosure proceedings. Id. The mortgagee named the condominium association as a party to the action but neglected to record a notice of lis pendens. Id. After the mortgagee's foreclosure action, a judicial sale was held on the condominium association's lien. Id. A purchaser purchased the property at the foreclosure sale and sold it to a subsequent purchaser. Id. The subsequent purchaser moved to set aside the judgment of foreclosure in favor of the mortgagee in its action. Id. The issue in the case was whether the subsequent purchaser took the property subject to the mortgage. Id. The subsequent purchaser argued that it took the property free of the mortgagee's mortgage because it acquired it during the pendency of the mortgagee's foreclosure action and a notice of lis pendens was not recorded. Id. at 1188. The court rejected the subsequent purchaser's argument noting that the filing of a lis pendens is not required to enforce a lien against a subsequent purchaser where the subsequent purchaser has actual or constructive notice. Id.

The lis pendens doctrine can be illustrated by considering the following example: An owner conveys land to a buyer who records. The owner initiates suit to have the deed set aside and records a lis pendens notice as required by state law. The buyer grants a mortgage on the land to a mortgagee. The court then renders judgment in favor of the owner and sets aside the deed. Because the mortgagee was on lis pendens notice of the owner's interest, the owner takes the property free from the mortgagee's mortgage. In those states that continue to follow the common law lis pendens doctrine, the owner would take free from the mortgage even if the owner had failed to file separate notice of the suit.

Because it is often difficult to discover the existence of pending litigation, statutes in most states limit the application of the lis pendens doctrine by requiring that a separate notice of the suit be filed. For example, in Rhode Island, a separate notice is required to be filed, and within seven days of the filing all parties named in the pending litigation must be mailed copies of the notice. R.I. Gen. Laws Ann. § 9–4–9 (2016). The statute in Connecticut states that the recorded notice of lis pendens is invalid and will not provide constructive notice unless the recording party serves a copy of the recorded notice within 30 days of the recorded notice. Conn. Gen. Stat. § 52–325(c) (2017). Kansas requires a 90-day notice of a pendency of the lis pendens action by summons or publication. Kan. Stat. Ann. § 60–2201(a) (2017). South Carolina's notice of lis pendens states that the notice is of no avail unless it is published or the defendant is served within 60 days after the filing. S.C. Code Ann. § 15–11–30 (2017).

H. MARSHALING

The equitable doctrine of marshaling assets does not deal so much with determining the priority of interests in the mortgaged property as with equitably preserving the value of each interest once priority has been established. The doctrine has two main facets: the two funds rule and the sale in inverse order of alienation rule. These principles of marshaling overlap somewhat; both may be applicable in certain situations. Matters are complicated further by conflict over what circumstances call for the application of each rule.

1. Two Funds Rule

The two funds rule is the most familiar principle of marshaling. It provides that when a senior mortgagee has a claim against two funds and a junior mortgagee has a claim against only one of them, the senior mortgagee must enforce its claim to best preserve the value of the junior mortgagee's security. Although the senior mortgagee may proceed at law against either or both funds, equity requires it to seek satisfaction first from the fund the junior mortgagee cannot reach.

The principle underlying the two funds rule is that a senior creditor with two funds to satisfy a debt, may not satisfy the debt in a manner to defeat the interest of another creditor who only has an interest in one of the funds. *In re* Szwyd, 394 B.R. 230, 236 (Bankr. D. Mass. 2008); Restatement (Third) of Property (Mortgages) § 8.6 cmt. a (1997). This means that the senior lienholder must first look to assets that are not available to the junior lienholder. *Szwyd*, 394 B.R. at 236. Once these assets or funds are exhausted, the senior mortgagee may proceed against the sole fund that the junior mortgagee has access. This prevents inequity to the junior lienholder by keeping the senior lienholder from unnecessarily eliminating the junior lienholder's security leaving the junior lienholder unable to satisfy its claim. Id. In *Szwyd*, the court notes that Massachusetts has three elements that a junior lienholder must prove to have this rule applied. Id. First, there must be a common debtor. Id. Second, it must be shown that there are two separate funds, one of which is available to both lienholders and one that is only available to the senior lienholder. Id. Finally, it must be shown that the senior lienholder will not suffer a detriment or be prejudiced if the senior lienholder is limited to one fund. Id. at 236–37.

In *Szwyd*, the debtor owned two parcels of real property. *Id* at 234. The debtor's residence was located on one parcel and it was encumbered by a mortgage. Id. The IRS held secured and unsecured claims against the debtor. Id. In liquidating the estate, the other parcel was sold resulting in net sales proceeds of $25,000 after a mortgage was satisfied. Id. The trustee in the bankruptcy action argued that because the IRS was the only creditor that could enforce its lien against the homestead property, the IRS should go after the residence first, leaving the $25,000 for the unsecured creditors to be paid in the debtor's bankruptcy. Id. at 234–35. The IRS argued that the marshaling doctrine was inapplicable against the government. Id. at 237. The court rejected the IRS's argument and held that the marshaling doctrine applied because IRS's claims could be satisfied from the residence, and the IRS would not be prejudiced. Id. at 237–38.

To illustrate another example of the two funds rule, assume that a mortgagor owns two parcels of land, lot A worth $10,000 and lot B worth $4,000. The mortgagor borrows $12,000 from a first mortgagee and grants the mortgagee a mortgage on both lots. The mortgagor then borrows $5,000 from a second mortgagee and gives the second mortgagee a second mortgage on lot A. The mortgagor defaults on both mortgages. The first mortgagee forecloses on lot A only, and the foreclosure sale brings $10,000. The first mortgagee claims the entire amount as first lienor. Although the first mortgagee's $12,000 mortgage was a first lien on lot A, under the two funds rule the first mortgagee receives foreclosure sale proceeds as if it had satisfied itself first out of lot B and then out of lot A. Under this principle, the first mortgagee receives $8,000 (the amount of its lien minus the value of lot B), and the second mortgagee is entitled to $2,000.

If you assume the same fact situation as in the immediately preceding illustration except that no default occurs and the first mortgagee releases its lien on lot B even though it knows of the second mortgagee's second mortgage on lot A. Under the two funds rule, the first mortgagee retains a first lien on lot A for only $8,000 (the amount of the original lien minus the value of lot B), and the second mortgagee has a second lien for $5,000.

2. Sale in Inverse Order of Alienation Rule

The doctrine of marshaling also applies when a large tract of mortgaged land is subdivided and sold in separate parcels to parties who pay the full purchase price for their lots without obtaining a partial release of the blanket mortgage. If the blanket mortgage was recorded, its lien follows each lot into the hands of the lot purchaser. (Payment of the full purchase price to the mortgagor does not discharge the mortgagee's lien.) Although the purchaser would not have consummated the deal if the purchaser had searched the title, the purchaser is not completely unprotected. Equity gives the purchaser the right to require that the land retained by the seller be sold at foreclosure before the purchaser's lot is sold. Because this concept favors purchasers in the order they acquired lots, it is called the sale in inverse order of alienation rule.

> *Illustration*: A mortgagor owns a ten-acre tract subject to a recorded mortgage in favor of a mortgagee. The mortgagor subdivides the tract into ten one-acre lots and sells lots A and B successively to purchasers who each pay the full sale price for their respective lots. The mortgagor defaults on the blanket mortgage, and the mortgagee forecloses. Under the sale in inverse order of alienation rule, equity requires the court to direct the sheriff to sell first the land retained by the mortgagor, next lot B, and finally lot A. The sale process ends whenever the cumulative proceeds are sufficient to satisfy the mortgage debt.

The sale in inverse order of alienation rule is limited in several respects. First, the rule is inapplicable when a purchaser pays a reduced purchase price for taking the property subject to the mortgage. Second, most purchasers making full payment search the records and demand a partial release of the mortgage. Third, the mortgagee may avoid application of the rule by placing an anti-marshaling clause in the mortgage.

3. Anti-Marshaling Clause

Courts generally will not apply marshaling in either of its forms in the face of a contrary agreement. Mortgagees, therefore, often insist on a mortgage provision giving them the right to release or foreclose and sell parcels of the mortgaged property free from any requirement to marshal assets.

CHAPTER 11

FORECLOSURE

Chapter 1 provides an overview of foreclosure and traces the evolution of its concept. This chapter provides a detailed discussion to promote an understanding of the procedure as it presently exists.

I. AVAILABILITY AND PURPOSE

Upon default, the mortgagee may have the mortgaged property sold to satisfy the unpaid mortgage debt. Although this process is customarily referred to as mortgage foreclosure, it is really the mortgagor's equity of redemption that is foreclosed.

The foreclosure process generally may be commenced by the mortgagee any time after default. Its purpose is to cut off the mortgagor's equity of redemption and the rights of all parties who acquired interests in the land after the mortgage was executed, so that whoever purchases the property at foreclosure receives title as it existed in the hands of the mortgagor immediately before the mortgage attached. An important corollary of this principle is that interests acquired by third parties prior to the execution of the mortgage survive foreclosure. As a result, the mortgagee obtains the full benefit of the security for which it bargained, but no more.

II. STATUTE OF LIMITATIONS

In most states, the mortgagee must foreclose within a certain statutory period after maturity of the mortgage. These statutes vary widely. *See, e.g.*, Idaho Code § 5–214A (2017) (providing a five-year statute of limitations from the maturity date of the obligation); N.H. Rev. Stat. Ann. § 508:2 (2017) (20-year statutory period); S.D. Codified Laws § 15–2–7 (2016) (foreclosure action on all real estate mortgages must be brought within 15 years after cause of action accrues).

Issues arise in foreclosure actions regarding whether the statute of limitations has closed, and mortgagees must carefully consider them to ensure that their foreclosure actions are not time barred. There are many statute of limitations issues that arise in cases. For example, the court in Wells Fargo Bank, N.A. v. Cohen, 80 A.D.3d 753 (N.Y. App. Div. 2010), considered whether the statute was closed when the mortgagee initiated a foreclosure action after a mortgagor defaulted on a mortgage debt. Id. at 754. The statute of limitations in New York for foreclosing on a mortgage is six years. *See* N.Y. C.P.L.R. 213 (Consol. 2017). The court stated that the running of the limitations period was based on the dates individual installment payments became due rather than the date in which the mortgagor made the last payment. Cohen, 80 A.D.3d at 754. In *Cohen*, even though the last payment was made outside of the six-year statutory period, the court determined that the statute had not closed for several payments because the due date of those payments occurred after the date that the mortgagor made the last payment. Id. at 754–755.

In Arizona, the statute of limitations for on an action on a debt is six years. Ariz. Rev. Stat. § 12–548 (2017). Although the Arizona statute does not expressly address mortgage foreclosure, case law has determined that foreclosure actions are included under the statute. In De Anza Land v. Leisure Corp. v. Raineri, 669 P.2d 1339 (Ariz. Ct. App. 1983), a mortgagee brought a foreclosure action against a debtor. The court stated that while the statute specifically referred to "an action for debt" and did not mention an action to foreclose a mortgage like statutes in other states that imposed the same limitations period for both remedies, the six-year period applied to foreclosure actions and actions on the underlying debt. Id. at 1343.

Because needless controversy arises when the statute of limitations on the mortgage and the underlying debt differ, several jurisdictions have enacted statutes that bar the enforcement of both simultaneously.

III. FEDERAL LEGISLATION AFFECTING FORECLOSURE

A. MORTGAGOR IN BANKRUPTCY

Following is a discussion of two significant ways that proceedings under the federal Bankruptcy Code may intrude on the foreclosure process. Various other aspects of bankruptcy law also may affect foreclosure.

1. Automatic Stay of Foreclosure Proceedings

The mortgagor's bankruptcy may significantly alter the mortgagee's right to foreclose. The filing of any form of bankruptcy petition automatically stays foreclosure proceedings against the mortgagor. 11 U.S.C.A. § 362(a) (2017). The Department of Housing and Urban Development, however, receives a limited exception from this automatic stay rule; it may still foreclose certain mortgages it holds on property containing five or more units. 11 U.S.C.A. § 362(b)(8) (2017). Moreover, the automatic stay principle is restricted in certain ways to deter its misuse via repetitive petitions. 11 U.S.C.A. § 362(c)(3)–(4) (2017).

The bankruptcy court may grant the mortgagee relief from the automatic stay in certain situations. First, relief may be granted for cause, which includes the "lack of adequate protection" of the mortgagee's interest in the property. 11 U.S.C.A. § 362(d)(1). *In re* Haydel Properties, LP, 2017 WL 1155690 (Bankr. S.D. Miss. 2017), is a case where a creditor sought a motion for relief from the automatic stay under this rule. The court stated that in applying the lack of adequate protection rule, the movant requesting relief from the stay has the burden to prove a prima facie case for relief, before the debtor's burden of persuasion arises. Id. at *2; *see* 11 U.S.C.A. § 362(g).

Further, the court stated that for the movant to meet this burden, the movant must show that it holds a valid claim that is a perfected security interest on the property and that the value of the security has declined or there is the threat of a decline, and the creditor is unable to protect its interest because of the automatic stay. Id. To determine if a creditor is adequately protected within the meaning of the statute, the court must analyze the property's "equity cushion," the value of the property after deducting the creditor's claim and all senior claims. Id. Most courts have held that an equity cushion of 20% or more represents adequate protection. Id. With respect to the meaning of "cause", the court noted that the Bankruptcy Code does not define the term. Id. at *3. It is determined on a case-by-case basis by looking at the all the circumstances. Id. A debtor's lack of good faith may constitute the requisite cause. Id.

Second, relief from the automatic stay may be granted when the mortgagor does not have any equity in the mortgaged property, and the "property is not necessary to an effective reorganization." 11 U.S.C.A. § 362(d)(2) (2017). The meaning of "equity" under section 362(d) is the difference between the value of the mortgaged property and all encumbrances on the property. *In re* Sutton v. Bank One, Texas, Nat'l Ass'n, 904 F.2d 327, 329 (5th Cir. 1990). For purposes of the meaning of equity, value is determined on a case-by-case basis with critical facts including the nature of the mortgagor's business, market conditions, the possibility of the mortgagor's rehabilitation and the nature of the security. Id. at 330. Once the movant has established that the mortgagor lacks equity in the mortgaged property, the mortgagor has the burden of establishing that the mortgaged property "is essential for an effective reorganization *that is in prospect."* Id. This means that there is "a reasonable possibility of a successful reorganization within a reasonable time." Id. (citations omitted).

Third, relief from the automatic stay will be granted when elements regarding a "single asset real estate" are met. 11 U.S.C.A. § 362(d)(3) (2017). A business is not a single asset real estate if a reasonable and prudent business person is able to generate substantial income from the operation activities. *In re* Scotia Pacific Co., LLC, 508 F.3d 214, 222 (5th Cir. 2007). Under the Bankruptcy Code, a single real estate asset is nonresidential property or residential property with five or more units provided that the mortgagor does not provide any substantial business other than operating the real property and activities incidental to such operation. *In re* River East Plaza, LLC, 669 F.3d 826, 828 (7th Cir. 2012). If the Bankruptcy Court is required to lift the automatic stay per section 362(d)(3)(A), the bankruptcy judge must lift the stay upon request unless within 90 days of the mortgagor's filing of the bankruptcy petition the mortgagor files a plan of reorganization that is reasonably likely of confirmation within a reasonable time. Id. at 831. In *River East Plaza*, the court dismissed a single asset real estate proceeding after refusing to consider the mortgagor's third reorganization plan. Id.

Finally, the automatic stay will be lifted when "the petition was part of a scheme to delay, hinder, and defraud creditors that involved either" a transfer of the mortgaged realty without the mortgagee's consent or a court's approval, or "multiple bankruptcy filings affecting such real property." 11 U.S.C.A. § 362(d)(4) (2017). The creditor seeking a lift from the automatic stay must establish a prima facie case pertaining to all of the above requirements. *In re* Tejal Investment, LLC, 2012 WL 6186159, at *4 (Bankr. D. Utah 2012). In *Tejal*, a creditor sought to have the automatic stay lifted pertaining to the debtor's property asserting that the debtor's bankruptcy petitions evidenced a scheme to hinder, delay, or defraud the bank that involved multiple bankruptcy filings. Id. at *1. The court noted that Congress enacted section 362(d)(4) under the Bankruptcy Technical Corrections Act of 2010 to limit the number of abusive filings. Id. at *4. Prior to filing the petition at issue in this case, the debtor had filed a bankruptcy action about two years before the current petition, but no plan was confirmed in that action and the case was dismissed. Id. The debtor filed the bankruptcy petition after the creditor had a receiver appointed. Id. at 5. Although the debtor argued that it had not engaged in a scheme to hinder, delay or defraud the creditor, the court rejected its argument and determined that it was a part of a scheme. Id. The debtor had filed the earlier bankruptcy petition the day before the creditor had taken actions to appoint a receiver, and the petition in the current case was filed a few days before the scheduled foreclosure sale. Id. The court concluded that these petitions showed that the debtor had a plan to delay or hinder the creditor's remedial efforts. Id.

Significantly, in *In re* Dorsey, 476 B.R. 261 (Bankr. C.D. Cal. 2012), the court determined that section

362(d)(4) did not require the debtor to have been the one to have created the "scheme" based on the passive language in this subsection and noted that at least one other court applied the same approach. Id. at 267.

2. Nullification of Prior Foreclosure Sale

Problems may arise even when the mortgagor enters bankruptcy after the foreclosure process has been completed. A bankruptcy trustee may set aside a prior foreclosure sale as a fraudulent transfer if the sale was held within two years of the bankruptcy petition filing at a time the mortgagor was insolvent, and the sale price did not constitute "reasonably equivalent value." 11 U.S.C.A. § 548 (2017). For many years, disagreement existed regarding how to determine "reasonably equivalent value." Ultimately the issue reached the Supreme Court where the justices concluded that the proceeds produced by a properly conducted state foreclosure sale satisfy the "reasonably equivalent value" standard. *See* BFP v. Resolution Trust Corp., 511 U.S. 531 (1994). While the Court in *BFP* expressly limited its decision to mortgage foreclosure sales, the same approach was applied in tax sales conducted in accordance to state law. *See In re* Tracht Gut, LLC, 836 F.3d 1146, 1152 (9th Cir. 2016). The court in *Tracht* held that California tax sales and mortgage foreclosure sales had identical "procedural safeguards;" therefore, the amount produced by a properly conducted California tax sale established "reasonably equivalent value." Id. at 1153.

Although courts are divided on the issue, a bankruptcy trustee may seek to avoid a prior foreclosure sale as a preference when a number of conditions are met. In general terms, a voidable preference may be found when the transfer was for the benefit of the creditor for an antecedent debt and the mortgagee purchases the mortgaged property at a foreclosure sale conducted within ninety days of the bankruptcy petition filing while the mortgagor was insolvent, and the mortgagee thereby received more value than it would have obtained in a hypothetical bankruptcy liquidation. 11 U.S.C.A. § 547(b) (2017). According to the House Report of section 547(b), a "preference is a transfer that enables a creditor to receive payment of a greater percentage of the creditor's claim against the debtor than the creditor would have received if the transfer had not been made and the creditor had participated in the distribution of the assets of the bankrupt estate." *In re* Tenderloin Health, 849 F.3d 1231, 1236 (9th Cir. 2017) (citing H. R. Rep. No. 95–595, at 177 (1977)). In *Tenderloin Health*, the court permitted a hypothetical preference within the hypothetical bankruptcy liquidation. Id. at 1236–1237. *See also In re* Save Home Energy, Inc., 2017 WL 1274921 (Bankr. D. Conn. 2017) (analyzing the section 547(b) requirements).

B. MORTGAGOR IN MILITARY SERVICE

The 2003 Servicemembers Civil Relief Act (SCRA), 50 U.S.C.A. § 3901 *et seq.*, grants special protection to mortgagors on active duty in the armed forces. The purpose of the SCRA is to strengthen the national defense by enabling U.S. servicemembers to focus on the country's defense needs and to temporarily suspend legal proceedings and transactions that may negatively impact servicemembers' civil rights during their military service. 50 U.S.C.A. § 3902 (2017). It suspends judicial and administrative proceedings and transactions for servicemembers during their military service. Under the SCRA, in an action filed during or within one year of the servicemember's service, the court can stay foreclosure proceedings or modify the underlying obligation but only if the servicemember continues to be bound by an obligation, the obligation is created before the servicemember's military service and the obligation is secured by a mortgage or deed of trust. 50 U.S.C.A. § 3953(a) & (b) (2017).

Generally, a foreclosure sale made during or within one year of the servicemember's military service is invalid. U.S.C.A. § 3953(c) (2017). After December 31, 2017, the foreclosure sale must take place within nine months rather than one year for it to be invalid. Honoring Americas Veterans and Caring for Camp Lejeune Families Act of 2012, 112 P.L. 154, 126 Stat. 1165 (2012). Significantly, if a person knowingly causes the property to be sold where the SCRA applies, that person has committed a misdemeanor punishable by a fine or not more than a year in prison. U.S.C. § 3953(d) (2017). The SCRA, particularly its default judgment and stay portions, should be consulted whenever a servicemember-mortgagor faces foreclosure.

In addition to the SCRA, there are sixteen states that have statutes to supplement the federal statute.

IV. FORECLOSURE BY JUDICIAL SALE

Foreclosure by judicially approved sale constitutes the backbone of our system of mortgage foreclosure. Where a mortgagee initiates a judicial foreclosure action and the mortgagee proves that the mortgagor is in default and the amount of the default, the court orders the sale of the mortgaged property to satisfy the mortgagor's debt. Coker v. JPMorgan Chase Bank, N.A., 364 P.3d 176, 178 (Cal. 2016). Such a proceeding is available in all states and the required method of foreclosure in a number of jurisdictions. Although court supervised foreclosure is the best way to ascertain the rights of the parties involved and thereby to produce the most marketable title, it is often a complex, protracted, and expensive procedure. Legal difficulties inherent in this process are analyzed in this section.

A. PARTIES DEFENDANT

A foreclosure decree affects only those persons before the court. Naming parties defendant, therefore, is a critical step in the foreclosure process. Parties defendant can be placed into two general categories—necessary parties and proper parties.

1. Necessary and Proper Parties

a. Proper Parties

A proper party defendant to a foreclosure action is one whose joinder is desirable, but not essential to achieve the purpose of foreclosure. Senior mortgagees and those who hold no interest in the property, but are personally liable on the debt are proper parties. A senior mortgage survives the foreclosure, and a purchaser at the foreclosure sale must take the property subject to it. Although an individual personally liable on the debt can be involuntarily joined, a senior mortgagee cannot be joined without the senior mortgagee's consent when the holder of a junior interest initiates foreclosure proceedings. *See, e.g.*, Garcia v. Stewart, 906 So. 2d 1117, 1120 (Fla. 4th Dist. Ct. App. 2005) (stating that a senior mortgagee cannot be forced to participate in the foreclosure action because the action does not terminate that mortgagee's interest). Although the holder of a senior lien cannot be compelled to join the foreclosure action, the foreclosing junior lienholder may want to join a senior mortgagee for the limited purpose of determining the amount of the senior mortgage debt. Restatement (Third) of Property, Mortgages § 7.1 cmt. a (1997).

In addition, a tenant of the mortgaged property whose lease was executed prior to the mortgage is a proper party because the lease and will survive the foreclosure. *See, e.g.*, Curtis v. U.S. Bank Nat'l Ass'n, 50 A.3d 558, 564 (Md. Ct. Spec. App. 2012) (stating that "[i]f the lease was created prior to the mortgage, the purchaser at foreclosure takes the property subject to the rights of the tenant"). But see Horizon Financial v. Giamo, 41 Pa. D. & C.3d 137, 141 (Pa. 1985) (concluding that tenant's lease was extinguished even though the lease was executed prior to the mortgage but the tenant's exercise of an option to renew the lease was subsequent to the mortgage).

b. Necessary Parties

A necessary party defendant to a foreclosure action is anyone who must be joined in order to accomplish the objective of foreclosure which, as previously noted, is to sell the mortgagor's interest in the property as it existed immediately before the execution of the mortgage. It is a person whose interest is subordinate to a foreclosing senior lienholder and includes everyone with an estate or possessory interest in the property. 1426 46 St., LLC v. Klein, 60 A.D.3d 740, 742 (N.Y. App. Div. 2009). A mortgagor is a necessary party even if the mortgagor is not the debtor of the note secured by the mortgage. *See* Sudhoff v. Fed. Nat'l Mortgage Ass'n, 942 So.2d 425 (Fla. 5th Dist. Ct. App. 2006).

All junior or subordinate interests may be extinguished upon foreclosure of a senior interest. The Third Restatement sets forth the prevailing rule:

> A valid foreclosure of a mortgage terminates all interests in the foreclosed real estate that are junior in the mortgage being foreclosed and whose holders are properly joined or notified under applicable law. Foreclosure does not

> terminate interests in the foreclosed real estate that are senior to the mortgage being foreclosed.

Restatement (Third) of Property, Mortgages § 7.1 (1997).

The mortgagor and anyone who holds a junior interest in the property may be joined in the foreclosure action without their consent. If a necessary party is not joined in the action, that party's interest cannot be extinguished and it survives the foreclosure. Holders of extinguishable interests include second mortgages, easements and leases.

> *Illustration*: Assume that a mortgagor owns land and grants a first mortgage to a first mortgagee. Subsequently, the mortgagor grants a second mortgage on the land to a second mortgagee, leases a part of the mortgaged land to a tenant and grants an easement over another part of the land to a friend. The mortgagor then defaults on the first mortgage, and the first mortgagee initiates foreclosure proceedings. In this action, the mortgagor, second mortgagee, tenant and friend are all necessary parties defendant because their interests must be extinguished if the foreclosure sale purchaser is to receive the mortgagor's interest as it existed immediately before the first mortgage was executed.

Significantly, during the subprime loan crisis, Congress enacted the Protecting Tenants at Foreclosure Act of 2009 (PTFA). Prior to the enactment of the PTFA, many residential tenants were losing their rentals because their leases were junior to the foreclosed mortgages. Many of the tenants had no idea that the mortgagor/landlord had defaulted on their mortgages until they were named as parties defendants to the foreclosure action. The PTFA protected tenants in residential leases by requiring eviction notices resulting from the extinguishment of the junior leases to provide tenants with at least 90 days' notice before they could be evicted from their rental dwelling. Moreover, unless the purchaser planned to occupy the property as a principal residence or if the lease was at will, tenants could remain in the residences until the end of their leases.

As originally enacted, the PTFA was scheduled to expire on December 31, 2012, but the Dodd-Frank Act extended the sunset date to December 31, 2014. While the federal government did not extend the PTFA, several state legislatures have enacted similar protections. *See, e.g.*, Fla. Stat. Ann. § 83.561 (West 2017) (requiring purchasers of residential property at the foreclosure sale to provide tenants with 30 days' notice before they can be evicted unless certain exceptions apply); Md. Real Prop. Code Ann. § 7–105.6 (2017) (providing 90 days' notice and other similar protections that existed under the PTFA).

2. Intentional Omission of Junior Lessees

When a junior lease is particularly favorable to the lessor, it is to the mortgagee's advantage to keep the lease alive through foreclosure and thereby enhance the sale value of its security. Because the rights of a junior interest holder not made a party defendant survive foreclosure, it would appear that a mortgagee could preserve a valuable junior lease by intentionally omitting the lessee from the foreclosure suit. Certain jurisdictions allow the mortgagee to keep a junior lease alive in this fashion. Elsewhere, however, foreclosure extinguishes an intentionally omitted junior lease, at least when the lessee does not want to preserve it. This approach may be justified on the ground that joinder requirements are for the protection of junior interest holders, not the mortgagee.

In view of the uncertainty that exists with regard to preserving intentionally omitted junior leases, a mortgagee sometimes will subordinate the mortgage to a valuable junior lease to ensure that the lease will survive foreclosure.

3. Lis Pendens

Under the doctrine of lis pendens, parties who acquire an interest in the mortgaged property with notice of the foreclosure proceedings are bound by the foreclosure decree just as if they had been named parties defendant. This doctrine was discussed in greater detail in Chapter 10.

B. CALCULATING PURCHASER'S BID

Because a senior mortgage is not extinguished in a foreclosure action, the bidder at the foreclosure sale must factor the balance of the senior mortgage debt into account in determining the amount to bid. *See*

Restatement (Third) of Property, Mortgages § 7.1 cmt. a (1997) (stating "in calculating an appropriate foreclosure bid a prospective purchaser should subtract any senior liens from the fair market value of the real estate"). For example, if the fair market value of property is $150,000 and the outstanding balance of the senior mortgage is $70,000, the maximum amount that the purchaser should bid at the foreclosure sale is $80,000 because the purchaser takes the property subject to the mortgage.

Conversely, if the $70,000 mortgage is junior to the mortgage that is being foreclosed, the bidder can bid up to $150,000 for the property because the junior mortgage will be extinguished.

C. SALE PROCEDURES

The judicial foreclosure sale procedure is governed by statutory law that varies from state to state. These statutes normally call for a public sale conducted by the sheriff or a court appointed official.

D. CONFIRMATION/ADEQUACY OF SALE PRICE

Foreclosure by judicial sale is not final until the sale is confirmed by the court. Absent fraud or chilled bidding, inadequacy of the foreclosure sale price is generally not a ground upon which courts withhold confirmation. This approach was discussed in Sewickley, LLC v. Chicago Title Land Trust, 974 N.E.2d 397 (Ill. App. 1 Dist. 2012). In *Sewickley*, a mortgagee initiated foreclosure proceedings against the mortgagor in Illinois, and the mortgaged property was eventually sold at a judicial sale for $300,000. Id. at 400. Under Illinois law, the court must conduct a hearing to confirm the sale, and the sale is finalized after the trial court approves the sale. Id. at 403–04. The court will not confirm the sale if proper notice is not given, the sale is unconscionable or fraudulent or justice will not be served. Id. at 404. The court determined that the $300,000 sale price was not grossly inadequate; however, the court stated that mere inadequacy of sales price alone will not warrant a court's refusal to confirm the sale. Id. at 406. According to the court, there must be inadequacy of the sales price coupled with other problems, including fraud or mistake. Id. 406–07. The court distinguished the facts in this case from a case where the sales price was only one-sixth of the property's fair market value "which tipped the scales of justice" for not confirming the sale. Id. at 407. In another Illinois case, the court explains that the rationale of requiring more than inadequacy of sales price is to provide a stable and permanent outcome to judicial sales and to recognize that it is expected that a forced sale will not result in a sale at full value. Deutsche Bank Nat'l v. Burtley, 861 N.E.2d 1075, 1082 (Ill. App. 1st Dist. 2006).

The case of Looper v. Madison Guar. Sav. & Loan Ass'n, 729 S.W.2d 156 (Ark. 1987), is an example where the court did not confirm the sale because the inadequate sales price was so great as to "shock the conscience." Id. at 157. In *Looper*, the foreclosed property sold for $1900 even though it was worth $42,500. Id. The court noted that whether the sale price shocked the conscience was not based on a mathematical formula; rather, the determination was based on circumstances such as the harm that might result if the sale was confirmed. Id.

Statutes in some states require that the sale price be a specified fraction of the appraised value of the property, e.g., two-thirds, but in certain of these jurisdictions, mortgagors commonly waive appraisal.

E. THE PURCHASER AT THE SALE

1. Purchaser's Title

The purchaser at a judicial foreclosure sale receives title to the property as it existed in the hands of the mortgagor immediately before the execution of the mortgage. Although the rights of the mortgagor, the mortgagee, and junior interest holders named parties defendant are extinguished, the rights of individuals who acquired interests prior to the execution of the mortgage survive foreclosure. For example, assume that a mortgagor grants an easement over the mortgagor's land to a neighbor. The easement is validly recorded. The morgagor then grants a first mortgage to a first mortgagee, a second mortgage to a second mortgagee, a third mortgage to a third mortgagee, and a lease on the property to a tenant. The mortgagor defaults on the second mortgage and the second mortgagee forecloses, naming all necessary parties in the suit. A third party submits the highest bid at the foreclosure sale and acquires title to the property. Although the interests of the mortgagor, third mortgagee, and tenant are extinguished, the purchaser takes the property subject to the first mortgage because it survives the foreclosure action.

In addition, because the foreclosure sale proceeds are used to satisfy the mortgage debt, the purchaser is subrogated to the rights of the mortgagee. This concept is important in determining the purchaser's position vis-à-vis a junior lienor omitted from the original foreclosure proceeding.

2. Purchaser Versus Omitted Necessary Party

As already noted, when a necessary party is not named as a party defendant, that party's interest survives foreclosure. However, the purchaser of the property at the foreclosure sale is not without remedy. The purchaser may eliminate the omitted junior lien by using any one of three methods—redemption, reforeclosure, or possibly strict foreclosure. As successor to the mortgagor's right of equity of redemption, the purchaser may extinguish the omitted junior lien by paying it off. The purchaser also is subrogated to the mortgagee's right to foreclose. The purchaser, therefore, may eliminate the omitted junior lien by reforeclosing the mortgage with the junior lienor now included or, in certain jurisdictions, by strictly foreclosing the rights of the junior lienor.

For example, in 6820 Ridge Realty v. Goldman, 263 A.D.2d 22 (N.Y. App. Div. 1999), the court stated that a purchaser had two remedies where a necessary party had been omitted from a foreclosure action—strict foreclosure or reforeclosure. Id. at 26. According to the court, both remedies permitted the purchaser to obtain a judgment that required the omitted party to either exercise redemption rights or foreclose within a certain period of time or lose all rights and interests in the property. Id. at 26. The necessary parties omitted from the foreclosure were tenants. The court determined that the purchaser had the right to strict foreclosure, the remedy chosen by the purchaser, against the tenants because the remedy could be used against anyone with redemption rights, including tenants under New York law. Id. at 27–28.

3. Purchase by Mortgagee

The mortgagee may purchase the mortgaged property at the foreclosure sale. Because the mortgagee is entitled to receive as much of the sale proceeds as is necessary to satisfy the mortgage debt, the mortgagee may bid up to that amount without having to produce any cash. As a consequence, the mortgagee frequently is the highest bidder at the foreclosure sale.

4. Purchase by Mortgagor

If the mortgagor or the mortgagor's agent purchases at the foreclosure sale, unpaid junior liens typically survive on the theory that the purchase was really payment of the senior lien. This is, of course, an exception to the rule that all properly joined junior interests are cut off by foreclosure.

F. DISTRIBUTION OF PROCEEDS AND SURPLUS

The proceeds of the foreclosure sale are used to pay the foreclosure expenses and then to discharge the mortgage debt. Any additional amount is known as "surplus." The surplus is used to satisfy junior liens, as well as other junior interests, in the order of their priority. After the surplus is paid to junior lienors, any additional surplus belongs to the owner of the equity of redemption, who in most cases is the mortgagor. *See, e.g.,* 735 Ill. Comp. Stat. § 5/15–1512 (2016); Nev. Rev. Stat. § 40.462 (2017).

The primary reason that surplus is used to satisfy junior mortgages is that these mortgages are extinguished upon the foreclosure of a senior mortgage provided that the junior mortgagee is a party to the foreclosure proceeding. It is important to understand that while the mortgage is extinguished, the underlying debt or obligation is not extinguished. Therefore, if the surplus does not cover the outstanding balance of the extinguished junior mortgage, the junior mortgagee can sue the mortgagor on the underlying obligation.

Even though the above rule is a widely-accepted principle, courts frequently address issues related to the distribution of foreclosure sale proceeds. For example, in Illinois, distribution of proceeds are first distributed to cover reasonable expenses of the foreclosure sale followed by reasonable expenses securing possession and maintaining the property before the foreclosure, including the payment of taxes and hazard and liability insurance. 735 Ill. Comp.

Stat. § 5/15–1512 (2016). In Midwest Bank & Trust Co. v. U.S. Bank, 859 N.E.2d 71 (Ill. App. Ct. 2006), the trial court had granted a motion from the purchaser at the foreclosure sale that a portion of the surplus should be paid to the purchaser for unpaid real estate taxes. Id. at 72–73. In its reversal, the court of appeals noted that the trial court abused its discretion by granting the request because a purchaser of property was required to take it subject to any prior liens, including the lien for unpaid real estate taxes. Id. at 76. The court of appeals found additional support for its decision in the "Notice of Sheriff's Sale" which stated that the property was conveyed "AS IS" and subject to prior mortgages of record and all general real estate taxes which were a lien on the property. Id. at 76.

Surplus is not paid to a senior mortgagee because the purchaser at the foreclosure sale must take the property subject to a senior mortgage. In Edler v. Regions Bank, 60 N.E.3d 288 (Ind. Ct. App. 2016), the mortgagee foreclosed on a second mortgage. Id. at 289. The mortgagor had not defaulted on the first mortgage, but the trial court directed a portion of the surplus to be paid to the first mortgagee. Id. at 290. The appellate court determined that the trial court abused its discretion by paying surplus to the first mortgagee because the statute clearly provided that the mortgagor was entitled to the surplus after payment of expenses and satisfaction of the second mortgage. Id. at 293. This rule applies irrespective of whether the first and second mortgages are held by the same mortgagee, which was the situation in the *Edler* case.

G. DEFICIENCY JUDGMENT

1. General

If the foreclosure sale proceeds are insufficient to satisfy the underlying debt, the mortgagee generally may obtain a deficiency judgment against the mortgagor and anyone else personally liable on the debt. This illustrate this principle, assume that a mortgagor executes a $10,000 promissory note and a mortgage on investment land to a mortgagee. Subsequently, the mortgagor conveys the land to a purchaser who assumes and agrees to pay the mortgage debt, but the purchaser eventually defaults when the outstanding balance of the debt remains $10,000 and the mortgagee forecloses. If the foreclosure sale produces $8,000 after expenses, the mortgagee receives the $8,000 and generally may obtain a deficiency judgment for $2,000 against the mortgagor and purchaser. Of course, the mortgagee may not recover more than $2,000 on these judgments.

2. Anti-Deficiency Legislation

Depression era legislation still restricts the recovery of deficiency judgments in a number of jurisdictions. Anti-deficiency statutes reduce the opportunity for a mortgagee to purchase the mortgaged property at a foreclosure sale for deflated amounts and then recover large deficiencies from the mortgagor. Bank of Am., N.A. v. Roberts, 217 Cal. App. 4th 1386, 1396 (2013). One statutory approach is to prohibit deficiency judgments in certain situations, such as in the case of purchase money mortgages. The standard purchase money transaction is where the seller retains an interest in the real estate sold to secure payment of the purchase price. *See, e.g.*, Cal. Civ. Pro. Code § 580b (2016); N.C. Gen. Stat § 45–21.38 (2016). Some jurisdictions consider purchase money mortgages to include not only seller financed situations but also security interests granted to lenders on the mortgagor's purchase of real estate and may prohibit deficiencies. *See, e.g.*, Ariz. Rev. Stat. § 33–729(A) (2016); Cal. Civ. Pro. Code § 580b (2016) (applies to one-to-four unit owner-occupied dwellings).

Another statutory approach prohibits deficiency judgments when the foreclosure is by power of sale. *See, e.g.*, Alaska Stat. § 34.20.100 (2016); Cal. Civ. Pro. Code § 580d (2016); Haw. Rev. Stat. § 667–38 (2016) (deficiency prohibited for nonjudicial foreclosure if the property is residential and owner-occupied); Or. Rev. Stat. § 86.797 (2016). Several states also limit deficiency judgments to the amount by which the debt exceeds the fair market value of the property. *See, e.g.*, Ark. Code Ann. § 18–50–112 (2016); Cal. Civ. Pro. Code § 726(b) (2016); N.Y. Real Prop. Acts. Law § 1371(2) (2016); Wis. Stat. § 846.165(2) (2016). For a full discussion of anti-deficiency legislation see generally Nelson, Whitman, Burkhart & Freyermuth, Real Estate Finance Law § 8.3 (West 2015).

Waiver of the protection provided by anti-deficiency legislation is generally considered ineffective as against public policy. *See, e.g.*, Parkway

Bank & Trust Co. v. Zivkovic, 232 Ariz. 286, 291 (Ariz. Ct. App. 2013) (holding that declarations in loan documents that waive the applicability of Arizona's anti-deficiency law violate public policy and are unenforceable); Coker v. JPMorgan Chase Bank, N.A., 364 P.3d 176, 188 (Cal. 2016) (concluding that the anti-deficiency statute that prohibited deficiency judgments in the case of purchase money mortgages applied to short sales and could not be waived); High Point Bank & Trust Co. v. Highmark Properties, LLC, 776 S.E.2d 838, 843 (N.C. 2015) (concluding that "because anti-deficiency legislation is so narrowly tailored to address specific instances of the public's vulnerability to lender overreach, waiver of this statutory protection as a prerequisite to receipt of a mortgage or as a condition of a guaranty agreement would violate public policy"); Borsheim v. Owan, 467 N.W.2d 95, 98 (N.D. 1991) (holding that the debtor's contractual waiver of the anti-deficiency statutes and its protections are ineffective and against public policy).

V. FORECLOSURE BY POWER OF SALE

Foreclosure by out-of-court sale is recognized in a substantial majority of states. Although foreclosure by power of sale represents a relatively expedient and inexpensive means of foreclosure, it is prohibited in a number of jurisdictions and where permitted, it exists as an alternative to foreclosure by judicial sale. This method of foreclosure is usually based on a mortgage provision authorizing sale of the property without court supervision. *See, e.g.*, Ala. Code § 35–10–1 (2017) (stating that where a power to sell is given in any mortgage, it is part of the security, and once the mortgaged property is sold under this power, legal title vests in the purchaser); Tex. Prop. Code § 51.002 (2015) (providing that a power of sale permitted by a deed of trust must be a public sale at an auction held between 10 a.m. and 4 p.m. of the first Tuesday of a month at the county courthouse); Wyom. Stat. Ann. § 34–4–101 (2017) (permitting power of sale authorized by the mortgage).

Power of sale foreclosures give mortgagors a shorter period of time to respond to the foreclosure notice, seek legal counsel, try to negotiate a loan modification, or obtain an alternative to foreclosure. Frank S. Alexander et al., *Legislative Responses to the Foreclosure Crisis in Nonjudicial Foreclosure States*, 31 Rev. Banking & Fin. L. 341, 344 (2011). It is more favorable to the mortgagees rather than the mortgagors because mortgagors are unable to raise issues related to the purported default or the validity of the power of sale foreclosure in a judicial action or hearing. Id.

A. COMPARISON TO JUDICIAL SALE

Foreclosure by power of sale serves generally the same purpose and produces essentially the same result as foreclosure by judicial sale. However, some significant differences exist.

1. Form of Security Device

Because the deed of trust is designed to be enforced by an out-of-court sale conducted by the trustee, it is a popular financing device in most states where foreclosure by power of sale is permitted. A standard mortgage, of course, may be drafted to include a power of sale provision.

2. Sale Procedures

The procedure for foreclosure by power of sale generally is regulated by statute. These statutes normally provide for a public sale conducted only after proper notice. For example, in Oklahoma, a mortgagor can elect to use a power of sale established in the mortgage but must first give appropriate written notice to the mortgagor and holders of other interests in the mortgaged property. Okla. Stat. tit. 46, § 45 (2017). In Vermont, a copy of the notice of nonjudicial sale must be served on the mortgagor by registered or certified mail, but the mortgagor may waive such notice. Vt. Stat. Ann. tit. 12 § 4965 (2017). This waiver must be recorded. Vt. Stat. Ann. tit. 12 § 4966(g) (2017).

Typically, the required notice must be by advertisement in a local newspaper for a prescribed period. For example, in North Carolina, a power of sale notice must be published once a week for a minimum of two consecutive weeks in a newspaper in which the property is located. N.C. Gen. Stat. § 45–21.17 (2016). In other jurisdictions, additional notice must be given to the mortgagor by personal service or mail. In New Hampshire, before a nonjudicial sale, notice must be published once a week for three consecutive weeks in the local newspaper and a copy of the notice must be sent to the mortgagor by certified mail at least 25 days for nonresidential mortgages and 45 days for residential mortgages. N.H. Rev. Stat. Ann. § 479:25 (2017). In addition, under Rhode Island law, notice by certified mail to the mortgagor in the power of sale is required, as well as notice by advertisement in the public newspaper for a minimum of three consecutive weeks. R.I. Gen. Laws § 34–11–22 (2016).

Junior interest holders usually are not entitled to such added notice. In Banc of America Leasing & Capital, LLC v. 3 Arch Trustee Services, Inc., 180 Cal. App. 4th 1090 (2009), a junior lienholder (who had recorded a judgment lien against the owner) filed an action against the trustee asserting a breach of statutory duties concerning a nonjudicial foreclosure sale. Id. at 1096. The court held that California's statute governing nonjudicial foreclosure sales specified the exact duties of a trustee concerning a nonjudicial foreclosure sale, which did not include searching for every possible judgment creditor. Id. at 1095. Therefore, a trustee was not required to provide notice to any party, including a junior lien holder, except in cases where the deed of trust or statute expressly required such notice. Id. at 1097. Furthermore, if a junior holder wanted to receive a notice of a nonjudicial foreclosure sale, the junior interest holder could file a "special notice request" that would have required that holder to be added to the notification list. Id. at 1098. However, the court provided that judgment lien holders were not entitled to receive automatic notice of sale under the nonjudicial foreclosure statute. Id. at 1100. The court noted that "trustees should not be saddled with the additional burden, risk, and costs associated with finding and providing notice to this type of lien holder." Id. at 1101. Therefore, unless a junior interest holder filed a special notice request, a trustee was not required to provide notice of sale concerning nonjudicial foreclosure sales.

3. Purchaser's Title

The purchaser at a power of sale foreclosure receives the same rights as a purchaser at a judicial foreclosure. Nonetheless, the title of the purchaser at a power of sale foreclosure generally is less secure because the sale has not been confirmed by a court and is, therefore, more likely to be the subject of future litigation. In Lee v. HSBC Bank USA, 218 P.3d 775 (Haw. 2009), because of a lack of communication, the mortgaged property was sold at a nonjudicial foreclosure sale even though the mortgagor had cured the default shortly before the sale. Id. at 776. The mortgagee's attorneys informed the purchaser that the mortgagor had properly cured the default prior to the sale and returned the purchaser's deposit. Id. at 777. The purchaser rejected the attempted rescission and sued for specific performance. Id. The court concluded that the nonjudicial foreclosure sale was invalid because the mortgagor was not in breach of a condition at the time of the foreclosure sale; thus, the sale did not abide with the Hawaii's power of sale statute. Id. at 779. Consequently, the purchaser could not enforce the sale and was only entitled to a return of his deposit and interest. Id. at 784.

4. Purchase by Lender

The form of the financing device authorizing foreclosure by power of sale determines whether the lender may bid at the sale. If a mortgage with a power of sale provision is involved, the mortgagee has a duty to conduct the sale in an impartial manner. Thus, the mortgagee may not purchase the property unless it has contractual or statutory permission to do so. If a deed of trust is used, the lender may freely bid because the trustee conducts the sale.

5. Deficiency or Surplus

Foreclosure by power of sale is conducted outside the judicial system. Consequently, the mortgagee may need to initiate a legal proceeding when there is either a deficiency or surplus. If the proceeds are insufficient to satisfy the mortgage debt, the mortgagee must bring suit to recover a deficiency judgment against a party personally liable on the underlying obligation. As discussed earlier in this chapter, deficiency judgments are subject to legislative prohibition or limitation in certain jurisdictions. If the proceeds exceed the amount of the mortgage debt, the mortgagee may file an interpleader action to guard against liability for paying the surplus to the wrong parties.

6. Judicial Review

Although the courts do not oversee foreclosure by power of sale, the process is always subject to later judicial scrutiny. This possibility reduces the value of the property to prospective purchasers and may cause the mortgagee to forego foreclosure by power of sale in favor of foreclosure by judicial sale.

B. CONSTITUTIONAL ISSUES

Foreclosure by power of sale has come under constitutional attack on the ground that the notice and hearing procedures used in the typical power of sale foreclosure do not meet the procedural due process requirements of the Fifth and Fourteenth Amendments. This attack really involves several issues.

1. Governmental Action

The Fifth and Fourteenth Amendments limit governmental action, not private activity. The first issue, therefore, is whether a power of sale foreclosure involves significant federal or state action.

The federal action question usually arises when the foreclosing mortgagee is connected to the federal government in some way. The few courts that have considered the question have tended to find federal action if the mortgagee is a branch of the federal government such as the U.S. Department of Veterans Affairs, but not if it is a private entity closely related to the federal government such as Fannie Mae and Freddie Mac.

In Dias v. Fed. Nat'l. Mortgage Ass'n, 990 F. Supp. 2d 1042 (D. Haw. 2013), the mortgagor alleged that the nonjudicial foreclosure was a violation of her constitutional right of due process. Id. at 1047. The

Federal Housing Finance Agency (FHFA), Fannie Mae's conservator, moved to dismiss this claim arguing that Fannie Mae was a private corporation and not a government actor. Id. In 1968, Congress privatized Fannie Mae, making it a private organization. Id at 1060. In 2008, Congress put both Fannie Mae and Freddie Mac into conservatorship of the newly formed FHFA to reorganize, rehabilitate or wind up their affairs. Id. The mortgagor argued that this conservatorship turned these entities into state actors since the conservator was a state actor. Id. The court rejected the mortgagor's argument and stated that the conservatorship did not make Fannie Mae a state actor; rather, FHFA merely took over their role as private actors while serving as the conservator. Id. at 1061. The court reasoned that the conservatorship did not give FHFA permanent control over Fannie Mae as required under precedent. Id. at 1062. *See* Lebron v. National Railroad Passenger Corp., 513 U.S. 374, 115 S. Ct. 961, 130 L.Ed.2d 902 (1995). The state of Michigan reached the same conclusion that state action was lacking in a case involving Freddie Mac. *See* Fed. Home Loan Mortgage Corp. v. Shamoon, 922 F. Supp. 2d 641 (E.D. Mich. 2013).

Although there is some authority that Ginnie Mae is not a federal instrumentality bound by due process restrictions, such a hybrid organization is difficult to categorize. Thus, the federal action question remains partly unresolved.

The state action question arises because power of sale foreclosure is recognized and regulated by the state. This issue is relatively well settled. The prevailing view is that power of sale foreclosure does not involve state action. Courts generally conclude that this method of foreclosure is established by private contract even though it may be recognized and regulated by state statute. *See* Apao v. Bank of New York, 324 F.3d 1091 (9th Cir. 2003). *See also* Grapentine v. Pawtucket Credit Union, 755 F.3d 29, 33–34 (1st Cir. 2014) (holding that there was no state action because state officials don't have a significant role in foreclosure proceedings and the power of sale statutes only confirm and regulate a common law right which exists because of an agreement between the parties); Parker v. BancorpSouth Bank, 253 S.W.3d 918, 924 (2007) (stating that the mere fact that the General Assembly passed the Arkansas Statutory Foreclosure Act does not constitute state action as the mortgagee is the actor in this foreclosure action that followed all the procedures); CitiMortgage, Inc. v. Drake, 410 S.W.3d 797, 804–806 (Tenn. Ct. App. 2013) (holding that Tennessee statutes which recognized, enforced, and regulated non-judicial foreclosures did not effectively convert such foreclosures into state action).

Unsuccessful arguments for state action have been based on encouragement, enforcement, and participation theories. The Supreme Court of Missouri in Fed. Nat'l Mortgage Ass'n v. Howlett, 521 S.W.2d 428 (Mo. 1975), rejected the mortgagor's argument that state action was present with Fannie Mae's foreclosure of her property. Id. at 432. The mortgagor argued that there was state action because the statute encouraged the clauses to be inserted into the deed of trust. Id. However, the court reasoned that the statutory authorization merely encouraged the contractual right and did not rise to the level of state action. Id. at 434. The statute did not compel the parties to include the clause in the contractual agreement.

2. Notice and Hearing

If a foreclosure by power of sale is considered to involve governmental action, procedural due process mandates that the mortgagor and other interested parties receive sufficient notice of the foreclosure and a presale opportunity to be heard. In order to determine whether these requirements have been met, it is necessary to examine the mortgage documents in question and the applicable local statutes. Power of sale foreclosure procedures rarely satisfy due process standards. Notice published in a newspaper often is inadequate. Moreover, an opportunity for a presale hearing normally is not provided.

3. Waiver

Even assuming that the requisite governmental action is present and that the local procedure violates either the Fifth Amendment or the Fourteenth Amendment, a power of sale foreclosure still may be conducted if the mortgagor knowingly and voluntarily waives the mortgagor's procedural due process rights. The validity of individual waivers, of course, only can be determined on a case-by-case basis.

VI. STRICT FORECLOSURE

Strict foreclosure was the method originally used to extinguish the mortgagor's equity of redemption. After default, an equity court would establish a time period within which the mortgagor was required to pay the debt or lose the mortgaged property to the mortgagee. This means of foreclosure generally was not accepted in this country. Today, strict foreclosure is available as a principal method of foreclosure in only a handful of states. Connecticut is one of the few states that permit strict foreclosure. Conn. Gen. Stat. Ann. § 49–15 (2016). However, in Connecticut any party may submit a written motion to have the mortgage foreclosed by sale. See Conn. Gen. Stat. Ann. § 49–24 (2016). In Vermont, unless requested by any party or ordered by the court, the state allows the court to issue a judgment and decree of foreclosure without a judicial sale of the mortgaged property. Vt. Stat. Ann. tit. 12, § 4941 (2017). In several other jurisdictions, however, strict foreclosure is authorized against necessary parties omitted from a prior judicial foreclosure suit.

Statutes in a few northeastern states provide for a special form of strict foreclosure that is accomplished by entry plus possession for a specified time period which ranges between one and three years. The effect is the same as the traditional form of strict foreclosure; the mortgagor's equity of redemption is extinguished without a foreclosure sale of any kind.

VII. STATUTORY REDEMPTION

A. AVAILABILITY

Although the equity of redemption expires at foreclosure, statutes in approximately one-half of the states establish a right to redeem the mortgaged property *after* the foreclosure sale. The primary goal of statutory redemption is to protect the mortgagor, as well as junior lienors, from sale of the property at a price far below its value. It allows a mortgagor to "prevent a bargain sale from becoming a *de facto* forfeiture" of the mortgagor's equity in the property. United States v. Wood, 658 F. Supp. 1561, 1567 (W.D. KY. 1987). These statutes also give the mortgagor more time to obtain the funds necessary to retain the property. Id.

Statutory redemption laws vary considerably, but each establishes a time frame, such as one year, within which redemption must be accomplished. In certain jurisdictions, the local statutory redemption scheme is inapplicable to power of sale foreclosure.

There is also a question of who is entitled to possession during the statutory redemption period. As a general rule, the mortgagor may retain possession of the mortgaged real estate during the statutory redemption period. *See, e.g.,* Iowa Code § 628.3 (2016) (providing a one-year redemption period and allowing the mortgagor to possess the real property); Ky. Rev. Stat. Ann. § 426.220 (2017) (stating that the mortgagor is entitled to possession until redemption period ends). *But see* Kan. Stat. Ann. 426.530 (2017) (allowing the purchaser to possession during redemption period, but the purchaser receives a deed with a lien reflecting the mortgagor's redemption right). Several states only allow for the mortgagor to possess the property in certain situations. *See, e.g.,* Mont. Code Ann. § 25–13–82 (2017) (allowing the mortgagor to possess the property during redemption if it is being occupied by the mortgagor as a home); Wash. Rev. Code 6.23.110 (2017) (allowing the mortgagor to possession if the property is used as the mortgagor's homestead or for farming purposes but allowing the purchaser to collect rent from a tenant who may continue to possess the property until the lease expires).

If redemption is not accomplished by the end of that period, the purchaser at the foreclosure sale receives title to and possession of the property.

B. PARTIES WHO MAY REDEEM

The mortgagor, the mortgagor's successors, and any junior lienor joined in the foreclosure may exercise a right of redemption under most statutes. The mortgagor and the mortgagor's successors frequently receive an exclusive right to redeem for a specified period. After the mortgagor's redemption period has elapsed, junior lienors usually have the right to redeem in the order of their priority. Certain states have adopted other procedures for exercising statutory redemption rights.

C. AMOUNT REQUIRED FOR REDEMPTION

The amount required for statutory redemption is generally the foreclosure sale price together with interest as specified in the statute.

D. RESULT OF REDEMPTION

1. By Mortgagor or Mortgagor's Successor

Statutory redemption by the mortgagor or the mortgagor's successor annuls the foreclosure sale and restores title to the redeemer. Authorities differ, however, as to whether unsatisfied pre-existing junior liens are revived.

2. By Junior Lienor

When a junior lienor redeems, the junior lienor generally receives the rights of the foreclosure sale purchaser. Other junior lien holders usually may redeem from the original redeemer.

E. WAIVER

States are divided on the question of waiver of the statutory right of redemption. Many states prohibit waiver of the statutory right of redemption. However, a few states allow the mortgagor to waive the statutory right of redemption. At the opposite end of the spectrum, certain jurisdictions allow mortgagors to waive their statutory redemption rights by mortgage provision. Other states permit waiver only in limited situations, such as when the mortgagor is a corporation. For example, mortgagors in Arkansas and Tennessee may waive their statutory redemption rights in the mortgage or deed of trust. A.C.A. § 18–49–106 (2016); Tenn. Code Ann. § 66–8–101 (2016). Other jurisdictions allow for a shortened redemption period in certain circumstances. In Minnesota, where the mortgaged property is agricultural use, the redemption period is shortened to six months if the mortgagor waives the 12-month redemption period. Minn. Stat. Ann. § 580.23 (West 2016).

F. COMPARISON TO EQUITY OF REDEMPTION

Statutory redemption is often confused with equity of redemption. Although both methods of redemption are designed to protect the mortgagor, they differ significantly. First, equity of redemption developed as a part of our common law and is available in all states. Statutory redemption is a legislative creation that exists in approximately one-half of the states. Second, the equity of redemption expires at foreclosure; statutory redemption rights then become operative after the foreclosure sale. An equity of redemption and a right of statutory redemption, therefore, cannot exist in the same party at the same time. Third, the equity of redemption is available until confirmation of the foreclosure sale. Statutory redemption, however, run from foreclosure sale to the end of the period established by statute. Fourth, the amount required to be paid to equitably redeem the property is the amount in default, usually the outstanding balance of the mortgage loan. The amount required for statutory redemption is based on the foreclosure sale price. Fifth, the right of equity of redemption may not be waived. It is a fundamental right in every mortgage. Statutory redemption, however, may be waived by mortgage provision in some jurisdictions.

G. CRITICISM OF STATUTORY REDEMPTION

Statutory redemption has been roundly criticized on the ground that it does not really achieve its intended purpose—to produce realistic bids at the foreclosure sale. *See* United States v. Stadium Apartments, Inc., 425 F.2d 358 (9th Cir.1970). Some critics have gone even further and suggested that statutory redemption is actually counterproductive. The fact that the purchaser must wait for a year or so before receiving the property may dampen bidding by outsiders and thereby depress the sale price. Moreover, this delay and its attendant risks may cause mortgagees to lend less or demand a higher rate of return in states that utilize a statutory redemption period to "protect" mortgagors.

CHAPTER 12

FINANCING COOPERATIVES AND CONDOMINIUMS

I. BACKGROUND

As the population of this country began to crowd our urban centers during the first half of the twentieth century, it became increasingly difficult for many people to realize the American dream of homeownership. Housing cooperatives and condominiums were developed in large part to meet the public's desire in this regard. Both offer individuals the opportunity to acquire a unit in a multi-unit building. Although cooperatives and condominiums are generally residential developments, either form of ownership may be used for a commercial project.

The cooperative and the condominium pose unique real estate finance problems. These issues are explored in this chapter, but first it is necessary to review the general legal principles underlying each form of development.

II. COOPERATIVES

A. COOPERATIVE CONCEPT

A cooperative is a type of ownership where individuals purchase ownership interests in the form of stock and enter into leases of units that they possess. Cooperative apartments became popular in New York City during the early 1900s and soon spread to other major metropolitan areas. Title to the cooperative apartment building, as well as the land upon which it is located, ordinarily is held by a corporation. Stock in the corporation is allocated among the cooperative apartment units based upon their relative size or value, usually value. Each cooperative member purchases the stock assigned to a specific apartment and receives a long-term "proprietary" lease to that unit. Rent payable under the lease is the cooperative member's proportionate share of the expenses the corporation incurs in operating the cooperative. Expenses include costs for taxes, insurance, maintenance, management, and, as discussed below, mortgage debt service. Under the Internal Revenue Code, cooperative members can deduct their proportionate share of allowable real estate taxes and mortgage interest on indebtedness for the acquisition, construction, improvement or maintenance of the building or for the acquisition of the land that the building is situated. IRC § 216(a) (2017).

B. FINANCING COOPERATIVES

1. Construction or Acquisition Financing

In order to finance the purchase or construction of the cooperative building, the cooperative corporation places a blanket mortgage on the property. Shareholders are not personally liable on this blanket mortgage. However, this general financing arrangement presents the individual cooperative members with certain financing problems.

2. Loans on Units

Lending institutions may be reluctant or unable to take a cooperative member's stock and proprietary lease as security for a long-term loan. Although such loans are more readily available today than they were some time ago, cooperative apartment purchasers still may face considerable difficulty in obtaining adequate financing in many areas of the country. As a result, the purchaser of a cooperative apartment unit may be required to have enough ready cash to pay for the stock allocated to the unit or find a seller who is willing to recover the seller's equity in installments over a number of years.

3. Default on Blanket Mortgage

The financial interdependence of the cooperative members is another source of concern. The existence of a blanket mortgage paid by rent receipts means that if some members fail to pay rent, the cooperative may not have sufficient funds to meet a mortgage loan installment. The entire membership is then faced with foreclosure unless they take action to cure the default. Although reserves and special assessments may be utilized to cover such a contingency, there is always the possibility that available funds will be inadequate and that all cooperative members will be at the mercy of the blanket mortgagee.

III. CONDOMINIUMS

A. CONDOMINIUM CONCEPT

Although cooperative apartment members are more than ordinary tenants, they do not hold title to their units. Condominium owners do. This idea of separate ownership of housing units in a multi-unit building originated long ago and was utilized throughout Europe in the Middle Ages.

Condominium development achieved prominence in the United States only relatively recently. Changes in economic, political, and social conditions precipitated dramatic condominium growth in this country since the early 1960s. The combination of a land shortage in populous regions, legislation in each state establishing guidelines for the creation of condominiums, and the possibility of insuring mortgages on individual condominium units caused condominium developments to spring up in such number that they now occupy a significant position in the overall housing picture. Commercial condominiums are also quite common. As might be expected, the cooperative dwindled in importance in the real estate marketplace as the condominium rose in popularity.

A condominium is created when a developer records a formal declaration that the developer submits certain real estate to the local condominium act. The property may consist of various kinds of development, such as a single high-rise structure, a number of garden apartment buildings, or a series of row houses. The contents of the declaration for a condominium is determined by the jurisdiction. For example, in North Carolina, the declaration must contain several items, including the name of the condominium (which must include the term "condominium"), the county, a legal description of the real estate, maximum units, use and occupancy restrictions, alienability restrictions, and allocation of common elements, expenses and votes. N.C. Gen. Stat. §§ 47C–2–105 & 47C–2–107 (2017). In every state, each condominium unit is identified in the declaration.

The purchaser of a condominium unit receives the fee simple to that unit and an undivided percentage interest in the common areas of the development as a tenant in common with the other unit owners. The common areas include the land and all aspects of the building not included within the description of individual condominium units. An owners association, usually formed as a corporation, manages the common areas and facilities.

The concept of individual ownership of part of a building has generated numerous legal problems. Litigation and legislation in the area is ever increasing. In 1977, the National Conference of Commissioners on Uniform State Laws approved the Uniform Condominium Act as a means to deal with unsettled condominium issues on a consistent basis throughout the country. Three years later the Commissioners amended and reissued the Act. The 1980 version of the Act has been enacted in a number of jurisdictions with modifications that vary among those states. *See, e.g.*, Ala. Code § 35–8A–101 (2017);

Minn. Stat. § 515A.1–101 (2017); Mo. Rev. Stat. § 448.1–101 (2017); N.C. Gen. Stat. § 47C–1–101 (2017); 68 Pa. Cons. Stat. § 3101 (2017); 34 R.I. Gen. Laws Ann. § 34–36.1–1.01 (West 2017); Tex. Prop. Code Ann. § 82.001 (West 2017).

This book is designed to present the fundamentals of real estate finance, not an exhaustive analysis of condominium law. Hence, the remainder of this section treats only the narrow area of condominium financing.

B. FINANCING CONDOMINIUMS

1. Construction Financing

Condominium construction lending is in many respects similar to financing subdivision development. In each case, the developer obtains a blanket construction mortgage loan to finance the contemplated improvements. The construction lender may require the developer to pre-sell a stated number of units before the construction lender advances construction funds. *See, e.g.*, Botai Corp., N.V. v. Comm'r, T.C. Memo. 1990–475 (1990) (developer was required to pre-sell at least 75% of the units with an aggregate sales price of at least $32 million to obtain construction loan); RJSG Props., LLC v. Marbella Condo. Developers, LLC, 2010 WL 2890307 (2010) (construction lender required developer to pre-sell at least 35 units). When construction is completed and a unit purchaser located, the purchaser obtains a permanent mortgage loan to pay the purchase price of the unit being acquired. The developer uses the money received from the purchaser to pay a proportionate share of the blanket construction loan. The construction lender in turn executes a partial release of the construction mortgage so that the developer can convey clear title to the unit in question. The end result is that the purchaser holds title to the unit subject only to the lien of the permanent purchase money mortgage. This process is repeated until no units are left in the hands of the developer. Thus, the transition from the construction loan to permanent financing is accomplished in a series of transactions as housing units in the subdivision or condominium are sold.

The condominium construction lender, however, faces a problem the subdivision financer does not. From a practical perspective, construction of the condominium building cannot be halted in midstream if the units are not selling well. Further, if the lender executes a partial release as each unit is conveyed, the lender may end up with a lien on only the least valuable portions of its original security. Many condominium construction lenders, therefore, will not execute any partial releases until the developer has obtained sales contracts for a certain percentage of the units. The lender also may require the developer to have a plan for converting the development into a rental project in the event many units do not sell.

2. Conversion Financing

Owners of rental apartment buildings or other structures often convert their property to condominiums as a means to profitably dispose of real estate. The condominium conversion process presents some financing problems. The existing mortgagee may be unwilling to cooperate with the conversion and grant partial releases as the condominium units are sold. In this event, the owner must obtain short-term mortgage financing from another source in order to bridge the conversion period. The proceeds of the new mortgage loan are used to satisfy the original mortgage debt. The owner then organizes the condominium and sells the units. The transition from the interim loan to permanent financing is accomplished as described in the preceding section on construction financing.

3. Loans on Units

a. General

The owner of a condominium unit may obtain financing on the unit in the same manner as the owner of a single-family dwelling. Thus, there is not the same financial interdependence among condominium owners as exists among cooperative apartment members. If one condominium unit owner defaults in the payment of the unit owner's mortgage loan, the unit owner faces foreclosure alone. The lender does not necessarily have a lien on any other unit. This availability of separate financing of individual units is the most striking advantage of condominium ownership over investment in a cooperative apartment.

b. Priority Vis-à-Vis Assessment Liens

Although condominium unit owners are less financially interdependent than are cooperative apartment members, they are far more so than are homeowners in a typical subdivision. This is because unit owners must work together to maintain the condominium common areas. To achieve this objective, the condominium homeowners association makes an assessment against each unit owner for the unit owner's share of the expenses of the condominium project. If a unit owner does not pay the assessment, the association receives a statutory lien against the delinquent owner's condominium unit. Under many condominium statutes, a lien for unpaid assessments is junior to an existing first mortgage on the unit. The Uniform Condominium Act, however, gives an assessment lien priority over an existing first mortgage for up to six months of unpaid assessments on the ground that such a limited preference is crucial to the financial well-being of the development. *See* U.C.A. § 3–116. Mortgage lenders indirectly benefit from fully-funded maintenance programs because the value of their security is thereby preserved. Moreover, lenders may shield themselves against loss of lien priority by requiring the unit owner to escrow funds for assessments just as they often require the unit owner to place monies in escrow for real estate taxes and insurance.

CHAPTER 13
ADVANCED TAX ISSUES

I. IN GENERAL

There are significant tax issues that impact real estate finance. Although it is beyond the scope of this book to address all of these issues, some of the most salient concepts will be discussed in this section to provide a basic understanding of these concepts. Other important tax principles were discussed in Chapter 2, including the deductibility of mortgage interest. Chapter 9 discussed the tax consequences of loan modifications, deeds in lieu of foreclosure and short sales.

This chapter explains the important concepts of adjusted basis, the tax shelter aspect of real estate, depreciation, choice of form for real estate holdings, limitations on deductions, like kind exchanges, installment sales, sale and leasebacks, sale of a principal residence and character of gain or loss. In addition, this chapter discusses the tax considerations of these concepts where the property is encumbered by a mortgage.

II. REAL ESTATE AS A TAX SHELTER

A. INCLUSION OF DEBT IN THE ADJUSTED BASIS—THE *CRANE* DOCTRINE

One of the most important concepts in tax law is adjusted or cost basis. The adjusted basis is important not only for commercial real property, but it is also important for property held solely for personal purposes, such as a principal residence or vacation cottage. Adjusted basis is instrumental in determining gain and depreciation. Generally, under the Internal Revenue Code, the adjusted basis is the cost of the property. IRC § 1012(a) (2017). If a person receives property by gift, that person's adjusted basis is the adjusted basis of the donor, also known as a carryover basis. IRC § 1015(a) (2017). However, if the fair market value of the real property is less than the donor's adjusted basis at the time of the gift and the donee disposes of the property for a loss, the donee's adjusted basis is the fair market value of the property at the time of the gift. Id. The purpose of this rule is to discourage individuals from giving or trading losses to someone who is better able to use them. Generally, the adjusted basis of property received from a decedent is the fair market value of the property at the time of the decedent's death, commonly known as a stepped-up basis. IRC § 1014(a) (2017).

There are significant tax issues that arise where a mortgage encumbers real property that has been conveyed by gift or sale. One significant issue is the impact of the mortgage on the transferee's adjusted basis. A second issue relates to the transferor's gain on the conveyance.

1. The *Crane* Doctrine and the Foundation of Tax Shelters

One of the most important cases in tax history is Crane v. Comm'r, 331 U.S. 1 (1947). In *Crane*, a woman was devised an apartment building under the terms of her husband's will, and she took the building subject to a mortgage. Id. at 3. At the time of the devise, the fair market value of the building equaled the outstanding balance of the mortgage. Id. One of the issues in the case was whether the nonrecourse mortgage debt should be included in the woman's adjusted basis. The Court determined whether the property that the woman acquired was the physical building or its equity, which would have been zero. The Court determined that the woman's adjusted basis was based on the physical property, the apartment building. Because the apartment building was acquired from a decedent, the adjusted basis was the building's fair market value at the time of the husband's death undiminished by the mortgage. Id. at 11. As a result, the woman was entitled to claim depreciation deductions on the apartment building. Id. at 12. Although the Court refused to address whether the woman would have been entitled to claim depreciation on the apartment building if the mortgage exceeded the fair market value of the building, the prevailing view is that the woman would not have been able to do so. *See* Estate of Franklin v. Comm'r, 544 F. 2d 1045 (9th Cir. 1976). In *Estate of Franklin*, the purchase price included a nonrecourse debt with a balloon payment due in 10 years, but the taxpayer did not establish that the fair market value of the property was about the same as the purchase price. Id. at 1048. The court noted that the purchase price exceeded the estimated fair market value. Id. In addition, subsequent payments toward the purchase price did not yield any equity.

Id. Based on the facts in the case, the taxpayer did not have any equity or investment in the property but attempted to claim depreciation deductions. Id. at 1049. The Ninth Circuit disallowed the claimed depreciation deductions. If a taxpayer is able to claim depreciation deductions where the purchase price in the form of a nonrecourse loan that exceeds the property's fair market value, it will encourage purchasers to overpay for the property with a nonrecourse loan in order to inflate the depreciation deductions.

In applying these principles, assume that a mortgagor purchases an office building worth $150,000 for $30,000 cash and takes it subject to an $120,000 mortgage debt. The mortgagor's adjusted basis is $150,000 per IRC § 1012. Under *Crane*, the mortgagor would be entitled to claim depreciation deductions based on the adjusted basis. However, if the mortgagor purchases the office building for a $150,000 nonrecourse debt only, and the fair market value of the building is worth $100,000 at the time of the acquisition, the mortgagor is not able to claim any depreciation deductions under *Estate of Franklin*, the prevailing view.

The Court in *Crane* also concluded that the mortgage was included in the woman's amount realized when she disposed of the building. *Crane*, 331 U.S. at 14–15. The rationale underlying the Court's decision was based on economic analysis. Because the woman had a small amount of equity in the apartment building, the mortgage was comparable to a recourse loan and treated as a personal obligation. For example, assume that a taxpayer owns property worth $100,000 that is subject to a $25,000 nonrecourse debt. If the taxpayer sells the property to a purchaser who pays $75,000 cash and takes it subject to the mortgage, the taxpayer's amount realized is $100,000 because it includes the $25,000 nonrecourse debt under the economic principles of *Crane.* Even though the taxpayer is not being relieved of a personal obligation, the taxpayer is de facto liable because the taxpayer will not merely abandon the property notwithstanding the nonrecourse nature of the debt in order to protect the $25,000 in equity.

The *Crane* Court in the famous footnote 37 indicates that there may be a different result where the taxpayer does not receive any additional consideration or "boot." Id. at 14. Hence, if the fair market value of the property is $75,000 and it is subject to a $80,000 nonrecourse debt, the *Crane* Court's economic analysis will not warrant inclusion in the taxpayer's amount realized because the taxpayer has no equity to protect. However, in Tufts v. Comm'r, 461 U.S. 300 (1983), the outstanding balance of the nonrecourse debt exceeded the fair market value of the property at the disposition, but the Supreme Court determined that the debt was included in the amount realized even though there was no equity to protect. Id. at 307. The Court determined that the fair market value of the property was irrelevant. Id. at 317. The Court's rationale was that the nonrecourse loan was a "true loan" which meant that it was not included in gross income at its inception because of the obligation to repay. Id. at

397. If it was not included in the taxpayer's income upon disposition, the taxpayer would have an accession to wealth without income recognition. Therefore, under *Tufts*, the amount realized includes nonrecourse debt even if the taxpayer does not receive any boot or additional consideration. For example, assume that the taxpayer disposes of property that is encumbered with a $140,000 nonrecourse loan. Assume also that the fair market value of the property is $125,000 and the taxpayer's adjusted basis is $130,000. In this example, the taxpayer will realize a $10,000 gain, the $140,000 nonrecourse debt less the $130,000 adjusted basis. The taxpayers in *Tufts* argued that they would have realized a $5,000 loss based on these facts, the $130,000 adjusted basis less the $125,000 fair market value of the property disposed. However, per *Tufts*, the property's fair market value is not relevant in the determination of gain or loss in this situation.

2. Part-Gift, Part-Sale Transfers

Under the tax code, a gift is excluded from the donee's gross income. IRC § 102(a) (2017). It is a nontaxable event. However, if a donor makes a gift of property that is subject to a mortgage, the transfer is a part gift, part sale. With a part gift, part sale, the donor has income to the extent that the amount realized exceeds the donor's adjusted basis. Treas. Reg. § 1.1001–1(e)(1) (2017). The amount realized is the donor's debt relief on the transfer. The donor is not able to recognize a loss on such a transaction. Id. The donee's adjusted basis in a part gift, part sale is the greater of the amount that the donee pays for the property or the donor's adjusted basis. Treas. Reg. § 1.1015–4(a) (2017). If the donee subsequently sells the property for a loss, the donee's adjusted basis cannot exceed the fair market value of the property. Id.

To illustrate these principles, assume that the donor owns an office building that is worth $250,000 and is encumbered by a $200,000 mortgage. Also, assume that the donor's adjusted basis in the building is $130,000. The donor gives the building to a donee who takes it subject to the mortgage. The donor's amount realized is $200,000, the debt relief per *Crane*. Therefore, the donor has gain totaling $70,000, the difference between the donor's amount realized and the donor's adjusted basis. The donee's adjusted basis is $200,000, the outstanding balance of the mortgage debt because it exceeds the donor's adjusted basis.

B. DEPRECIATION

An owner is entitled to claim a depreciation deduction for real property that is used in a trade or business or held for the production of income. IRC § 167(a) (2017). Depreciation is a method of cost recovery. It doesn't determine the actual reduced valued of the property but represents an artificial mechanism of cost recovery. An owner can claim depreciation once the property is placed in service and must stop claiming depreciation when the property is no longer in service. Treas. Reg. § 1.167(a)–10(b) (2017). Therefore, depreciation is not allowed while a building is being constructed nor is it allowed when an owner begins using the property for personal purposes. In addition, an owner is not allowed to claim depreciation on land or inventory because property must be subject to exhaustion or wear and tear to be depreciable. Treas. Reg. § 1.167(a)–2 (2017). This means that a developer who subdivides land, builds houses and sells them to homeowners is not able to claim depreciation on these houses.

Depreciation is computed based on the owner's basis in the property. The basis must be reduced by "allowable" depreciation even if the owner does not claim it. *See* IRC § 1016(a)(2) (2017). This reduction is to prevent the owner from claiming a double benefit in the form of a deduction and reduced gain upon the disposition of the property.

Tangible property placed in service after 1980 must be depreciated under IRC § 168. Residential rental property and nonresidential real property must be depreciated under the straight line method. IRC § 168(b)(3) (2017). Under the straight line method, an equal amount of depreciation is claimed each year other than the year the property is placed in service and the year that it is disposed. The depreciation rules under section 168, known as ACRS or MACRS, require depreciation deductions to be based on certain conventions. For residential and nonresidential real property, the convention that applies is the mid-month convention. IRC § 168(d)(2) (2017). This means that all real property is presumed to have been placed in service or disposed during the middle of the month. IRC § 168(d)(4)(B) (2017).

Therefore, even if an owner places an apartment building in service on June 1, for purposes of depreciation it is considered to have been placed in service on June 15. Finally, MACRS determines depreciation based on an applicable recovery period. The applicable recovery period is 27.5 years for residential rental property and 39 years for nonresidential real property. IRC § 168(c) (2017).

The Internal Revenue Service has made it very easy to compute depreciation by issuing various publications and revenue procedure that help owners compute the depreciation deductions. *See* Rev. Proc. 87–57, 1987–2 C.B. 687 (1987) and Pub. 946 available on the IRS website. They include depreciation tables that determine the depreciation deduction. For example, assume that in February 2017 a mortgagor acquires an apartment building for $300,000 (including $50,000 for the land). The mortgagor makes a down payment of $60,000 and takes out a $240,000 nonrecourse loan. The mortgagor's basis is $300,000 per IRC § 1012. The basis includes the nonrecourse debt pursuant to the *Crane* case. The $50,000 cost that is allocated to the land is not depreciable because it is not subject to exhaustion or wear and tear. Hence, the mortgagor's depreciable basis is $250,000. Per Table 6 of Rev. Proc. 87–57, the mortgagor can depreciate $7,955 ($250,000 times 3.182%). In 2018, the mortgagor can claim $9,090 ($250,000 times 3.636%).

III. FORM OF OWNERSHIP

A. INDIVIDUAL OR CONCURRENT OWNERSHIP

Individual investors of real property may acquire it in their own names. This is the simplest form of business ownership. But, the investors are not shielded from limited liability. Hence, if a loan is recourse, the mortgagee may be able to collect a deficiency judgment against the investors. Of course, if the loan is nonrecourse, the mortgagee will not able to pursue a deficiency judgment against the investor. For tax purposes, the investor must report income and deductions (including mortgage interest) on Part I of Schedule E of the Form 1040 tax return.

Individuals may own real property concurrently as joints tenants, tenants in common, tenants by the entireties or community property. Other than spouses filing a joint income tax return, concurrent owners report income, expenses, and losses on their individual tax returns. Types of expenses include mortgage interest, insurance, repairs, utilities, depreciation and property taxes.

B. REGULAR C CORPORATIONS

1. Taxation of Corporations—In General

If a corporation owns income-producing real estate, income and expenses are reported on its corporate income tax return, Form 1120. A corporation is a taxpayer separate from its shareholders. Under IRC § 11(a), tax is imposed on a corporation's taxable income. Currently, the maximum corporate income tax rate is 35%. *See* IRC § 11(b)(5) (2017). However, in April 2017 President Donald Trump proposed that the maximum corporate income tax rate be reduced to 15%. While Congress has yet to consider President Trump's proposal, if the corporate tax is drastically cut in this manner, there will be significant advantages to owning income producing real property in the corporate form because the tax rate will be much lower than the maximum individual rate, which currently is 39.6%. *See* IRC § 1 (2017).

2. Disadvantages of Corporate Form for Owning Commercial Real Estate

Traditionally, a corporation was not the choice of form for real estate holdings. One of the biggest disadvantages is that corporate taxation results in the so-called "double tax." The corporation pays taxes on its taxable income, and distributions or dividends from earnings and profits are included on the shareholders' tax returns.

The other significant disadvantage of using the corporate form arises when it realizes a taxable loss. The shareholders are not entitled to claim the loss on their individual tax returns. This is the primary reason that corporations were infrequently the form used during the tax shelter era in the 1980s. Many residential and nonresidential rental property during that time generated substantial losses. If it had been owned in the corporate form, shareholders would not have been able to use these losses to offset their income on their individual income tax returns.

C. PARTNERSHIPS, S CORPORATIONS AND LLCs

1. Taxation of Partnerships—In General

Entities taxed as partnerships have very different tax consequences than entities taxed as corporations. Partnerships must file a Form 1065 to report income, gains, losses and other items. It is an informational return only. The partnership is a pass-through entity and is not subject to income taxes. *See* IRC § 701 (2017). The partnership issues Schedule Ks to partners that provide them with their distributable share of partnership items, including income, deductions and credits reportable on their tax returns. Generally, this distributable share is determined by the partnership agreement, although special allocations are allowed. IRC § 704(a) & (b) (2017). The partners are then required to report these items consistently on their individual income tax returns. A partner can deduct losses only to the extent of the partner's adjusted basis in the partnership interest. A partner may include in the partner's adjusted basis an allocable share of the partnership's nonrecourse debt. However, a limited partner is not entitled to include a debt in the limited partner's adjusted basis if another partner, such as the general partner, has personal liability on that debt.

2. Advantages of Owning Commercial Real Estate in the Partnership Form

Unlike entities taxed as corporations, losses and deductions are deductible on the partners' individual tax returns. As a result, during the tax shelter era, it was uncommon for investors to own residential and nonresident rental property that generated losses in the corporate form. Instead, the limited partnership was the choice of form. As noted in the next section, partners' ability to claim these losses has been limited. However, there are several significant exceptions to these limitations. Moreover, as long as a real estate activity is profitable, the income can still be sheltered by deductions, including depreciation. A further advantage is that taxable income is not subject to double taxation because it is only taxed on the partners' tax returns.

IV. LIMITATIONS ON DEDUCTIONS

One of the tax advantages of owning rental real property is that an owner can claim depreciation deductions. As already noted, the analysis for determining whether an owner may claim depreciation deductions related to a real estate holding starts with the determination of the adjusted basis which is based on how the owner acquires the property. For example, under IRC § 1012, an owner's adjusted basis is the cost of the property. After determining the adjusted basis, the owner must compute any allowable depreciation deductions under the Internal Revenue Code. After computing the depreciation deduction, it must be determined whether the owner has a sufficient amount at risk. Assuming the owner has a sufficient amount at risk, it must be determined whether the loss is deductible under the passive activity limitation rules. This section discusses the at risk and passive activity limitation rules.

A. AT RISK RULES

1. Purpose of the At Risk Rules

Prior to the enactment of the Tax Reform Act of 1986, the at risk rules did not apply to real estate. The rules were made applicable to real estate after the explosion of tax shelters. This explosion was made possible because the Supreme Court in *Crane* determined that nonrecourse indebtedness was included in an owner's adjusted basis. The real impact of *Crane* did not take effect until Congress accelerated depreciation deductions which allowed for higher deductions in the earlier years after the property was placed in service. As a result, many individuals began investing in real estate for its tax benefits rather than the income derived from the real estate holding.

2. General Rules

IRC § 465(a)(1) provides that any deductible loss is limited to the amount that the owner has at risk. To the extent that the loss is disallowed, it is carried forward to the following taxable year. IRC § 465(a)(2) (2017). The at risk rules apply to individuals and closely held C corporations. *See* IRC § 465(a)(1)(B) (2017).

An owner's initial amount at risk is the sum of the owner's cash contributions to the activity, the adjusted basis of property contributed by the owner to the activity, and amounts borrowed for use in the activity for which the owner is personally liable or has pledged property that is not used in the activity as security. IRC § 465(b) (2017). In general, the amount at risk is the owner's investment and the owner's risk of loss. A recourse debt is always added to the amount at risk because the owner bears the risk of loss. However, an owner will be considered at risk with respect to a nonrecourse debt if it "qualified nonrecourse financing" related to an activity of holding real property. In order to meet this exception: 1) the owner must borrow money from a "qualified person" or from the government or guaranteed by it, 2) no one can be personally liable on the loan, and 3) the loan cannot be a convertible debt. IRC § 465(b)(6) (2017). A "qualified person" is a lender who is not related to the owner (unless the financing is commercially reasonable), the seller of the real property or the promoter of the venture. IRC § 49(a)(1)(D)(iv) (2017).

The owner must determine the amount at risk annually to account for changes made during the tax year. For example, if an owner repays a nonrecourse loan, the amount at risk increases. If an owner claims a loss, the amount at risk is lowered.

To illustrate these concepts, assume that an investor purchases a duplex for $10,000 cash and a $90,000 recourse loan. The investor rents the duplex to tenants. During 2017, the investor realizes a

$15,000 loss (including $2,000 in depreciation). The investor's initial at risk amount is $100,000 because it includes the $10,000 cash investment and the $90,000 recourse debt. Hence, the investor can claim the entire loss. After claiming it, the investor's at risk amount is reduced to $85,000 (the initial $100,000 at risk less the $15,000 loss). If the $90,000 debt is nonrecourse rather than recourse and the qualified nonrecourse indebtedness exception does not apply, the investor's deduction for the loss is limited to $10,000. The additional $5,000 loss is then carried forward to 2018. In order for the investor to claim the carryforward loss in 2018, the investor must pay down the nonrecourse loan with funds outside of the duplex's rental income or contribute additional property or cash to the duplex investment.

B. PASSIVE ACTIVITY LIMITATION RULES

1. Purpose and General Rules

The passive limitation rules were enacted under the Tax Reform Act of 1986 to reduce the increased numbers of tax shelters that had grown during the 1980's. Upon the enactment of accelerated depreciation, wealthy investors increasingly invested in unprofitable ventures, including real estate investments, that generated losses to offset their high income from other sources. The advantageous depreciation rules incentivized investing in activities that generated losses. For example, in Tufts v. Comm'r, 461 U.S. 300 (1983), the partners in the limited partnership had invested a mere $44,212 but claimed ordinary losses and depreciation deductions from the partnership's construction and ownership of an apartment complex in two years totaling $439,972 from their distributable share of the partnership losses. Id. at 302. The inclusion of a $1,851,500 nonrecourse loan entitled the partnership to the high depreciation deductions. *See* id.

Under IRC § 469(a)(1), a passive activity loss (PAL) is disallowed during a taxable year for individuals, estates, trusts, closely held C corporations and personal service corporations. IRC § 469(a) (2017). A PAL is defined as the aggregate passive losses over the aggregate passive income for the tax year. IRC § 469(d)(1) (2017). A disallowed loss is carried forward to the next taxable year. IRC § 469(b) (2017). The taxpayer is also able to deduct the loss upon the disposition of the entire interest in the activity in a fully taxable transaction. IRC § 469(g)(1) (2017).

It is important to note that the taxpayer must apply the at risk rules before applying the passive activity limitation rules. If the taxpayer does not have a sufficient amount at risk in order to claim a loss, the taxpayer is unable to claim the loss even if the taxpayer has a sufficient amount of passive income to offset the loss.

A passive activity is one in which the taxpayer does not "materially participate." IRC § 469(c)(1)(B) (2017). Material participation is defined as regular, continuous and substantial involvement in an activity. IRC § 469(h)(1) (2017). The treasury regulations set forth several tests for determining whether there is material participation, including one that requires the taxpayer to participate in the activity more than 500 hours during the tax year. *See* Treas. Regs. § 1.469–5T (2017). Generally, a taxpayer does not meet the material participation test if the taxpayer is a limited partner in a limited partnership, and a taxpayer's investment in rental activities does not satisfy the material participation test. IRC § 469(c)(2) & (h)(2) (2017). Conversely, portfolio income, gross income from interest, dividends, annuities and royalties, is active income. IRC § 469(e)(1)(A) (2017). These types of income have elements of passive income, but this rule is necessary to prevent a clear loophole.

To the extent that a taxpayer has passive income and passive losses, the losses will offset the passive income dollar for dollar. As a result, a passive loss can be used as a tax shelter if the taxpayer has passive income. For example, assume that a limited partner realizes a $20,000 loss from an investment during 2017. If the limited partner does not have any passive income during 2017, the $20,000 loss is carried forward to 2018. Alternatively, if the limited partner has at least $20,000 of income from a passive source, such as from the rental of an apartment building, the $20,000 passive loss is fully deductible. If the limited partner has $5,000 rental income and $20,000 passive activity loss, $5,000 of the loss is deductible and the $15,000 balance is carried forward to 2018. In 2018, if the limited partner realizes $7,000 of rental income, $7,000 of the $15,000 carryover loss is deductible and the balance, $8,000 is carried forward to 2019.

Returning to the *Tufts* facts, the limited partners would not have been able to deduct the $439,972 ordinary losses and depreciation during the tax years at issue if they did not have any passive income. The passive activity losses would have been carried forward until they disposed of the apartment complex. In *Tufts*, however, the carryover loss would have been deductible within two years because the limited partnership disposed of the entire interest.

2. Exceptions

a. The Real Professional Exception

Under the Internal Revenue Code, if more than one half of a taxpayer's personal services are devoted to real property trades or businesses that the taxpayer materially participates and the taxpayer performs more than 750 hours of service, then the passive activity limitation rule does not apply to the taxpayer's rental real estate activities for the year. IRC § 469(c)(7) (2017). Under this exception, each of a taxpayer's interest in rental real estate is treated as a separate activity unless the taxpayer elects to treat all real estate activities as one activity. Id. *See also* Treas. Reg. § 1.469–9(e)(1) (2017).

b. The Active Participant Exception

The active participant exception entitles the taxpayer to deduct passive losses up to $25,000 in rental real estate activities against nonpassive income. IRC § 469(i)(1) & (2) (2017). In order to fall under the active participant exception, the taxpayer must own at least a 10% interest in the activity. IRC

§ 469(i)(6)(A) (2017). A taxpayer meets the active participation exception if the taxpayer participates in a significant and bona fide manner in the management decisions, such as approving new tenants, making repairs, deciding rental terms or hiring third parties to make repairs. Moss v. Comm'r, 135 T.C. 365, 371 (2010). The active participant test is distinguishable from the material participant exception because it can be satisfied without regular, continuous, and substantial involvement in operations.

The $25,000 maximum deduction is phased out by 50% of the amount that the taxpayer's adjusted gross income (AGI) exceeds $100,000. IRC § 469(i)(3) (2017). Consequently, the deduction is phased out completely once the AGI reaches $150,000. To illustrate this principle, assume that the taxpayer owns a duplex and actively participates in the rental of one unit to tenants. Assume also that the taxpayer realizes a $12,000 loss in the rental activity and has AGI of $140,000 during 2017. The taxpayer's maximum $25,000 deduction will be reduced because the taxpayer's AGI exceeds $100,000. The maximum $25,000 deduction will be reduced by $20,000 ($140,000 less $100,000 times .50). Consequently, the taxpayer is not entitled to claim the entire $12,000 loss; rather the PAL deduction for 2017 is $5,000 ($25,000 maximum deduction less $20,000 reduction). In this example, the $7,000 disallowed loss will be carried over to 2018.

V. LIKE KIND EXCHANGES

Under the tax code, if a taxpayer exchanges property solely for like kind property, the taxpayer does not recognize any gain or loss on the exchange if the property exchanged and received are used in the taxpayer's trade or business or held for investment purposes. IRC § 1031(a)(1) (2017). One of the key exceptions to the like kind rule is that it does not apply to inventory or property held primarily for sale to customers. IRC § 1031(a)(2)(A) (2017). It is not necessary for both parties to the exchange to meet the requirements. That is, one party in the transaction may qualify for the nonrecognition treatment while the other party must recognize gain. In determining whether property is like kind, you look to the nature or character of the property rather than its grade or quality. Treas. Reg. § 1.1031(a)–1(b) (2017). In the context of real property, improved property is like kind to unimproved property. Id. An apartment building is like kind to an office building. An exchange of rental real property of 30 years or more is like kind to a fee interest (a sale and leaseback). Treas. Reg. § 1.1031(a)–1(c) (2017). However, although the lease in real property is like kind to a fee interest, the transaction must be an exchange rather than a sale.

In Leslie Co. v. Comm'r, 539 F.2d 943 (3rd Cir. 1976), the IRS disallowed a loss arguing that the sale and leaseback was a like kind exchange because the taxpayer had conveyed land and leased it back for a 30-year term. Id. at 945. The court cited a regulation that defined an exchange as "a reciprocal transfer of property" rather than a transfer of property for money only. Id. at 947 (*citing* Treas. Reg. § 1.1002–1(d)). The court determined that the transaction was a sale and allowed the loss because the money received equaled the fair market value of the property; hence, the lease had no capital value. Id. at 949. The court rejected the Eighth Circuit's approach that determined that a similar arrangement was an exchange by looking solely at whether the sale and leaseback were reciprocal. Id. at 948. *See* Century Elec. Co. v. Comm'r, 192 F.2d 155 (8th Cir. 1951), *cert. denied* 342 U.S. 954, 72 S.Ct. 625 (1952). Rather, the court adopted the Second Circuit's approach in Jordan Marsh Co. v. Comm'r, 269 F.2d 453 (2d Cir. 1959). *Leslie*, 539 F.2d at 949.

If a taxpayer receives "boot" which is cash or nonqualifying property, the taxpayer must recognize gain (but not a loss) not exceeding the boot. IRC § 1031(b) & (c) (2017). Significantly, mortgage relief is treated as cash received by the taxpayer under the like kind exchange rules. *See* IRC § 1031(d) (2017). For example, assume that the taxpayer has investment land that is encumbered by a $20,000 nonrecourse mortgage, has a fair market value of $100,000 and the taxpayer's adjusted basis is $60,000. The taxpayer exchanges it for a duplex worth $80,000 that the taxpayer plans to use in the taxpayer's trade or business, and the exchanger takes the land subject to the mortgage. In this example, the taxpayer's amount realized is $100,000, the $80,000 fair market value of the duplex (per IRC § 1001(b) (2017)) and the $20,000 of debt relief per *Crane*. Hence, the taxpayer's realized gain is $40,000 (amount realized of $100,000 less adjusted basis of $60,000). The taxpayer must recognize $20,000, the amount of the boot or mortgage relief. The balance of the gain is deferred until the taxpayer disposes of the duplex.

The tax consequences change if both parties to the exchange are being relieved of debt. Under the regulations, consideration received in the form of debt relief is offset against consideration given in the form of debt assumption. Treas. Reg. § 1.1031(d)–2(b) (2017). Therefore, in the above example, if the property that the taxpayer receives in the exchange is subject to a $5,000 debt, the taxpayer is considered to have received $15,000 of boot and must recognize gain in that amount. Conversely, the other person in the exchange does not need to recognize any gain because that person has taken on more debt than debt relief.

In addition, there are several significant rules or factors that must be considered before anyone contemplates a like kind exchange. First, the like kind exchange rules are strictly construed. Second, the nonrecognition rule is mandatory when the section 1031 requirements are satisfied. Therefore, if a taxpayer has a loss in the property to be exchanged, the taxpayer should avoid a like kind exchange because the loss will not be recognized. Third, it is not a like kind exchange if the taxpayer conveys investment real property, receives cash and uses the cash to purchase investment real property. Instead, the taxpayer has engaged in a sale rather than an exchange. Fourth, the nonrecognition of the gain or loss is generally deferred because the adjusted basis of the property received in a like kind exchange is the adjusted basis of the property transferred with certain adjustments to reflect the taxpayer's after-tax consequences (e.g., the adjusted basis is decreased by any cash received, including mortgage relief). IRC § 1031(d) (2017). Fifth, the taxpayer may enter into a deferred exchange (a so-called *Starker* exchange) and qualify for nonrecognition treatment. Frequently, a taxpayer may have found someone to acquire the taxpayer's property, but that person doesn't own real property that the taxpayer wants to acquire. For a transaction to qualify as a deferred exchange, the taxpayer must identify the property to be received in the exchange within 45 days from the date that the taxpayer transferred the relinquished property and must receive the identified property within 180 days after the transfer of the relinquished property or the due date of the tax return, whichever is earlier. IRC § 1031(a)(3) (2017). *See also* Treas. Reg. § 1.1031(k)–1 (2017). Finally, the taxpayer may enter into a three-cornered exchange, a transaction that involves multiple properties. For example, the taxpayer owns Blackacre and wants to acquire Whiteacre but A, the owner of Whiteacre doesn't want to acquire Blackacre. Rather, the owner of Whiteacre wants to acquire Pinkacre and that owner, B, wants to acquire the taxpayer's property, Blackacre. The taxpayer conveys Blackacre to B, B transfers Pinkacre to A, and A conveys Whiteacre to the taxpayer. If the holding requirements are satisfied, it qualifies as a like kind exchange. The transaction also qualifies as a like kind exchange for the taxpayer even if one of the parties receives cash instead of property. For example, the taxpayer owns Blackacre that is worth $100,000 and wants to acquire Whiteacre that is owned by B, but B doesn't want to acquire Blackacre. The taxpayer can convey Blackacre to A. A pays $100,000 to B for Blackacre. B conveys Whiteacre to the taxpayer. The taxpayer is the only person who is eligible for the nonrecognition treatment in this example.

VI. TAX CONSIDERATIONS OF INSTALLMENT SALES

A seller who engages in an installment sale can obtain a tax advantage by using the installment method to spread any realized gain over the term of the contract. This tax treatment also applies where the seller provides purchase money mortgage financing. A seller who provides purchase money mortgage financing or enters into an installment land contract is taxed under the installment sale rules of the Internal Revenue Code. Under IRC § 453(b)(1), an installment sale occurs where the seller receives at least one payment after the end of the year in which the sale takes place. The installment method is inapplicable to several items, including inventory, property held primarily for sale to customers in the ordinary course of business and losses. IRC § 453(b)(2) (2017).

A seller may elect out of the installment method. IRC § 453(d) (2017). Ordinarily, it is more favorable for a taxpayer to defer taxes based on time value of money principles. However, there are several reasons why a seller may decide to elect out of the installment method. If the property that the seller has disposed is taxed as a capital gain, the seller may have a capital loss that offsets that gain. Under the tax code, a capital loss is deductible dollar for dollar against capital gains. IRC § 1211(b) (2017). Noncorporate taxpayers are also able to deduct up to $3000 of capital losses against ordinary income. Id. For example, if the seller realizes a $25,000 capital gain from an installment sale, has a $28,000 capital loss (such as from the sale of stock), and has at least $3,000 in wages, the seller will be able to deduct the entire $28,000 loss against the $25,000 capital gain and $3,000 in wages. As a result, it will beneficial for the seller to elect out of the installment method. Conversely, it may be more beneficial for a seller to take advantage of the installment sale rules if the seller does not have the $25,000 loss.

Another reason that a seller may decide to elect out of the installment method is where the seller's income is modest, and the capital gain from the sale will be taxed at the zero percent rate. Under the tax code, capital gains are taxed at zero percent for sellers with ordinary income taxed at the 10% or 15% income rate tax brackets. IRC § 1(h)(1)(B) (2017). Based on the 2017 rate schedules, the zero percent rate applies where taxable income does not exceed $37,950 (single taxpayers) or $75,900 (married taxpayers filing a joint return).

If a seller does not elect out of the installment method, the seller must compute the "gross profit ratio" to determine the amount of each installment that is taxable. See IRC § 453(c) (2017). This ratio determines how much of each payment is taxable and how much is considered to be a return of the seller's basis. Under the installment method, mortgage relief is considered a return of the seller's adjusted basis. If the purchaser takes the property subject to a mortgage or assumes a mortgage and the mortgage exceeds the seller's adjusted basis (e.g., seller's cost), the seller is taxed on the excess in the year of the installment sale. Treas. Regs. § 15a.453–1(b)(3)(i) (2017). In such a case, the gross profit ratio will be 100%. This means that 100% of each payment will be taxed as it is received. Consequently, whenever the mortgage relief equals or exceeds the seller's adjusted basis, all payments that the seller receives will be taxed along with any excess mortgage relief over the seller's adjusted basis.

VII. SALE AND LEASEBACK TRANSACTIONS

The general tax ramifications of a sale and leaseback are easily understood. The seller-lessee realizes a capital gain or loss on the sale of the property and may deduct all rent paid and mortgage interest. The investor-lessor must include rental income in gross income but is entitled to claim depreciation deductions on the building and other improvements.

The elaborate plans of the parties, however, will collapse if the substance of the transaction is found to be a security arrangement rather than a genuine sale and leaseback. The landmark decision in Frank Lyon Co. v. United States, 435 U.S. 561 (1978), establishes the standard that is applied in determining whether the sale and leaseback will be upheld for tax purposes. In *Frank Lyon*, a state bank wanted to construct an office building to be used as the bank's headquarters. Id. at 563. However, because of certain regulatory constraints, the bank could not take title to the improvements. Id. at 564. As a result, it entered into a sale and leaseback arrangement. Id. at 565. The lessor/buyer (Lyon) used $500,000 of its own money and loan proceeds to finance the venture. Id. at 567. The bank was obligated to pay a leaseback rental equal to the principal and interest payments on the permanent mortgage. Id. at 566. The bank also acquired the option to repurchase the building at various times at prices equal to the unpaid balance of the long-term mortgage plus the lessor's initial investment ($500,000) compounded at a 6% annual rate of interest. Id. at 567. The IRS argued that based on substance over form principles, the sale and leaseback arrangement was a mere financing device rather than a true sale and leaseback. Id. at 573.

The Court applied a facts and circumstances analysis in determining whether the substance of the transaction was a sale and leaseback arrangement. While there were facts indicating that the transaction was a sham, such as the fact that total rent payable under the building equaled the principal and interest payments of a mortgage loan, there were other factors that indicated that the form should be upheld. Some of the facts that supported a sale and leaseback were: 1) Lyon alone was personally liable for repayment of the mortgage loan; 2) the lease was for a noncancelable term of at least 25 years (i.e., definite rental term); hence, the bank was unconditionally obligated to pay the rent, even if lessor had stopped making the mortgage payments; 3) if the bank stopped making rental payments, the lessor was required to continue making mortgage payments; 4) regulatory constraints precluded the bank from owning the improvements; and 5) although the lessor was related to the bank, independent investors were interested in the deal. The Court upheld the form of the transaction because there was a "genuine multiple-party transaction with economic substance which is compelled or encouraged by business or regulatory realities, is imbued with tax-independent considerations, and is not shaped solely by tax-avoidance features that has meaningless labels attached." Id. at 583–84.

In the event the transaction is found to be a hidden security arrangement instead of a legitimate sale and leaseback, significant tax consequences will result. The parties must readjust their tax positions to reflect reality and pay any resulting tax deficiencies. If the transaction is recharacterized as a disguised mortgage, the purported seller/lessee does not recognize gain or loss on the transfer to the purported purchaser/lessor. Also, the seller/lessee is entitled to claim depreciation and property tax deductions as the true owner of the property and mortgage interest deductions on the disguised mortgage. The purported purchaser/lessor must include mortgage interest in income instead of including the entire rental income in gross income.

VIII. SALE OF A PRINCIPAL RESIDENCE

An owner who sells or exchanges a principal residence the owner may be able to exclude up to $250,000 realized gain on the transaction. IRC § 121(a) & (b) (2017). To qualify for the exclusion, the owner must have owned and used the residence as the owner's principal residence for two of the last five years. IRC § 121(a) (2017). For or a couple filing a joint return, the exclusion is $500,000 provided that both spouse used the residence as a principal residence and at least one spouse owned it for two of the last five years. IRC § 121(b)(2) (2017). An owner can take advantage of this exclusion more than once. However, an owner cannot exclude gain under section 121 more than once every two years. IRC § 121(b)(3) (2017).

An owner who does not meet the ownership and use requirements or has previously excluded principal residence gain within the last two years is able to exclude a portion of the gain if the sale or exchange is caused by a change in place of employment, health or unforeseen circumstances. IRC § 121(c) (2017). Under the regulations, unforeseen circumstances include death of the owner or the owner's spouse, involuntary conversion of the residence or divorce or legal separation. Treas. Reg. § 1.121–3(e)(2) & (f) (2017).

With appropriate tax planning, an owner can maximize tax savings related to the sale or exchange of a residence. But, if the owner sells the principal residence for a loss, the loss is disallowed because personal losses are not deductible under the Internal Revenue Code. *See* IRC § 165(c) (2017).

IX. CHARACTERIZATION OF GAIN OR LOSS

The character of gain or loss from the disposition of real property depends on the nature of the ownership and the length of time that the seller holds the real property. Capital gains (assuming the seller has "net capital gain" as defined under IRC § 1222(11)) are taxed at favorable tax rates and are generally taxed at 15% or 20%, depending on the seller's income. *See* IRC § 12(h)(1)(C) & (D) (2017).

The deductibility of capital losses is limited. Under IRC § 1211 (a) and (b), capital losses are deductible dollar for dollar against capital gains, but the seller's ability to deduct capital losses against ordinary income, including wages and business income, is limited. Corporate sellers can offset capital losses against capital gains. IRC § 1211(a) (2017). Noncorporate sellers can only offset up to $3,000 against ordinary income. IRC § 1211(b) (2017). Conversely, ordinary losses are deductible against all types of income. For example, assume that in 2017 a seller has $300,000 income from the seller's dental practice and realizes a $50,000 loss from the sale of real property. If the loss is an ordinary loss, the seller can deduct the entire loss in 2017. However, if the loss is a capital loss and the seller does not have any capital gains, the seller can offset only $3,000 against the dental income. Without capital gains, it will take the seller over 16 years to deduct the entire $50,000 loss. Based on time value of money principles, the seller will have greater tax savings by deducting the entire loss in 2017 rather than deducting it over time.

A. THE HOLDING REQUIREMENT

To the extent that the seller has held the real property for a year or less, the seller is required to recognize ordinary income or ordinary loss. It is important to note that this determination is based on the time that the seller has "held" rather than "owned" the real property. Under IRC § 1223, a seller may be considered to have held real property longer than the seller has actually owned it. Section 1223 provides several holding period rules. For example, if a seller exchanges real property in a like kind exchange, the holding period for the property received in the like kind exchange includes the period in which the seller held the property transferred in the exchange. *See* IRC § 1223(1) (2017). The policy underlying this rule is that the gain or loss from the property transferred in the exchange is deferred and will be recognized when the property received in the exchange is disposed. Therefore, it is reasonable to include the exchanged property's holding period with the time that the seller holds the property received in the exchange. The same principle applies for property that is acquired by gift. Under the tax code, if the donee's basis is determined in whole or in part based on the donor's basis, the donee includes the time in which the donor has held the gifted property. IRC § 1223(2) (2017). A gift is a nontaxable event; hence, gain or loss is based in part on that deferred gain or loss.

B. DEALER TRANSACTIONS

The definition of a capital asset excludes property held "primarily for sale" to customers in the ordinary course of the owner's trade or business and inventory. IRC § 1221(a)(1) (2017). As a result, if an owner's interest in real property falls under this rule, the owner will recognize ordinary income or ordinary loss on its disposition. The Supreme Court has defined the term "primarily" within the meaning of section 1221(a)(1) as "of first importance" or "principally." *See* Malat v. Riddell, 383 U.S. 569, 572 (1966). This determination is a question of fact. Rockwell v. Comm'r, 512 F.2d 882, 884 (9th Cir. 1975). Courts will consider several factors, including the reasons the owner acquired or subsequently held the property, the number and frequency of sales, whether the owner improved the property, the owner's efforts in trying to find buyers for the property and the owner's ordinary business. Maddux Constr. Co. v. Comm'r, 54 T.C. 1278, 1284 (1970).

C. PROPERTY HELD AS AN INVESTMENT

If an owner sells or exchanges property held for more than a year for the production of income or for investment rather than for use in a trade or business, it is a capital asset entitling the owner to capital gain treatment. For example, if an owner has a vacation cottage that is used solely for personal purposes, the owner receives capital gain treatment because it is a capital asset. The same conclusion is reached where the owner owns a condominium unit and rents it to tenants, but the rental does not rise to the level of a trade or business under the facts and circumstances test of *Maddux*.

In addition, an owner's principal residence is a capital asset. Any gain exceeding the section 121 exclusion amount or gain that is ineligible for the exclusion because the owner does not satisfy the use and ownership requirement is included on the owner's tax return as capital gain.

D. PROPERTY HELD AS A TRADE OR BUSINESS

If an owner uses real property in a trade or business, it is not considered to be a capital asset. *See* IRC § 1221(a)(2) (2017). However, this property may receive treatment that is significantly more favorable than being classified as a capital asset. Real property used in the trade or business that is held more than a year is section 1231 property. Briefly, section 1231 gains must be netted with section 1231 losses. IRC § 1231(a) (2017). The items to be netted under this rule are those from the sale or exchange of trade or business property, condemnation of property used in the trade or business and condemnation of capital assets used in the trade or business or a transaction entered into for profit. IRC § 1231(a)(3) & (4) (2017). These items must also be held more than a year. Gains and losses from other casualties must also be netted if the gains exceed or equal the losses after netting these items. IRC § 1231(a) (4)(C) (2017). If the gains exceed the losses, all gains and losses are treated as long-term capital gain and losses. IRC § 1231(a) (1) (2017). Once they are treated as long-term capital gains and losses, they are netted with any other capital gains and losses. On the other hand, if the section 1231 losses equal or exceed the section 1231 gains, the gains are treated as ordinary income and the losses are treated at ordinary losses.

The key advantage to section 1231 is that if the gains exceed the losses, they may be taxed at the favorable capital gain rates. However, if the losses equal or exceed the gains, these gains and losses will be taxed as ordinary income and losses. While the ordinary income is taxed at higher rates than capital gains, the ordinary losses will fully offset the ordinary income. Further, the excess ordinary losses will offset the owner's ordinary income from other sources, such as wages, interest and business income.

INDEX

References are to Pages